CONTENTS

CONTENTS

UMAR IBN AL-KHATTAB

THE CROWN OF CALIPHS

Amongst the nations before your time, there have been inspired people (who were not Prophets), and if there is one amongst my Ummah, he is Umar.

– Prophet Muhammad

MOIN QAZI

ABOUT THE BOOK

In the vast corridors of history, we come across a parade of diverse human characters that symbolise the enormous, vast plethora of our surrounding canvas. This romance of history is not just fascinating but also genuinely inspiring. Every age has been a model for a succeeding one. Thus, the history of either the kingdoms or the human race, or, for that matter, the history of religion or science, has basically been the history of the evolution of man from a cave dweller to a visitor to the moon. In its vast penumbra, history extols only a few individuals whose lives shine in luminescence and whose ideals are living models of shimmering stars that make up the glory of this civilisation. These great men have been the pathfinders and torchbearers of ideals that shaped and glorified civilizations, which glue people into a rich and glimmering heritage.

Men of genius are meteors who had a genuine desire to glow the light of this efflorescence into a more glittering glimpse of our civilisation, prescience, and culture that would keep growing through the ever-twilight of history. There were men from diverse spheres of life, men who were kings, philosophers, scholars, rulers and generals who could grasp the true purpose of life quite early and did not have to share the disgrace of many others who could not catch the luminescence of this truth. The noble souls, whose teachings have survived the driftwood of history and whose names still carry an aura of greatness, were men driven by a ceaseless urge to open out their hearts to others, those who changed society by liberating segments of the population and seep out the prejudice. All great men—whether social reformers, thinkers, politicians, sages, or patriots—differ from ordinary men only in one respect. They dare to dream and also work to transmute that dream into reality. They give life meaning and purpose and devote themselves single-mindedly to that purpose. The truly great men are not the men of wealth or possession, not men who gain name and fame, but those who testify to the truth in them and refuse to compromise whatever the cost.

In the seventh century, the envoy of the Roman Emperor set out for Medinah, accompanied by a large entourage, flaunting the pageantry of adornments for which the Roman Empire was famous. On arrival in the metropolis of Islam, he enquired from a passer-by: "Tell me please, where is the palace of the Caliph?"

The Arab looked around and was confused by the absence of any sign of royalty. He was amazed and prompted by a curious emotional thought. He hinted to the Arab commoner, "What do you mean by a palace?" retorted the Arab." I mean the palace of Umar, the Caliph of Islam," added the envoy. "Oh! You want to see Umar. He took him inside the palace.

To his amazement, the Caliph was lying on the floor shorn of any trappings of royalty, which the envoy felt embarrassed at the humble sight. His report of the observation Impressed the Roman Emperor.

Converting to Islam in the 6th year after Prophet Muhammad's first revelation, Umar spent 18 years in the companionship of the Prophet. He succeeded Caliph Abu Bakr on 23 August 634 and played a significant role in Islam. His reign saw the transformation of the Islamic state from an Arabian principality to a world power, controlling the whole territory of the former Sassanid Persian Empire and more than two-thirds of the Eastern Roman Empire. His legislative abilities, his firm political and administrative control over a rapidly expanding empire and his brilliantly coordinated attacks against the Sassanid Persian Empire that resulted in the conquest of the Persian Empire in less than two years marked his reputation as an astute political and military strategist. Throughout this remarkable expansion, Umar closely controlled general policy and laid down the principles for administering the conquered lands. The structure of the later Islamic empire, including legal and administrative systems and financial architecture, is essentially a result of his farsightedness and wisdom. A strong ruler, stern toward offenders, and ascetic to the point of harshness, he enjoyed enormous respect for his commitment to justice and authority.

Umar despised the trappings of kingship and wealth. Foreign visitors were always amazed to find that there was no protocol for gatekeepers, court chancellors or bodyguards. Simplicity, poverty, and justice—these are three qualities of the brave and energetic man who led the Arabs out of the confines of the Arabian Desert into the lush lands of the age-old Fertile Crescent. Umar's extraordinary virtues catapulted the young Muslim community onto the map of world history in an effulgent blaze of glory and power.

Umar personified what the Arabs called *amuruwwa*, the virtue of being a man. It connotes a cluster of virtues: bravery, generosity, practical wisdom, and honour, all of which are highly valued and praised in the Arab tribal culture.

Throughout his reign, Umar remained a legendary Puritan, a stern, austere man who came down hard on any public display of vulgarity, gambling, improper dress, misuse of state property or abuse of delegated powers. He expected those who had been entrusted with high office to have a morality that matched their exalted responsibilities.

Umar was the architect of Islamic civilization. Humankind has a tryst with destiny to realize its sublime nature in the matrix of human affairs. Umar turned out to be a significant figure in the development of Muslim civilization who supervised the installation of Abu Bakr as the first Caliph and also masterminded the victories over both Byzantine and Persian empires. He was an implacable puritan and the architect of the whole political geography of the Islamic empire. Umar was a member of the Umayyah clan of the Makkan Quraysh tribe – thus, the name of the empire he founded was the Umayyad Empire. After the death of

Prophet Muhammad, Umar made sure that the community leadership went to Abu Bakr. This effort ensured that the group did not splinter according to differing loyalties between those from Makkah and those from Medinah. Abu Bakr, in turn, designated Umar as his successor when he was on his deathbed.

TIMELINE OF THE LIFE OF CALIPH UMAR

577: Umar born in Makkah to Khattab ibn Nufayl and Hantama bint Hisham.

616: Umar's conversion to Islam.

634-644: Umar (b 577 CE – d 3 November 644 CE)) reigns as the second Caliph. The Muslims subjugate Egypt, Palestine, Syria, Mesopotamia and Persia. There was a necessity for garrisons to be built in the conquered lands, and the Muslim rulers began to take control of the financial organisation.

635: Muslims begin the conquest of Persia and Syria.

635: Arab Muslims capture the city of Damascus from the Byzantines.

636: Battle of Yarmuk (also: Yarmuq, Hieromyax): Following the Muslim capture of Damascus and Edessa, Byzantine Emperor Heraclius organizes a large army that manages to take back control of those cities. However, Byzantine commander Baänes was defeated outright d by Muslim forces under ibn Walid in a battle in the valley of the Yarmuk River outside Damascus. This left all of Syria open to Arab domination.

636: The Arabs under Saad ibn Abi Waqqas defeat a Sasanian army in the battle of Qadisiyya (near Hira), gaining Iraq west of the Tigris. A second victory follows at Jalula, near Ctesiphon.

637: The Arabs occupy the Persian capital of Ctesiphon. By 651, the entire Persian realm would come under Islam's rule, which continued its westward expansion.

637: Syria is conquered by Muslim forces.

637: Jerusalem falls to invading Muslim forces.

638: Caliph Umar marries Umm Kulthum and enters Jerusalem.

639-42: Conquest of Egypt (642 taking of Alexandria) by 'Amr ibn al-'As. Muslims captured the seaport of Caesarea in Palestine, marking the end of the Byzantine presence in Syria.

Timeline of the Life of Caliph Umar

641: Islam spreads into Egypt. The Catholic Archbishop invites Muslims to help free Egypt from Roman oppressors.

641: Under the leadership of Abd-al-Rahman, Muslims conquer southern areas of Azerbaijan, Daghestan, Georgia, and Armenia.

641/2: Under the leadership of Amr ibn al-As, Muslims conquer the Byzantine city of Alexandria in Egypt. Al-As created the first Muslim city in Egypt, al-Fustat, and built the first mosque in Egypt.

644: The death of Umar and succeeded by Uthman.

1. THE FOUNDATION OF ISLAM

Islam is a major world religion founded by Prophet Muhammad in Arabia in the early 7th century CE. The Arabic word *islām* means "surrender"—specifically, surrender to the will of the one God, called Allah in Arabic. Islam is a strictly monotheistic religion, and its adherents, called Muslims, regard the Prophet Muhammad as the last and most perfect of God's messengers, including Adam, Abraham, Moses, Jesus, and others. The sacred scripture of Islam is the Qur'ān, which contains God's revelations to Muhammad. The sayings and deeds of the Prophet recounted in the Sunnah are also an essential source of belief and practice in Islam.

The religious obligations of all Muslims comprise the Five Pillars of Islam, which include the profession of faith (*shahādah*) in God and his Prophet, prayer (*ṣalāt*), charity (*zakāt*), pilgrimage (hajj), and fasting (*ṣawm*). The fundamental concept of Islam is the Shari'a —its law, which embraces the total way of life commanded by God. Observant Muslims pray five times a day and join in community worship on Fridays at a mosque, where an imam leads worship. Every believer is required to make a pilgrimage to Mecca, the holiest city, at least once in a lifetime, barring poverty or physical incapacity. The month of Ramadan is devoted to fasting. Alcohol and pork are always forbidden, as are gambling, usury, fraud, slander, and the making of images. In addition to Eid al-Fitr, which celebrates the breaking of the fast of Ramadan, Muslims celebrate Muhammad's birthday and his ascension into heaven. Eid al-Adha marks the culmination of the pilgrimage to Mecca.

Divisions occurred early in Islam, brought about by disputes over the succession to the leadership of the Muslim community (*ummah*).

The Shi'ah argued that Muhammad had designated his son-in-law, 'Ali ibn Abī Ṭālib, as his successor. The Sunnis, who today make up the majority of Muslims, claimed he did not appoint a specific successor. Another significant element in Islam is mysticism, also known as Sufism. The encounters with the West in the 19th and 20th centuries prompted the rise of fundamentalist movements that have voiced grievances they attribute to colonialism and a perceived decadence of Islamic society. In the early 21st century, there were more than 1.5 billion Muslims in the world. A comprehensive perspective is required to explain the history of today's Islamic world. This approach must enlarge upon conventional political or dynastic divisions to draw a comprehensive picture of the stages by which successive Muslim communities, throughout Islam's 14 centuries, encountered and incorporated new peoples so as to produce an international religion and civilization.

In general, events referred to in this article are dated according to the Gregorian calendar, and eras are designated bce (before the Common Era or Christian Era) and ce (Common Era or Christian Era), terms which are equivalent to bc (before Christ) and ad (Latin: *anno Domini*). In some cases, the Muslim reckoning of the Islamic era is used, as indicated by ah (Latin: *anno Hegirae*). The Islamic era begins with the date of Muhammad's migration (Hijrah) to Medina, which corresponds to July 16, 622 ce, in the Gregorian calendar.

In what follows, the terms Islamic world and Islamdom are used interchangeably. The term Islamic describes aspects pertaining to Islam as a religion, while Muslim as an adjective describes aspects related to Islam's adherents. The term Islamicate refers to the social and cultural complex that is historically associated with Islam and Muslims, including the function and participation of non-Islamic and non-Muslim individuals and groups within that complex.

2. THE CALIPHATE

Caliph is the term or title for the Islamic leader of the *Ummah,* nation or community of Islam. It is an Anglicized/Latinized version of the Arabic word *Khalīfah* (listen, which means "successor," that is, successor to the prophet Muhammad. Some Orientalists (non-Muslim Western scholars) wrote the title *Khalīf,* which remains the preferred term among scholars, although the more common "caliph" will be used in this article. The caliph was usually designated as *Ameer al-Mumineen* or "Prince of the Faithful," where "Prince" is used in the context of "commander." The title has been defunct since the abolition of the Ottoman Sultanate in 1924.

A Brief History of the Caliphate

A caliphate is an Islamic form of government in which political and religious leadership is united, and the head of state (the caliph) is a successor to the Prophet Muhammad. The first Muslim empire—the Caliphate—began with the conquests of the mid-seventh century CE and fragmented in the mid-tenth century. This chapter outlines the Caliphate's political and economic history, its organizational structures, the Middle East were transformed by the formation of new elites, by a new transregional coinage economy, by the rapid expansion of new cities and settlements, and by an agricultural revolution. The religion that became Islam was crucial in uniting the conquerors of the empire and then as the idiom for the expression of the conquered peoples' political ambitions. Eventual widespread conversion among the conquered populations meant that as the Caliphate collapsed, it left behind Muslim successor states, as well as new linguistic and ethnic identities—notably the Arabic and New Persian *linguae France,* and a transregional "Arab" ethnicity first four caliphs (also known as the "rightly guided caliphs," or RasProphet hidden) led from Medina in modern-day Saudi Arabia. In the earliest years of the caliphate, Muhammad's family and disciples ruled the Muslim community—or ummah—implementing the same system he had created. The period of the rightly-guided caliphs ended in 661, when Ali, the fourth of the rightly guided caliphs, was killed, and Mu'awiya ibn Abi Sufyan, seated in Syria, proclaimed himself caliph. Some Muslims consider all four of the rightly guided caliphs to be legitimate successors to the Prophet, whereas others accept only Ali. This disagreement led to a split in Islam and the emergence of its two main branches, Sunni and Shia. Historically selected by a committee, the holder of this title claims temporal and spiritual authority over all Muslims but is equal to a possessor of a prophetic mission, on par with Prophet Muhammad, as the final prophet. For centuries, the caliphate represented the ideal that all Muslims, regardless of race, are equal members of a single, global entity, the ummah. It also stood for the integration of the spiritual with the political, ensuring, at least in theory, harmony between the law of the state and divine law. In practice, too, much of the Islamic world, even if governed by autonomous Sultans, maintained a sense of unity, and the life experiences of Muslims were similar regardless of where they lived. The law was more or less the same throughout the territory of which the caliph was, if only nominally, the head. The caliphate was an attempt to create a single, God-fearing community of all humanity.

Although the caliph was not invested with spiritual authority possessed by Prophet Muhammad, the caliph presided over a state governed under Islamic law (Sharia) whose territories constituted the "abode of Islam" (*dar al-Islam*). Thus, the caliph served as the symbol of the supremacy of the Sharia, as commander of the faithful (*amir al-mu'minin*) in his capacity to both defend and expand these lands and as leader of prayers (Imam), thereby clothing the caliphate with religious meaning. Sunni Islam holds that Muhammad left no instructions regarding his successor, who was to be elected, with the decision of the community regarded as infallible.

Modern understandings of the title of caliph are varied. Some movements in modern Islamic philosophy have emphasized a protective dimension of Islamic leadership and social policy from an understanding of *khalifa* that equates roughly to "render stewardship" or "protect the same things as God." This derives from the use of the term for humanity in the Qur'anic creation narrative at Q2:30.' Sayyid Abul A'la Maududi (1903- 1979), founder of the Jamaati-Islam, took this view. Some consider the modern absence of a single Muslim head of state to be a violation of the Islamic legal code, the Shariah. Scholars came to view the caliphate as a 'necessity in the world.' Others insist that after the four rightful caliphs, the office ceased to exist—meaning that those who claimed after to be "khalifa" were actually "melik" (king), as suggested by Ibn Khaldun (1332 – 1406). Islamist movements (who argue for the restoration of authentic Islamic governance) have argued for the necessity of re-establishing the institution of a single office whose occupant, as successor to Muhammad, would possess clear political, military, and legal standing as the global leader of the Muslims. Such an initiative has yet to gather much practical support in the Muslim world.

The first Muslim empire—the Caliphate—began with the conquests of the mid-seventh century CE and fragmented in the mid-tenth century. This chapter outlines the Caliphate's political and economic history, its organizational structures, and forms of coercive and ideological power. During the long eighth century, the Mediterranean and the Middle East were transformed by the formation of new elites, by a new transregional coinage economy, by the rapid expansion of new cities and settlements, and by an agricultural revolution. The religion that became Islam was crucial in uniting the conquerors of the empire and then as the idiom for the expression of the conquered peoples' political ambitions. Eventual widespread conversion among the conquered populations meant that as the Caliphate collapsed, it left behind Muslim successor states, as well as new linguistic and ethnic identities—notably the Arabic and New Persian *linguae francae*, and a transregional "Arab" ethnicity

he caliphate was established as the succession to Muhammad and became a defining institution of Muslim societies. It was, however, an evolving institution with a different political and religious meaning in successive eras. The first phase, the period of the Rightly Guided Caliphs (632–61; known as Rashidun), was the religious chieftainship of a community and the political leadership of a coalition of nomadic conquerors. In the succeeding early Umayyad period (661–85), the caliphate was recalibrated as a Syrian-Arab monarchy. In the later Umayyad (685–750), the caliphate was transformed into a new form of Middle Eastern empire defined and legitimized both in older imperial and Islamic terms.

Accordingly, following Muhammad's death, Abu Bakir was elected based on his close association with the Prophet, his righteousness, and his leadership ability. The Shi'a Islamic tradition, on the other hand, asserts that the community made a grievous error in electing Abu Bakr rather than Muhammad's cousin and son-in-law, 'Ali ibn Abi Talib, whom they believe was chosen by the Prophet. These partisans of 'Ali consider Abu Bakr's succession to be illegitimate, claiming that infallibility was limited to the Prophet's family through 'Ali, 'Ali's sons through his marriage with the Prophet's daughter, Fatima, and their descendants. Thus, Shi'ite Islam rejected the Sunni notion of rightly guided (Rashidun) caliphs, a term used for the first four caliphs, acknowledging instead the rightful succession of 'Ali and his descendants. The Rashidun Caliphate (632–661) followed the Umayyad Caliphate (661–750) established by Mu'awiya in Damascus, Syria. The dynastic succession established by Mu'awiya lasted until a rival clan of the Quraysh tribe, the Abbasids, successfully revolted. The Abbasid Caliphate (750–1258) established a dynasty with its capital in Baghdad, though its control over the state was severely reduced during its last three centuries by rival secular rulers, including the Buyids and Seljuks along with the Fatamid Caliphate (909–1171) in Egypt and the Umayyad Caliphate (929–1031) of Spain. The Ottoman conquest of the Mamluk state led to the establishment of the Ottoman Caliphate (1517–1924).

A History of Heterogeneity

Analysts scouting for the meaning of the caliphate usually consider its political style, economy, leadership and territorial conflict. Beyond its geopolitical identity, what are the historical pillars of the Islamic empire? What has been the reality on the ground in terms of social structure, culture and daily life? If the Islamic State, the Taliban, al Qaeda, and other political perversions of Islam knew the rich cultural history of Muslim caliphates, they would run in the opposite direction.

A caliph is a successor to the Prophet Mohammed, who died in 632, leaving the election of leadership in the hands of his close companions. The caliphate -- a society ruled by the caliph -- has been in flux ever since. Following the reign of the first four caliphs, dynasties were in the race for the new empire. The Baghdad-based Abbasids took power from the Damascus-based Umayyad dynasty in 749. They ruled for over 500 years until Hulagu Khan and his Mongol armies destroyed the capital in 1258. During that time, emirates and sultanates -- including surviving Umayyads who maintained a rival caliphate from Andalusia on the Iberian Peninsula from 929 to 1031 -- threatened Abbasid leadership from time to time. From 909 to 1171, the Fatimid dynasty ruled from Cairo, taking on invading Crusaders from the north for nearly a century.

The Makings Of A Caliphate

The caliphate -- a society ruled by the caliph -- has been in flux ever since. Following the reign of the first four caliphs, dynasties emerged to rule an expanding empire. The Baghdad-based Abbasids took power from the Damascus-based Umayyad dynasty in 749. They ruled for over 500 years until Hulagu Khan and his Mongol armies destroyed the capital in 1258. During that time, emirates and sultanates -- including surviving Umayyads who maintained a rival caliphate from Andalusia on the Iberian Peninsula from 929 to 1031 -- threatened Abbasid leadership from time to time. From 909 to 1171, the Fatimid dynasty ruled from Cairo, taking on invading Crusaders from the north for nearly a century.

Shifting imperial boundaries in what we now call the Middle East is nothing new. Claims on this fertile and prosperous region that connects continents date back to Alexander the Great, 300 years B.C. As Peter Frankopan illuminates in *The Silk Roads: A New History of the World*, after Alexander's campaigns,

"The intellectual and theological spaces of the Silk Roads were crowded, as deities and cults, priests and local rulers jostled with each other. The stakes were high. This was a time when societies were highly receptive to explanations for everything from the mundane to the supernatural and when faith offered solutions to a multitude of problems. The struggles between different faiths were highly political. In all these religions -- whether they were Indic in origin like Hinduism, Jainism and Buddhism, or those with roots in Persia such as Zoroastrianism and Manichaeism, or those from further west such as Judaism and Christianity, and, in due course, Islam -- triumph on the battlefield or at the negotiating table went hand in hand with demonstrating cultural supremacy and divine benediction. The equation was as simple as it was powerful: a society protected and favoured by the right god, or gods, thrived; those promising false idols and empty promises suffered.

There were strong incentives, therefore, for rulers to invest in the proper spiritual infrastructure, such as the building of lavish places of worship. This offered a lever over internal control, allowing leaders to form a mutually strengthening relationship with the priesthood, who, across all the principal religions, wield substantial moral authority and political power. This did not mean that rulers were passive, responding to doctrines laid out by an independent class (or, in some cases, caste). On the contrary, determined rulers could reinforce their authority and dominance by introducing new religious practices.

An Un-Islamic Caliphate

Although Mustafa Kemal Ataturk officially put the kibosh on the caliphate in 1924 with the fall of the Ottoman Empire, its restoration has been an ongoing conversation among Muslim peoples searching for identity, security and self-determination in the wake of post-Word War I colonialism.

During the life of the prophet in Medina, Muslims lived in a community with Jews and Christians. Although there were tensions among them, each religious group was governed by its own scriptural civil and penal codes: worship and marriage, birth and death, theft and murder. Intrareligious disputes were often brought to Mohammed for arbitration. Medina was an oasis, an agricultural economy, and men and women both farmed the fields. Its large markets were renowned for produce, leather, woven baskets and blankets made and sold by women. The superintendent of the market under the second caliph, Umar, was a woman. There were schools and courts—women-owned property and inherited from their parents and husbands.

There were battles, mainly with the powerful families of Mecca bent on persecuting the nascent Muslim community that posed a threat to their pre-eminence and the profitability of their markets. The battles of Badr and Uhud mark triumph and defeat, respectively, that live in legend and allegory today. Raids on passing caravans supplemented the economy with goods and earned a reputation for fierceness. Perhaps it was not a perfect governance structure, but by and large, peace reigned in Medina until the prophet's death, at which time political rivalries began unravelling Muslim unity. Nevertheless, respect for people of other faiths, particularly within the Abrahamic tradition, remained.

Historically, the tremendous Muslim-administered civilizations contained populations that varied linguistically, culturally and religiously. From the Iberian Peninsula to the Malay Peninsula, from the outskirts of Vienna to the outlying islands of Indonesia, heterogeneity prevailed even if equality did not. Taxes were higher on non-Muslims in some economic structures in which only Muslims were allowed to enter into military service. (The taxes were considered payment for security.) Churches and synagogues welcomed worshippers on their prescribed days. People were buried in cemeteries according to local religious traditions and culture. In the Jewish cemeteries of Toledo, Spain, headstones facing Jerusalem are inscribed in Hebrew and Arabic. The Metropolitan Museum of Art's "Art of the Arab Lands, Turkey, Iran, Central Asia and Later South Asia" describes the multicultural nature of these societies: Artisans and craftspeople of different faiths made the windows, doors and sacred artefacts for great houses of worship, libraries and palaces across continents and centuries, as well as household objects and books, sacred and secular alike.

The caliphates and empires of Islam are rich in culture, gender equity (especially as compared with contemporary non-Muslim societies), literacy and the arts. They also fought with one another as furiously as they had fought the Crusaders. Safavids and Ottomans from the 16th to 19th centuries. Arabs and Turks during and after World War I. Syria's rebels and government today, as well as Libya's, along with the Islamic State and those it hopes to subjugate.

Muslims and non-Muslims, superpowers and small powers, powerbrokers and pawns alike must recognize that the extreme behaviours of politically motivated Muslims are not synonymous with Islamic values or the cultures of the caliphates.

What's happening today is tribal and political. It's about land, resources, trade routes and trading partners. It's about power, control of women, managing neighbouring states and creating a new status quo. The next time you read "revive," "restore," "Islamic" and "caliphate," remember: It's not about religion.

Allowance for alternate forms of worship, lifestyle and religious legislation is woven into Islamic scripture and jurisprudence. Where, then, did the horrific massacres of Muslims and people of other faiths in the Islamic State's so-called caliphate come from? The multiconfessional nature of Islamic civilization is something the Islamic State does not understand. Nor does it comprehend the broad range of social and cultural expressions that historically inhabit a caliphate. Therefore, it is essential to distinguish between calling for the restoration of a caliphate and the goals of the Islamic State.

The origin and history of the caliphate's empire.

Some Muslims hold that Muhammad had neither appointed a successor nor legislated how the community should be governed after his death, but that the *ijma* (consensus) of the community, which Prophet Muhammad said 'would not agree in error', decided on the caliphate. The caliph would lead the community but would have no privileged ability to interpret Islam. On the other hand, the caliphs were initially chosen for their purity and knowledge of Muhammad's *sunnah* (for example, sayings and acts), and their views would have carried weight. It is believed that the early caliphs used the title 'deputy of the Prophet of God' but that later they dropped 'the Prophet' and used only 'deputy of God.' Patricia Crone and Michael Cook (1997) argue that the caliphs saw themselves as ruling directly on behalf of God and that they did claim privileged authority. In fact, once *Shariah* had been codified, it took priority (in theory) over any rulings that a caliph or a political authority appointed or designated by the caliph, such as a Sultan, might decree. Effectively, jurisprudence or *fiqh* was the preserve of professionally trained religious scholars. At the same time, administration and politics (*siyasah*) were the preserve of the caliph (and of the sultans, who technically deputized for him). One must remember that no human ruling can override the word the Qur'an,

In practice, there has often been a struggle between these two distinct spheres of authority. Caliphs and sultans could issue decrees (*qanun,* or *kanun*) that, in their view, either dealt with matters not covered by the *Shariah* (which leaves certain areas to '*urf,* local custom) or which they said were necessary for the safety of the realm. Over time, two parallel legal systems emerged. One, the *Shariah* court system, presided over by religious scholars, dealt with matters related to religion, including marriage, divorce, and inheritance.

Some parallels have been drawn between the offices of the caliphate and the papacy, a position which, like that of the caliph, has embraced spiritual, political and military leadership at different times over the centuries and seen disputes over individual holders and the nature of the role itself. The two major traditions of Islam, Sunni and Shi'a, differ profoundly in the critical question of who the first Caliph of Islam should have been and the subsequent legitimacy of all later officeholders.

The Rightly Guided Caliphs

The bare outlines of the historical record suggest a very uncertain and contested beginning. At the death of the Prophet, there was no instruction from him and no agreement among his followers that there should be a succession at all. 'Umar and other Muslims persuaded a partial gathering of the community to accept Abu Bakr as caliph. Abu Bakr (632–34), the first of the Rashidun caliphs, was named *Amir al-mu'minin* (commander of the believers), a *shaykh* or chief who led the collectivity, arbitrated disputes, and followed the precedents set by Muhammad. His authority derived from tribal tradition, his connection to the Prophet, and the community's election of him. According to tradition, when assuming office, Abu Bakr said that he would obey the precedent (sunna) of the Prophet and that people should obey him as long as he obeyed it.

Umar ibn al-Khattab's Visits to Bayt al-Maqdis

The discussion regarding the reasons behind the arrival of Umar Ibn al-Khattab in Bayt al-Maqdis and his historic visit involves a number of issues. Such issues revolve around whether this visit was a special visit paid to Bayt al-Maqdis by Umar, whether his arrival into Syria from Madinah had been for reasons connected with Bayt al-Maqdis, or this visit took place for other reasons which had nothing to do with Bayt al-Maqdis. Furthermore, we may ask if this visit took place in order to meet certain conditions that were laid down by the inhabitants of Bayt al-Maqdis, which made it necessary for Umar to come to them. Such questions are, in turn, connected with many other issues, such as: what was the first place that Umar reached at the beginning of his visit and what were the tasks

that he carried out during this visit and other visits to the region, in the light of the classification of the stages of the Islamic conquest of Syria? In other words, what were the circumstances surrounding each of Umar's visits to Syria? Any researcher who tries to examine the reasons behind the arrival of Umar in Bayt al-Maqdis will face significant problems. This is because the Islamic sources significantly differ in identifying these reasons. They vary even with regard to the work Umar carried out while he was there. For instance, Islamic sources contain an enormous number of accounts narrated by narrators with different political affiliations and areas, as mentioned earlier. Although Islamic sources, or indeed most sources, arrive Umar personally in the walled part of Bayt al-Maqdis, a condition laid down by its inhabitants in return for their surrender, some other sources link the arrival of Umar in the region to military reasons explicitly required by the Palestinian front. He arrived after the Muslims asked for his help in dealing with the inhabitants of Palestine in general and Bayt al-Maqdis.

This brief study aims to examine historical accounts relating to Umar Ibn al-Khattab's visit to Bayt al-Maqdis by focusing on the reasons, aims and objectives. Multiple historical sources with diverse accounts have posed a challenge to modern researchers in determining the accuracy and validity of issues surrounding Umar's visit to Bayt al-Maqdis. Therefore, in this paper, the authors gather all the available reasons, compare them and try to link them with the surrounding situation. At the same time, the authors provide explanations of the reasons for the great contradictions among the Islamic sources and accounts. In addition, the reasons behind Umar's different visits to Syria and the work he carried out during each visit are reported and explained. Through the analysis of the early sources.

3. UMAR'S BIOGRAPHY

History bends to the will of man when driven by faith and steadfastness. Umar was one such extraordinary man. He bent history to his will, leaving a legacy that successor generations have looked upon as a model to copy. He was one of the greatest conquerors, a wise administrator, a just ruler, a monumental builder, and a man of piety who loved God with the same intensity that other conquerors of his calibre loved gold and wealth. The Prophet planted the seed of Tawhid. At its most elemental level, Tawhid means belief in one God. In its historical sense, it connotes a God-focused civilization, where the entire human effort focuses on seeking divine pleasure. Abu Bakr (r), with his wise intercession at a historic moment, ensured that the seed did not perish with the death of the Prophet.

Umar ibn al-Khattab was the second Rashidun caliph and ruled from 634 to 644. He was a senior companion and father-in-law of the Islamic prophet Muhammad. Umar's reign is known for its vast conquests, including the incorporation of present-day Iraq, Iran, Azerbaijan, Armenia, Georgia, Syria, Jordan, Palestine, Lebanon, Egypt, and parts of Afghanistan, Turkmenistan, and southwestern Pakistan into the Caliphate. It was during the Caliphate of Umar that the seed grew into a full-blown tree and bore fruit. Umar shaped the historical edifice of Islam, and whatever Islam became or did not become in subsequent centuries is primarily due to the work of this historical figure. Indeed, Umar (was the architect of Islamic civilization.

Regarded as the epitome of the just ruler, Umar (or Omar)—the second caliph—is one of the most significant figures in early Islamic history. His rule (634-44 CE) laid the foundations of an empire that has since defined, both culturally and geographically, the heartlands of the Islamic world. Shibli Numani's classic account links the military conquests of the period with Umar's reforms in law, government, and public administration. It describes Umar's strengths, skills, and character and evaluates his contribution to the ethos of Islam.

. Umar was born in Mecca around 581 to the Adi clan of the Quraish tribe. Umar belonged to an average-class family, but he was able to become literate and well-known for his physical strength, becoming a champion wrestler. When Muhammad first declared his message of Islam, Umar believed Islam was heretical rhetoric against the Quraish and his ancestors, and he resolved to kill Muhammad. He was stopped on his way to Muhammad's house. However, with news of his sister's conversion to Islam, Umar was initially calm but then became calm calmed.

Umar was part of the first emigration to Medina and became an essential companion of Muhammad. He participated in all of the Muslim battles against the Quraish. Upon the death of Muhammad, Umar was in such a state of despair that he threatened to decapitate anyone who said that Muhammad was dead.

Abu Bakr became the first successor to Muhammad. During Abu Bakr's short reign as caliph, Umar was a vital advisor to him, and Abu Bakr selected Umar as his successor prior to his death. Umar reigned as caliph from 633 until his assassination in 644. Umar's time as caliph saw the Islamic empire grow at an unprecedented rate, taking Iraq and parts of Iran from the Sassanids, thereby ending that empire, and taking Egypt, Palestine, Syria, North Africa and Armenia from the Byzantines. Umar also codified Islamic law and was known for his simple lifestyle and modest living. A famous story tells of him arriving in Jerusalem and walking beside his camel upon which his servant was sitting.

Umar was murdered in 644 by an enslaved Persian who had a personal quarrel with Umar. He stabbed the caliph six times as Umar led prayers in Masjid al Nabawi. Umar died two days later and was buried alongside Prophset Muhammad and Abu Bakr. Prior to dying, he appointed a council of six men to elect his successor from amongst themselves, choosing Uthman ibn Affan. Umar is broadly acclaimed for institutionalising most of the major political institutions of the Muslim state and stabilizing the rapidly expanding Arab empire.

Noble lineage

Umar came from an impeccable pagan stock. His father expelled his half-brother, Zayd (one of the four *hanif*), from Makkah many years earlier because of his apparent lack of respect for the old gods. The pedigree of Umar is Umar, the son of Khattab, the son of Tufail, the son of Abd al-Uzza, the son of Ribah, the son of Abdulla, the son of Qurat, the son of Zurah, the son of Adi, the son of Ka'b, the son of Lovayy, the son of Fahr, the son of Malik.

The people of Arabia are primarily descendants of Adnan or Qahtan and owe their origin to Ismail. Removed to the eleventh degree from Adnan, Fahr, the son of Malik, was a person of significant influence and power, and the famous tribe of Quraysh is his descendant. Ten individuals acquired great eminence among the Quraysh because of their strong capabilities and were the founders of several separate clans named after them. These were Hashim, Ommayya, Naufal Abd al-Dar, Asad, Taim, Makhzum, Adi, Jamah, and Samah. Umar is a descendant of Adi in the direct line. He was a prince among the Quraysh, a man who liked his wine as much as his hunting and was well educated.

Babyhood

Like Prophet Muhammad, Umar's rearing was by Bedouin foster parents. One example is when Umar rode through Dajnan in the desert east of Makkah, its familiar landscape. A memory of these distant childhood days among the Bedouin stirred in him. 'There was a time, he recalled to his Companions, 'when I roamed the desert as a camel herd, dressed in a fleece jacket, and whenever I sat down tired, my father would beat me. Now I live in a time when I need reckon none as my superior except God.'

It was the custom of all the great families of Arab towns to send their sons into the desert soon after their birth to be suckled and weaned and spend part of their childhood amongst one of the Bedouin tribes. It was not just the desert's fresh air that they wished their sons to imbibe. That was for their bodies, but the desert also had its bounty for souls. One learned self-discipline, nobility, and freedom in the desert. A vacation in the desert also offered an escape from the domination of time and the city's corruption.

Moreover, it provided the opportunity to become a better speaker through exposure to eloquent Arabic spoken by the Bedouin, which helped renew the bonds with the desert life for city dwellers of every generation. Like Prophet Muhammad, Umar also spent his babyhood in the Arab countryside.

One of the most striking facts about Arabian society was that the spoken language was kept in its purest form by the nomadic tribes. It is almost as if the lack of material objects and written forms kept the joy and vitality of the language at its most acute. It alone maintained the breathless virility and inventiveness. Nobility and freedom were inseparable, and the nomad was free. In the desert, a man was conscious of being the lord of space, and in virtue of that lordship, he escaped from the domination of time.

Early life

Umar was born in Mecca to the Banu Adi clan, which was responsible for arbitration among the tribes.[His father was Khattab ibn Nufayl and his mother was Hantama bint Hisham, from the tribe of Banu Makhzum. In his youth, he used to tend to his father's camels in the plains near Mecca. His merchant father was famed for his intelligence among his tribe. Umar himself said: "My father, al-Khattab, was a ruthless man. He used to make me work hard; if I didn't work, he used to beat me, and he used to work me to exhaustion.

Despite literacy being uncommon in pre-Islamic Arabia, Umar learned to read and write in his youth. Though not a poet himself, he developed a love for poetry and literature. According to the tradition of Quraish, while still in his teenage years, Umar learned martial arts, such as horse riding and wrestling. He was tall, physically powerful and a renowned wrestler. He was also a gifted orator who succeeded his father as an arbitrator among the tribes.

Umar became a merchant and made several journeys to Rome and Persia, where he is said to have met various scholars and analyzed Roman and Persian societies. As a merchant, he was unsuccessful. Like others around him, Umar was fond of drinking in his pre-Islamic days.

When Abu Bakr died, he was careful not to leave the same type of succession crisis as they had faced at the Prophet's death. He knew what he wanted to do. He named Umar his successor, and he became the caliph by virtue of being his successor. Umar (successor also got the additional title of Commander of the Faithful. He lived for another ten years, sometimes leading the armies himself and always living simply and according to strict Muslim law. He had his son publicly whipped for drunken behaviour, although the whipping wounded him to death. Ali ibn Abi Talib worked closely with Umar as his second-in-command, filling the power vacuum if Umar left Medina. Most of the news from Umar's reign is about the intense decade of conquest that began under Abu Bakr but really took off now.

Let's review Umar's biography. He had been an early Meccan convert to Islam but with a twist. When his sister began following the brand-new strange cult, he grew furious. He assaulted her. Then, when she shamed him, he set out to kill the Prophet. When he heard the soulful verses of the early Qur'an, he was overwhelmed and immediately converted. So, he was a very early convert and friend to the Prophet and clearly was Abu Bakr's closest companion as well. But Umar was a violent man. Stories about him always include his calling for someone's head to roll. He was in charge of forcing Ali to submit to Abu Bakr, so either he put his shoulder to Ali's door, injuring Fatimah, or he ordered one of his bodyguards to do it.

Umar had two wives in Mecca, but in Medina, he married a local woman to create alliances. He may have married or at least fathered children by several more, the total coming to as many as nine. But the most exciting story is about the wife he married around the time he succeeded Abu Bakr as Caliph.

Atiqah was a child in Mecca when Muhammad's revelations began, and her guardian was an early convert. She married a much older man who took her to Medina with the other Muslims, but they must have divorced, so she married Abu Bakr's son Abdullah next. Atiqah was a poet! She was renowned in the community for the poetry she recited; note that she did not need to be literate since all poetry was memorized, like the Qur'an. Abdullah ibn Abi Bakr doted on his wife, although she bore no children. They say Abu Bakr was angry because Abdullah listened to his wife too much, both in obeying her and in literally hanging around talking to her when he should have been out leading armies or collecting taxes. He tried to make Abdullah divorce her. But in the end, she remained Abdullah's wife. Abdullah doted on her so much that he made her promise not to remarry. He willed her a large property since she had no son to inherit.

When her husband died a year after Muhammad, she turned down several marriage offers. But Umar was a suitor who was not to be denied. He ordered her guardian to marry her to him. Then he argued with her until she finally gave in. A'isha sent her a bitter message asking for their family property back since Atiqah broke her vow. But Atiqah finally bore a child to Umar.

The remarrying cross-overs get dizzying. Umar also married a widow of the Battle of Ajnadayn: Umm Hakim, first wife of Ikrimah, a leading Meccan. But Ikrimah himself married two women who were almost the wives of Muhammad. They probably had been intended brides during his last year of life. One arrived just after his death, and they decided not to return her to her father—but the failure of the marriage alliance to the Prophet may have contributed to her clan's part in the Ridda Wars rebellion. Ikrimah may have been a big shot in Mecca, but the Prophet wasn't.

The other girl might have been the bride that A'isha boasted she got rid of because it's not clear how this Asma was (or wasn't) a wife of Muhammad. In that story, A'isha said she told this new bride that it would really turn Muhammad on if she pretended to be afraid and said to her new husband, "I take refuge from Thee in Allah!" The girl (Asma?) didn't realize this was a formula for divorce until Muhammad left the room. Whatever happened, now married and divorced without consummation, Asma was a logistical problem for the Muslims. She was married to another man first but ended up with Ikrimah. We don't know why Umar didn't choose to marry one of these Ikrimah widows, and I don't think we know what will happen to them next.

Abu Bakr left a widow, another Asma. She had been married to Ja'far, Ali's brother. After he died in the first doomed invasion of Syria, Abu Bakr married her. She bore him a son along the road to Mecca, the infant Muhammad. But now, in 634, she was a widow again. This time, *Ali* married her, so he became the stepfather to his brother's children and Abu Bakr's toddler. As if Muslim names were not confusing enough, eventually, the story will feature this Muhammad, son of Abu Bakr and technically A'isha's half-brother, but emotionally the son of Ali. He didn't have an easy life; he was a walking divided allegiance.

There's one more tangled marriage story, this time for Umar again. After he became the Caliph, he asked to marry Ali's daughter, who was known as Umm Kulthum. Shi'ites do not believe this marriage happened, and everyone agrees that Ali intended to marry his daughters to their cousins, Ja'far's sons. Sunni sources say Umar insisted, but one twist was the girl's age. It hadn't been many years since her mother, Fatimah, died, and the child was not yet the age of puberty. Sunni sources say Ali agreed to the match on Umar's promise that he would be the best husband ever and that Umm Kulthum lived as a queen in Medina, sending a gift of perfume at one time to the Empress in Constantinople. If this marriage did happen, it's another example of what ridiculous age gaps they were willing to accept, basing a marriage's value on rank and wealth, not on age suitability. Umar likely wanted a public sign of Ali's support to quell possible rebellions.

Umar's youth

'Umar was born into a respected Quraysh family thirteen years after the birth of Muhammad. In his youth, he used to tend to his father's camels in the plains near Makkah. His father was famed for his intelligence among his tribe. He was a middle-class merchant, a ruthless man, and an emotional polytheist who often mistreated Umar. During his later political rule, Umar would comment about his father, "My father Al-Khattab was a ruthless man. He used to make me work hard; if I didn't work, he beat me and worked me to exhaustion."

Umar's family was known for its extensive knowledge of genealogy. When he grew up, 'Umar was proficient in this branch of knowledge and swordsmanship, wrestling, and speaking. He also learned to read and write while still a child, a scarce thing in Makkah then. 'Umar earned his living as a merchant. His trade took him to many foreign lands, and he met many people. This experience gave him an insight into the affairs and problems of men. 'Umar's personality was dynamic, self-assertive, frank, and straightforward. He always spoke whatever was in his mind, even if it displeased others.

Umar was twenty-seven when the Prophet proclaimed his mission. The ideas Muhammad was preaching enraged him as much as they did the other notables of Makkah. He was just as bitter against anyone accepting Islam as others among the Quraysh. When his enslaved individual girl accepted Islam, he beat her until he was exhausted and told her, "I have stopped because I am tired, not out of pity for you." Later, after he had embraced Islam, he became the most ardent votary of the Prophet.

The transformation of Umar

When the enemies of Islam heard the name of Umar, their knees would tremble. When Satan saw Umar walking down the street, he would turn the other way. Even Umar's friends would sometimes find his presence intimidating, and they, too, feared his anger. However, this man of strength and power cried quickly and had a soft and compassionate heart. Umar was humble without being weak. Umar combined two opposing character traits, which made him unique among the men around Prophet Muhammad (peace be upon him). Umar's path to the truth began with a vehement hatred of Muhammad (peace be upon him) and the religion of Islam, but that hatred soon turned into a fierce love. Umar ibn Al Khattab strengthened Islam.

Umar belonged to a middle-class family, neither rich nor poor, of the Adi clan, which was part of the tribe of Quraish. He had a strict upbringing. His father was a harsh man who worked his son to exhaustion and beat him when he considered it necessary. Despite this, Umar was literate, which was an uncommon skill in pre-Islamic Arabia. Born approximately 11 years after Prophet Muhammad, Umar was a relatively fair-skinned boy who grew into a tall, well-built, muscular man known for his fierce demeanour and wrestling skills.

Umar began his working life as a shepherd for his father and aunts, and he got a minimal stipend, often only a handful of dates for a full day's work. He supplemented his income by engaging in wrestling competitions, but as he grew into manhood, he became a successful trader and respected businessman. Umar was known as a man of strength. His posture and bearing denoted strength, and his voice was loud and commanding. When Mohammad's teachings became a problem for the men of Makkah, Umar pronounced his hatred for Islam openly and took part in the abuse and torture of many of the weaker converts to Islam.

Turning point

A turning point in Umar's life was his interaction with his sister, Fatima bint Khattab. On his way to suppress people who had embraced Islam, he heard the news of his sister's reversion to Islam. Then, with the intention of punishing his sister and brother-in-law, Umar rushed to Fatima's house and started beating Fatima. Fatima was stern and adamant and uttered the *Kalimah* – I pledge that there is no God other than Allah, and Muhammad is the Messenger of Allah. Umar was a man of prudence and high thinking. His devotion was sincere. Once he believed something true, he acted for that. As an enemy of Islam, he worked for the Quraish, and as a follower of Islam, he worked for it.

In fact, the Prophet had prayed to Allah for the reversion of either Abu Jahl or Umar bin Khattab to Islam. Allah guided Umar to hold the torch of the Islamic faith.

Umar's miracle

History narrates that 'Umar objected to slaughtering the riding camels, saying: "How can we slaughter the camels and then fight the enemy on foot"? 'Umar's advice was it was as if a shroud *(ghiṭā')* covering the Prophet was lifted *(kashaya)*. After the miracle occurred, the Prophet uttered the two testimonies.

In this tradition, it is 'Umar who initiates the miracle and guides the Prophet, step by step, to perform it. It is as if 'Umar knew in advance that a miracle would occur and what its outcome would be. The Prophet only follows 'Umar's guidance without realizing his power to perform miracles. As a matter of fact, the miracle occurs out of 'Umar's sight. Moreover, by objecting to the slaughter of the camels 'Umar is represented as the only one who really cares for the ensuing battle, for without their mounts, the military strength of Muslim warriors' would be seriously damaged. 'Umar is an actual military commander who comprehends the different aspects of battle. In this 'Umar is obviously remembered as the leader under whose command the Islamic community achieved its most significant military expansion into Persia, Syria and Iraq. Another significant element in this tradition is the self-confidence that 'Umar's advice infuses into the Prophet's behaviour. 'Umar's words lifted a "shroud" that was covering the Prophet's judgment. This renewed self-confidence brings Muḥammad to reiterate the two testimonies.

Umar's role

The rule of Umar(ruled 634–644) had not so much to stimulate conquests as to organize and channel them. He chose as leaders skilful managers experienced in trade and commerce as well as warfare and imbued with an ideology that provided their activities with a cosmic significance. The total numbers involved in the initial conquests may have been relatively small, perhaps less than 50,000, divided into numerous shifting groups. Yet few actions took place without any sanction from the Medinan government or one of its appointed commanders. The fighters, or *muqātilah*, could generally accomplish much more with Medina's support than without. 'Umar, one of Muhammad's earliest and staunchest supporters, had quickly developed an administrative system of manifestly superior effectiveness. He defined the *ummah* as a continually expansive polity managed by a new ruling elite, which included successful military commanders like Khālid ibn al-Walīd. Even after the conquests ended, this sense of expansiveness continued in the way Muslims divided the world into their zone, the Dār al-Islām, and the zone into which they could and should expand, the Dār al-Ḥarb, the abode of war. The norms of 'Umar's new elite were supplied by Islam as was perceived by the prevalent times. Taken together, Muhammad's revelations from God and his Sunnah (precedent-setting example) defined the cultic and personal practices that distinguished Muslims from others: prayer, fasting, pilgrimage, charity, avoidance of pork and intoxicants, membership in one community centred at Mecca, and activism (jihad) on the community's behalf.

The Second Caliph 'Umar & Extending Civil Liberties to Non-Muslims

During 'Umar's caliphate, the dhimmis (religious minorities in the Islamic State) enjoyed complete religious freedom and civil liberties. They had the full right to practise their religious rituals and rights. They played their bugle, punctually held their socio-religious fairs, and carried the cross in procession. As for the issue of enforcing conversion to Islam, Caliph 'Umar and his administrators never adopted such policies, and they always maintained the Quranic principle that there is no compulsion in religion.

Not only did non-Muslims have the right to complete religious freedom, but they also enjoyed the right to equal citizenship. During the reign of 'Umar, Learning of this incident, 'Umar ordered the demolition of the mosque and restored the land to its original owner. A Lebanese Christian scholar, Professor Cardahi, wrote in 1933 that "this house (with the above piece of land) of the Jew, known as Bait al Yahudi, still exists and is well known".

One of the highlighting examples of tolerance and coexistence occurred during the reign of 'Umar when the city of Jerusalem was freed from the Roman forces. The Patriarch of Jerusalem refused to give the city's keys to anyone except the Caliph. Therefore, 'Umar travelled to Jerusalem and met the Patriarch at the gate, and they went together to visit the historical Church of Resurrection. When the time of prayer came, the Patriarch courteously requested that the Caliph offer his prayer in the church. 'Umar kindly declined his invitation and said, "If I do so, the Muslims may sometime in future infringe upon your rights by pretending to follow my example." Instead of praying inside the cathedral, he offered his prayers at its steps outside.

The atmosphere of coexistence was disseminated during the whole reign of 'Umar's caliphate, during which adherents to all religions enjoyed full and sedulous rights and protection. Non-Muslims continued to have their properties and land possessions, and a ban was imposed on Muslim citizens of the State with regard to the purchase of lands belonging to the dhimmis. Such policies were put into effect during the pact of Ileliyah in which Caliph 'Umar pledged the following,

"This is a peace granted by God's servant, Amir al-Muminin, 'Umar, to the people of Ileliyah extending to their life, property, churches, healthy, diseased and their co-religionists. Their churches will not be made into residential places, nor shall they be destroyed. Neither shall their territories be damaged, causing the loss. The number of their crosses and their assets will not be reduced, and they will not be asked to become Muslims..."

The interests of the non-Muslims were highly regarded in areas where Islam spread, such as in Syria, Mah Dinar, Jurjan, Azerbaijan, and Moqan. All non-Muslim subjects were assured of a pledge for the safety and security of their lives, properties, religion and customs. When Syria was conquered, 'Umar ordered Abu 'Ubaidah "to prevent Muslims from oppressing the dhimmis, from causing any loss to them, from dispossessing them without reason, and finally stick tenaciously to the fulfilment of the promises given to them."

In Homs, Muslims took the jizyah from the Christian and Jewish population in exchange for their protection from the Roman forces. To the surprise of Abu 'Ubaidah, the supreme commander, the Roman forces intensified their military forces, and the Muslim army had to retreat, as he was not going to be able to protect the city of Homs. Abu 'Ubaidah returned the tax money that the people of Homs paid due to their failure to keep their pact of security and safety intact. Such a generous act moved the people of Homs, and they pledged that they would protect their city and would not let the Romans conquer them in the hope that Muslims would return.

Another example is that of the Patriarch of Alexandria, who suffered severe persecution from the Romans in 20 A.H. The Muslim forces divested the Romans from their authority over Egypt and restored the fugitive Patriarch to his former post. It was during these days that one of the distinguished ecclesiastical heads remarked, "Today I witness in this city of Alexandria salvation and contentment reigning after a long period of persecution by the Roman rulers."

The second righteous caliph 'Umar bin al-Khattab, followed the leading example of the Prophet Muhammad and the Caliph Abu Bakr in dealing with religious minorities who resided within the boundaries of the Muslim state. If the credit for extending social security to non-Muslims was given to the first caliph, the second caliph went even a step further in developing both safety and prosperity of the lives of the non-Muslims living in the Muslim communities through setting fine examples of social behaviour and administrative attitudes toward religious minorities.

During 'Umar's reign, extreme leniency and liberality were shown to minorities even when they committed dangerous acts against the Islamic state. For example, the inhabitants of Arbasus, a town near the frontiers of Syria, agreed with the victorious Muslim army, which guaranteed peace and protection to them in exchange for their loyalty. While this pact was still intact, the Christian residents of Arbasus worked for the Romans, who were political opponents of the Muslims. The commander 'Umair bin Sa, consulted the Caliph on this issue of treason and 'Umar responded with the following, "The commander should ask the offenders to resettle elsewhere, offering them double cost for their flocks and property or that he should wait for one year to see if they change their conduct for the better." The final decision was to banish the dangerous elements of Arbasus from the Islamic state for dishonouring their agreement with the Muslims and for committing treason, an act which barred them from becoming citizens of the Islamic state.

In another incident, the governor of Yemen sent multiple complaints to the Caliph about the conspiracies of some minority groups and sought his direction. The governor suggested their banishment from the Islamic territory. Caliph 'Umar refused the governor's proposal of banishing the defaulters for fear that this action might adversely affect innocent families. Hence, he suggested instead that these groups should be resettled in some other part of the Islamic state. However, they were to be provided with better housing arrangements and compensation for their properties in cash. This group preferred to settle in Syria, and the government accepted their choice and gave them both lands and houses.

Caliph 'Umar integrated non-Muslims into his administration. In the famous history book titled "Al-Ansab", it was reported by al-Baladhuri that 'Umar wrote to his Syrian governor asking him to send a Greek who could adequately assess the accounts of the revenue department. Therefore, a Christian was appointed as the head of the accounts portfolio in the Prophet's city. The non-Muslim communities used to be consulted in economic, administrative, and military matters of the state, especially when they were directly pertinent to them. Non-Muslims also served in the Muslim armies, but they were not obligated to do so, and those who chose to do so were recruited on a voluntary basis.

'Umar introduced an equitable inaugurated economic system based on equal opportunity. The religious minorities were free to enter transactions, make agreements in business, spend and keep money and have a total share in commercial prosperity. No specific taxation was introduced to harass them. As for the jizyah, it was introduced as a taxation for maintaining protection and security in exchange for not being recruited into the Muslim army. The jizyah tax was not levied upon the needy, the oppressed, women, children, religious heads and the sick people of the non-Muslim communities. When it came to collecting tax revenues on land, revenues were collected leniently, and the terms of the agreement with the landlords were lenient.

It is a known fact that during the reign of Caliph 'Umar, poor Jews and Christians were maintained at the expense of the State and on the alms and donations collected from the Muslims. It is reported that 'Umar encountered an old Jewish man begging, so he gave him some money from the government treasury and directed the cashier to give him monthly financial support.

The spirit of love, compassion, and sympathy were significant elements of Islamic society among all different religious votaries. Abdullah ibn 'Umar, the son of the second Caliph, would not eat the meat of a goat slaughtered for him until he had sent some of it to his neighbours. The tradition of feeding one's neighbours was a common Prophetic tradition that was widespread among the companions.

When it came to war booty, Muslim soldiers were not despoilers and were not aiming at looting booties. 'Umar had always been very cautious when it came to war spoils and always warned the soldiers not to indulge in worldly gains. The famous speech of 'Umar that he delivered to a dispatched army shows the true essence of jihad,

"Do not show cowardice in an encounter. Do not mutilate when you have the power to do so. Do not commit excess when you triumph. Do not kill an older man, a woman or a minor, but try to avoid them at the time of the encounter of the two armies, at the time of the heat of victory and at the time of expected attacks. Do not cheat over booty. Purify jihad from worldly gains. Rejoice in the bargain of the contract that you have made with God, and that is the great success."

Muslim armies marched to war with a high sense of morality and ethical conduct, as they were commanded not to destroy lives and destroy properties. Landowners whose crops or produce were damaged due to the movement of the troops received ample compensation for what they had lost. At one time, the Caliph satisfied a tiller by giving him 10,000 dirhams from the State Treasury because the army had spoiled his harvest. Before the advent of Islamic conquests, non-Muslim populations suffered the brunt of Roman and Persian colonization of their lands.

Sir William Muir, the Scottish Orientalist, said, "The people of Syria, too, apart from the religious persecution to which they had been subjected, suffered from increased taxation, and in consequence remained passive spectators of the invasion of their country, hoping more, indeed, from an occupation by the Arabs, who abstained from pillage, and whose rule was mild and tolerant, than from the continuance of the status quo" (The Caliphate, p. 65).

To sum up the treatment of non-Muslims during the reign of 'Umar, we can honestly say that Islam, with its moral principles, introduced to the world a much-needed sense of justice, moderation and coexistence among world religions and predominantly minority religious groups within Muslim nations. Encouraging religious pluralism was a new phenomenon in ages whose annals were stained with episodes of religious persecution and where religious discord and strife were only suppressed with much bloodshed.

Islam brought a new dawn of civil liberties and religious freedom to all religious communities when it gained political prominence, which revolutionized conditions in the conquered countries.

"This is the safety given by a servant of God, the leader of the faithful, Umar ibn al Khattab, to the people of Ilia. This safety is for their life, property, church, and cross, for the healthy and the sick, and all their co-religionists. 1. Their churches shall neither be used as residences nor any harm done to them. 2. There shall be no decrease in their crosses or riches. 3. There shall neither be any compulsion in religion nor shall they be harmed."

The document speaks for itself. The Muslim armies were fighting for the freedom of worship, not for religious conversion. They considered it their mission on earth to free humankind from the yoke of exploitation and abuse. The conquered people were referred to as *dhimmis* (from the word *dhimana*, meaning trust or responsibility). They were part of a bond of trust and would not be harmed, as had happened time and again in history. Umar stayed for a few days in Flem and, after inspecting the army positions in Syria, returned to Medina. The Byzantines tried to regroup in Egypt and use it as a base to recover Syria. In 641, Umar (r) sent an expedition under Amr bin al-As to Alexandria. The Copts were neutral in this test of strength between the Byzantines and the Muslims. Alexandria fell, and the Muslim armies continued their advance as far as Tripoli in Libya.

Meanwhile, the eastern front with Persia was active. The Persians did not take lightly their losses in the border areas west of the Euphrates River. They reorganized, put their western defences under the famous Khorasani General Rustam and reinforced him with the services of two able officers, Narsi and Jaban. The withdrawal of Khalid bin Walid from the Iraqi front to Syria had weakened Muslim defences. So, Al Muthannah went to Medina and sought additional troops. Caliph Umar permitted him to raise a new army, allowing for the first time the recruitment of men from the Arab tribes that had at one time become apostates. Abu Obaid Saqafi was selected to lead this new army. Skirmishes started immediately between the opposing forces. Abu Obaid met the Persian officer Jaban at the Battle of Namaraq and defeated him. He followed it up with a victory over Narsi at the Battle of Maqatia. Undaunted, the Persian commander Rustam sent a new army under Mardan Shah and reinforced it with a hundred war elephants. The Arabs had no experience fighting elephant-mounted troops. In the ensuing battle, Abu Obaid was trampled under one of the elephants, and the Arab forces suffered severe setbacks across the Euphrates.

The War between the Muslim and Persian Empire

It was now evident that what had started as a border war had become a test of strength between the Muslims and the Persian Empire. Umar (r) called a meeting of all the Arab nobles for consultation and offered to personally lead a campaign to Persia. However, upon the advice of Ali ibn Abu Talib, the Caliph chose Sa'ad ibn Waqqas to lead an army of 20,000 towards Persia. Sa'ad ibn Waqqas was a Companion of the Prophet and a veteran of the Battle of Badr. Among those embarking on the mission were seventy Companions of the Prophet who had fought at the Battle of Badr. The inclusion of *Badri* Companions increased the enthusiasm of Muslims to a feverish pitch. Even some of the Christian tribes in the border areas offered to support the Muslim army. On the opposing side, the Persian General Rustam was at the head of 50,000 seasoned soldiers.

As directed by the Caliph, Sa'ad ibn Waqqas sent a peace mission to Rustam headed by Muthannah ibn Harith. Rustam, mindful of the motivation of the Arab soldiers, directed the Arab delegation to Emperor Yazdgard. The Persian Emperor received the Muslims with great pomp and offered to pay them a rich bounty, provided they returned to their homeland. In reply, Muthannah ibn Harith offered the Emperor three choices. One, accept submission to God, become a Muslim and a brother in faith. Two, take the protection of the Muslim state and pay *jizya*. Three, if the first two were unacceptable, face war. The Emperor was upset at these suggestions, told them he would have them killed were they not on a peace mission, and sent them back with a handful of dust from the Persian soil, admonishing that the Arabs would get no more than that pitiful amount of dust from Persia.

Umar's nomination

The responsibility of the successor went to the new caliph caliphs (literally substitutes), who were considered the prophet's heirs. Following the prophet's death in 632, great unrest stirred in the Islamic world. This period saw bloody warfare that brought about the murder of three of the first four caliphs.

Since Prophet Muhammad did not set rules for appointing his successors, four men who were considered the most righteous of Muslims, were close to the prophet and shared family ties with him were given this arduous task. These continued to rule as caliphs from Medina and were the Muslim people's spiritual, political and military leaders. The first caliph was Abu Bakr, a close friend of Muhammad and the father of `Aisha, the favourite of the prophet's nine wives. Abu Bakr wanted to ensure that no differences should divide Muslims after his death.

As his sickness grew, Abu Bakr seriously considered identifying his successor. After careful thought, he chose to nominate Umar. He put his proposal before the leading Companions. Most of them appreciated and endorsed the

During a fragmentary moment of dissent by weak opponents, Ali said he would acknowledge no other Caliph save Umar. Abu Bakr was very impressed with Ali's selflessness in not pressing his claim and for putting the interests of the Muslim community above personal interests. Turning to Ali, Abu Bakr said:

"You are indeed a prince in the most exalted sense of the term, for others are mere men."

On 22 August, Caliph Abu Bakr died. On the same day, Umar assumed the office of the caliphate. After taking office as the Caliph, Umar I (ruled 634–644) addressed the Muslims in his Inaugural address:" O ye faithful! Abu Bakr is no more amongst us. He is satisfied that he has successfully piloted the ship of the Muslim state to safety after negotiating the stormy sea. He successfully waged the apostasy wars, and thanks to him, Islam is now supreme in Arabia. After Abu Bakr, the mantle of the caliphate has fallen on my shoulders. I swear before God that I never coveted this office. I wished that it would have devolved into some other person more worthy than me. But now that in the national interest, the responsibility for leading the Muslims has come to vest in me, I assure you that I will not run away from my post and will make an earnest effort to discharge the onerous duties of the office to the best of my capacity by the injunctions of Islam. Allah has examined me from you and you from me. In performing my duties, I will seek guidance from the Holy Book and follow the examples the Holy Prophet and Abu Bakr set. I seek your assistance with this task. If I follow the right path, follow me. Correct me if I deviate from the right direction so we do not go astray."

Umar believed that the actual traits of a great leader must be that he is firm but not overbearing; he is soft but not weak; he is generous but not extravagant, and he is thrifty but not miserly. Umar was humble without being weak. He combined two contrasting character traits, making him unique among the men around Prophet Muhammad.

Umar initially opposed Muhammad, his distant Qurayshite relative and later son-in-law. Following his conversion to Islam in 616, he became the first Muslim to pray at the Kaaba openly. Umar participated in almost all battles and expeditions under Muhammad, who bestowed the title *al-Fārūq* upon him for his judgements. After Muhammad's death in June 632, Umar pledged allegiance to Abu Bakr (r. 632–634) as the first caliph. He served as the closest adviser to the latter until August 634, when the dying Abu Bakr nominated Umar as his successor.

The two Umars

Although not known by his given name of Umar, there was another strong, determined man opposed to Islam. This man was initially known as Abu Hakim (the father of wisdom), but history remembers him as

Abu Jahl (the father of ignorance), the avowed enemy of Islam. Prophet Muhammad (may the mercy and blessings of God be upon him) gave him the name Abu Jahl to denote his total ignorance in not recognizing the truth of Islam. Traditional accounts reveal that Prophet Muhammad, on one occasion, raised his hands in supplication and begged God to strengthen Islam by whomever of the two Umars he loved most. To the enemies of Islam and the companions of Prophet Muhammad Umar ibn Al-Khattab, embracing Islam was an unthinkable notion.

Umar's hatred of Islam was so intense that he volunteered to kill Prophet Muhammad. Without a second's hesitation, he strode down the streets of Makkah, intent on drawing his sword and ending the life of the Prophet of God. One of the men of Makkah, who was secretly a Muslim, saw the look on Umar's face and immediately knew that his beloved Prophet was in danger. Without fear for himself, he approached Umar and asked him where he was going so quickly. Umar replied that he was going "to the man who has disunited our people, cursed our gods and made fools of us", and he said, "I am going to kill him".

The young Muslim man named Nu'aim felt terror rush into his heart and tried to engage Umar in a discussion to divert him, but Umar was intent on his mission and continued to stride along the street. Nu'aim reluctantly spoke the words that led Umar to Islam. He said, "Why don't you take care of your own house first." Umar stopped short and asked him what he meant by those words. Umar's beloved sister and her husband had secretly embraced Islam, and Nu'aim revealed their secret in order to save the life of Prophet Muhammad.

Umar turned around immediately and walked with determination toward his sister's house. As he approached, he could hear the sound of the Qur'an being recited. Umar knocked on the door. Inside, the inhabitants scrambled to hide their copies of the Qur'an, but Umar entered and demanded to know what the "humming" sound he had heard was. Umar's sister replied that it was nothing, just the sound of them talking, but Umar knew the sound of the Qur'an and asked menacingly, "Have you become Muslim?" Umar's brother-in-law answered in the affirmative, saying that Umar had fallen upon him and wrestled him to the ground. Umar's sister tried to defend her husband, and in the scuffle, Umar hit her face, drawing blood.

Umar's sister seemed to have the strength her brother was so famous for. She stood up and faced her angry brother, saying, "You enemy of God! You would hit me just because I believe in God. Whether you like it or not, I testify that there is no god but Allah and that Muhammad is His slave and messenger. Do whatever you will!" Umar saw the blood running down his sister's face; her words echoed in his ears, and he stood up. Umar demanded that the words of the Qur'an he had heard as he approached the house be recited again for him.

"We have not sent down the Qur'an unto you (O Muhammad) to cause you distress, but only as a reminder to those who fear (God)—a revelation from Him who has created the earth and high heavens. The Most Beneficent rose over the (Mighty) Throne (in a manner that suits His Majesty). To Him belongs all that is in the heavens and all that is on the earth, and all that is between them, and all that is under the soil. And if you (O Muhammad) speak aloud, then certainly, He knows the secret and that which is yet more hidden. No one has the right to b override the Qur'an! To Him belong the Best Names." (Qur'an 20:2-8)

Umar ibn Al Khattab was a strong and assertive man. His heart filled with burning hatred for Islam. The supplications of Prophet Muhammad (may the mercy and blessings of God be upon him) and the sublime beauty of the Qur'an changed his mind, his heart, and his life. When Umar accepted Islam, he became a man devoted to the Ummah of Muhammad. As a Muslim, he was pleased when the Ummah was pleased and displeased when the Ummah was displeased.

Ummah is an Arabic word, roughly translated to mean nation, but as with many Arabic words, it does not translate well into English.

In English-speaking and Western countries, the word nation usually defines the nation-state, whose members live between a set of predefined borders often set by religious, racial or ethnic differences. This is not the definition of Ummah. Ummah means the community of believers bound together with a purpose — to worship God. Together, they are strong. Divided, they are weak. Each member is united with all of the others in a spiritual way that can even have physical manifestations. When one part of the Ummah is in pain, the whole Ummah hurts. (A Hadith)

"And verily this Ummah of yours is One Ummah, and I am your Lord and Cherisher: therefore fear Me (and no other)." (Quran 23:52)

When Umar ibn Al Khattab accepted Islam, he wanted to be part of his community and wanted to proclaim his membership of this unique nation. Umar wanted to join the Ummah in their happiness and their pain. At the time of his conversion, the weaker members of the Ummah suffered systematic abuse and oppression, often by Umar himself, but his heart now felt their pain, and he wanted to experience it. Umar did not want his Islam to go unnoticed; he immediately informed the enemies of Islam that he was Muslim.

At first, the men of Makkah who had not embraced Islam were shocked and did not react to Umar's conversion, but as word spread, they came together at the House of God and attacked Umar. Eventually, Umar, the robust and muscular wrestler, sat in the midst of his attackers, and they beat him. Umar recovered from his beating, and because of him, Islam became strong. The heart of Umarr overflowed with love for his brothers and sisters in Islam.

Abu Bakr Siddiq and Umar were the two closest companions to Prophet Muhammad (peace be upon him). Ali Ibn Abu Talib said that Prophet Muhammad went out in the morning with Abu Bakr and Umar, and he would return at night with Abu Bakr and Umar. The Prophet himself called Abu Bakr and Umar his eyes and ears and said they were his advisers from the inhabitants of the earth. Umar stood beside

Prophet Muhammad in all of the trials and tribulations that faced the Muslim Ummah.

When the Muslims of Makkah migrated to the city of Madinah, they were all left in a well-planned, secret migration, but not Umar. He was the only Muslim to make the migration openly. In fact, he proclaimed that he was leaving and invited any man who thought he was strong enough to challenge him. Umar flung his sword around his neck and strode through the streets of Makkah with his head held high and his heart, which was no longer filled with hate, burning with a fierce love for God, His Prophet Muhammad and his fellow believers.

Although remembered for his strength, Umar was also known to be a pious and generous man. He would spend the nights in worship, often waking his family in the last part of the night to join him in his devotions. He was a staunch believer, confident in God's promise of Paradise, and he readily spent his wealth for the sake of God and to benefit the believers. One of Prophet Muhammad's companions narrates that Umar once distributed 22,000 dirhams to people in need and had a habit of giving away bags of sugar. When Umar was asked about it, he said, "Because I love it, and God said in the Qur'an, "By no means shall you attain piety, unless you spend (in God's Cause) of that which you love; and whatever of good you spend, God knows it well." (Qur'an 3:92)

Umar was one of ten men to whom Prophet Muhammad gave the joyous news that they would be admitted to Paradise. However, this did not stop him from working tirelessly all of his life to please God. He was a man of knowledge, a man known for his generosity and tireless devotion to the worship of God, and perhaps above all, he was devoted to the Ummah of Prophett Muhammad. Prophet Muhammad counselled us all when he said, "A man is not a true believer until he loves for his brother what he loves for himself." Umar wanted paradise, but he also wanted it for every man, woman, or child who believed that there was no god but God and that Muhammad was His messenger. This was Umar, who distinguished truth from falsehood; he was a man of the Ummah. Umar's eyes filled with hot tears. "Is this what we were against?" he asked. "The One who has spoken these words needs to be worshipped." Umar left his sister's house and rushed to Muhammad. Those with Prophet Muhammad were afraid, but they admitted Umar and restrained him until he was in Muhammad's presence. Prophet Muhammad grabbed him and said, "Why did you come here, son of Khattab?"

Umar faced Prophet Muhammad with humility and joy and said, "O Messenger of God, I have come for no reason except to say I believe in God and his Messenger." Prophet Muhammad became overjoyed and cried out that God was Great! Within days, Umar led a procession of Muslims to the House of God, where they prayed openly. It was on this occasion that Prophet Muhammad gave him the nickname Al Farooq. It denotes one who is able to distinguish truth from falsehood. Islam became stronger with Umar. His fierce hatred melted into a love that knew no bounds. His life and his death were now for the sake of God and his Messenger.

The challenges for Umar

Upon his election to the Caliphate, Umar faced the immediate geopolitical situation in West Asia. The Arabian Peninsula is a vast desert, except for its southwestern tip near Najran and Yemen, where the monsoons bring in rain from the Indian Ocean and make the area fertile. To the north, the desert is closed by the Jordan River, which separates it from the hills of Palestine and Lebanon. To the east, its boundaries are closed by the Euphrates. The area between the Rivers Euphrates and Tigris is called the Jazira (island). This area, known in ancient times as Mesopotamia, was called *Iraq and Arab* in the early Islamic period. The waters of the two rivers irrigate this area and have made it the cradle of civilizations. East of the River Tigris, the land gradually rises into the Persian Plateau, leading into the heartland of ancient Fars. The Arabs called this area *Iraq e Ajam*, and it included the Farsi (Persian) speaking areas of Khuzistan, Hamadan, Fars, Persepolis, Isfahan, Azerbaijan, Khorasan, Makran and Baluchistan.

Umar was the first Muslim leader to expand the Islamic empire to non-Arabian regions; during his reign as caliph, he helped to conquer Mesopotamia and some of Persia from the Sassanids and took Syria, Egypt, Palestine, Armenia and North Africa from the Byzantine Empire. Umar's conquest of Jerusalem was famously peaceful, leaving intact the Christian holy sites and permitting Jews to reenter the city and settle near the Western Wall. It was an event that signified the dramatic shift of Jerusalem from a Christian-dominated city to a part of the Islamic empire. Umar's cleared the Temple Mount to build a rough-hewn wooden mosque on the spot, a precursor to Al Aqsa Mosque. The reign of Umar ended abruptly in 644 A.D. when a Persian prisoner of war assassinated him, and wars of succession frayed the close-knit fabric of the empire. But in spite of the chaos that ensued after Umar's death, Muslim sovereignty in Jerusalem was to flourish for centuries to come.

The Persian and Byzantine empires held the balance of power in the region, with the Euphrates River as the historical divide between their respective areas of influence. Persia also controlled Yemen and the territories along the Red Sea, north of Mecca and Medina. The emergence of Islam and the unification of the Arabs altered this balance of power. It was a situation that neither the Byzantines nor the Persians could ignore. Khosroe, the emperor of Persia, was on record as having ordered an assault on Medina. The Byzantines had attacked on the northern frontier and had killed the Muslim general Zaid bin Haris (632). Border clashes had begun during the Caliphate of Abu Bakr between the newborn Islamic state and the two superpowers. The triumph of Umar over the mighty empires of Persia and Byzantium within a brief span of ten years is one of the most remarkable stories in military history.

The expansive Muslim empire had a sense of mission taught by Islam. It was a matter of faith, Which dictated that humankind is born into freedom and is accountable only to the transcendence of God. Islamic civilization is God-centered, and its mission is to establish divine patterns on this earth. From this perspective, any social or political system that imposes subservience to a despotic ruler or an oppressive empire detracts from this transcendence and needs a decisive confrontation and challenge.

When Umar became the Caliph, the campaigns in Syria were ongoing. The Battle of Yarmuk (636) broke the resistance of the Byzantines, but Palestine was not yet subdued. Umar commanded Amr bin al-As to proceed from Yarmuk to Jerusalem. Since resistance was hopeless, the Patriarch of Jerusalem offered the keys to the city provided the Caliph himself came up to accept them. When the Caliph heard of this, he appointed Ali ibn Abu Talib (r) as the acting Caliph and set out north from Medina. Umar ibn al Khattab was now the Caliph of all of Arabia and surrounding territories. He could have travelled as a conqueror in pomp and luxury. But he, like the other Companions, had received his training from the Prophet Muhammed (p). Theirs was the kingdom of heaven and not of this earth. They held the key to the treasures of the world but only as a Divine Trust as servants of the Lord.

Equity in Umar's policies

Equity in Umar's policies, public treasury (Baitul mal), Army bureau, department of Records (Diwan), and Hisba were all initiated during his time, which led to signifying recruitment. This comprehensive paper explores the subject of recruitment and selection during the reign of Umar ibn Khattab, the second caliph of the Rashidun Caliphate. The reign of Umar bin Khattab from 634 to 644 AD saw notable progress in administrative structures, such as the implementation of a well-organized recruiting and selection procedure.

It is most of an issue for utilizing reputable print encyclopedias, nonfiction books, academic journals, and dictionaries. This study offers a comprehensive examination of the historical backdrop, selection criteria, and the influence of Umar bin Khattab's approach on the governance of the caliphate. The method used in this research is a descriptive approach. The recruitment policy and its processes are arrived at through three ways: gh, the collection of data from secondary sources; The study found that his employment of experts, regardless of closeness or any other factor, was the main characteristic of the era, and recruiting policies and procedures can be used to establish an Islamic recruitment policy and structure.

The Era of Umar Ibnul Khattab is considered the golden age in the history of Islam. The public treasury *(Baitul mal)*, Army bureau, department of Records (*Diwan*), and Hisba were all initiated during his time, which led to signifying recruitment. This comprehensive paper explores the subject of recruitment and selection during the reign of Umar ibn Khattab, the second caliph of the Rashidun Caliphate. The reign of Umar bin Khattab from 634 to 644 AD saw notable progress in administrative structures, such as the implementation of a well-organized recruiting and selection procedure. This study examines the strategies used by Umar bin Khattab to find and choose persons for essential roles within the Islamic state. We can utilise reputable print encyclopedias, nonfiction books, academic journals, and dictionaries. This study offers a comprehensive examination of the historical backdrop, selection criteria, and the influence of Umar bin Khattab's approach on the governance of the caliphate. The method used in this research is a descriptive approach; the recruitment policy and its process and data collected from secondary sources have yielded productive results. The study found that his employment of experts, regardless of closeness or any other factor, was the main characteristic of his era. His recruiting practices establish an Islamic recruitment policy and structure.

The Politics of Islamic Education in The Caliphate of Umar Ibn Khattab

This study aims to reveal the political system of education in the reign of the second caliph, Umar ibn Khattab. The method used in this study is qualitative research with a literature study. The process of data collection was conducted through documentation and observation techniques so that the available literature sources were then studied, compared, and presented in words by the researcher. The results of the study are that political policies in the early period of Islam helped determine the development and progress of education in the area of the central government to the conquered regions, such as al-Quds (Palestine), Sham, Sassanid (Persia), Egypt and others. The system is accessible with appropriate educators (teachers and lecturers), the emergence of a bilingual learning method, the periodic payment of teacher salaries, and the tiered education system, starting from the basic to the madrasah level. Furthermore, it was noticeable that since the reign of Umar ibn Khattab, Islamic education has been widely accessible to society regardless of race, social status, or economic status.

A study of Umar bin Kharab's Ijtihad in an effort to formulate Islamic law reform

These laws include the collection of zakat, which is a type of charitable giving, and the distribution of this money to those who are in need. 8 Another significant effect is the ideology of stewardship or Khilafa. The Khulafa-e-Rashideen promulgated that. According to this school of thought theorized by Al Sehlawi, leaders should act as protectors and caretakers of the people they govern. This study examines Umar bin Khatab's Ijtihad in an effort to formulate Islamic law reform. Umar is known as the Imam Al-Mujtahidin and is also a brilliant contributor to the development of Islamic law. Modern Islamic intellectuals widely adopt a visionary approach to finding new legal rulings whose values are in accordance with present times. Even today, Umar's Ijtihad practices are a source of inspiration for the development of Islamic law. He dared to take policies that were no longer in accordance with the literal understanding of the verses of the Qur'an or the Sunnah. This research method is qualitative and is commonly called library research. Library research examines data by exploring, observing, analysing, and identifying existing knowledge in the literature to obtain a dependable conclusion, both philosophical and empirical. This study concludes that, in principle, Umar bin Khattab's Ijtihad continues to hold the Qur'an and Hadith as sources of Islamic law. However, his views are not technically the same as the textual provisions of the texts, which practical fiqh scholars judge as qath'iy texts, such as not giving the right to receive zakat to converts, not cutting off the hands of thieves, not taking spoils of war (Khaimah), as well as adding caning punishment for alcohol drinkers. What Umar bin Khattab did in some of these cases did not mean he was against the law t set by the Prophet Muhammad SAW and other companions; however, it was to achieve a law that will be able to fulfil Al-Mashlahah which is Maqashid Al-Shari'ah or the goal of Shari'ah, specifically preserving human mind, achievement of benefit and prevention of harm.

The Politics of Islamic Education in The Caliphate of Umar Ibn Khattab

We must understand the political system of education in the reign of the second caliph, Umar ibn Khattab. The process of data collection was conducted through documentation and observation techniques so that the available literature sources were then studied, compared, and presented in words by the researcher. The results of the study are that political policies in the early period of Islam helped determine the development and progress of education in the area of the central government to the conquered regions, such as al-Quds (Palestine), Sham, Sassanid (Persia), Egypt and others. The system can be grasped by the application of educators (teachers and lecturers), the emergence of a bilingual learning method, the periodic payment of teacher salaries, and the tiered education system, which starts from the basic to the madrasah level. Furthermore, it was noticeable that since the reign of Umar ibn Khattab, Islamic education has been widely accessible to all sections of society regardless of race, social and economic status.

4. UMARS'S TRYST WITH JERUSALEM

Capture of Jerusalem

Jerusalem (al-Quds in Arabic) represents the heart of three world religions: a holy place for Islam, Judaism and Christianity, yet it is also a dangerous flashpoint to one of the world's most intractable conflicts, the Palestine-Israel issue.

Jerusalem is Islam's third holiest site and home to the al-Aqsa mosque (Muslims worldwide faced this mosque in prayer before the direction was changed to the mosque in Makka).

It also holds the Dome of the Rock, where the Prophet Muhammad ascended on his night journey to heaven. The al-Haram al-Sharif, or the Noble Sanctuary as it is also called, is held by Jews and Muslims alike to be the place where the Prophet Ibrahim was prevented from sacrificing his son Ismail (or Isaac to Christians and Jews) by God's intervention.

But for many people throughout history, Jerusalem has been a prized possession and much fought over. Archaeological work in the area suggests that the city was inhabited as far back as 4000 BC. Its earliest known name may be Jebusite, the translation of a Canaanite town. Together with the later-arriving Philistines, they are the earliest known ancestors of present-day Palestinians.

"Philistinians" settled along the stretch of the Mediterranean coast that extended approximately from Jaffa to the Gaza Strip and was within the land of Canaan for many centuries. Having left such an indelible mark, the land of Philistia, or Palestine as it became known, has remained to this day.

David invades

In 1000 BC, the Israelite king, David, invaded Jerusalem and walled and fortified the city against further invasion. Later, when King Solomon built the temple, Jerusalem became a spiritual capital, first for the Jews and later for Christians and Muslims.

In 586 BC, it fell to the Babylonians, and their Nebuchadnezza destroyed them, but later himself it. They rebuilt it. Alexander the Great also captured the whole of Palestine in 332 BC, and in the subsequent years, the Egyptian Ptolmies and Syrian Seleucids ruled Jerusalem.

Towards the approach of the 1st century, the city was the ruling capital of the Maccabean empire of Simon Maccabee before giving way to the long rule of the Romans. During the Roman era, the town of Bethlehem near Jerusalem witnessed the birth of Jesus Christ, a prophet in Islam and, in the Christian belief, the son of God.

Jerusalem is a spiritual capital for Jews, Christians, and Muslims who preached the importance of worshipping one God in the towns of Nazareth and Galilee, where he lived. He was tried in Jerusalem by the Roman official Pontius for his misdeed sof of a rebel and false prophet.

The sentence he received was death, and Christians believe he was then crucified. This act became the central pillar of Christianity, and the place of his (alleged) crucifixion in Jerusalem became the holiest site in Christendom. His followers flocked to the site on pilgrimage, and a church, the Church of the Holy Sepulchre, was built around it. Biblical Palestine became a holy land for Christians.

After the Romans conquered Jerusalem, it became the capital of the Herod dynasty, which ruled under the direction of Rome. In AD70, the Roman emperor Titus destroyed the Temple to punish and discourage the Jews who had rebelled against his rule.

In 135, the Roman emperor Hadrian rebuilt the city, giving it new walls and officially naming the land Palestine while renaming Jerusalem as Aelia Capitolina in honour of his pagan God, Jupiter. From 313, with the widespread acceptance of Christianity by Rome, Jerusalem underwent a revival, greatly aided by St Helena (wife of Emperor Constantine), who sponsored much re-building of the city in the early 4th century. It became a centre for Christian pilgrimage.

By 638, with the rapid spread of a new religion in the region, Islam, the city was captured by an army led by Abu Ubaydah under the caliphate of Umar ibn al-Khattab, and Islam came to Palestine.

Ever since the time of Muhammad, Muslims have considered Jerusalem to be an essential place for pilgrimage after Makka due to its religious significance as the place of the prophet's miraculous journey to heaven.

Between 688 and 691, the Dome of the Rock mosque was constructed by al-Walid ibn Abd al-Malik. Two years later, the al-Aqsa mosque was built on the same site, commemorating the place of the prophet's prostrations. The two mosques and their surroundings became known as al-Haram al-Sharif, and they became the third holiest site for Muslims.

By the 11th century, Islam had been in the region for more than 500 years. The city gained a worldwide reputation as a city of the three faiths. But with the Fatimids in power, their empire fighting Christian expansionism, the rulers began to restrict the flow of Christian pilgrims. The Fatimid ruler al-Hakim destroyed the Church of the Holy Sepulchre (later rebuilt) in response to an uprising. This act contributed to the onslaught brought by the coming Crusaders.

In AD1095, Pope Urban II preached for a crusade against Muslims in Palestine. Those who will fight, he said, are promised heavenly redemption for their sins and booty for what they capture or conquer.

In 1099, Jerusalem was conquered by the Crusaders and its inhabitants were slaughtered (Muslims, Christians and Jews alike). For much of the 12th century, it became the capital of the Latin Kingdom of Jerusalem.

In 1187, under the leadership of Salah al-Din, Muslims recaptured the city, and, much to the relief of the Christian inhabitants, there was no revenge killing. Those who wanted to leave were permitted to do so, with all their goods and belongings, and those who wanted to stay were guaranteed protection for their lives, property, and places of worship. Before he departed to reconquer Muslim lands, Salah al-Din appointed Diya al-Din Isa al-Hakkari as governor and protector of the city.

After that, under Mamluk and then Ottoman rule, Jerusalem was rebuilt and restored, mainly by Sulayman II (also known as Sulayman the Magnificent), building walls, gates, towers, and aqueducts for the city.

His most notable work is the beautiful tile work commissioned for the exterior of the Dome of the Rock. With the incomparable skills of Persian master ceramicists, 40,000 tiles were fired and put into place, crowned by the inscription of verses from the Quran. They remain to this day.

By 637, Muslim armies began to appear in the vicinity of Jerusalem. In charge of Jerusalem was Patriarch Sophronius, a representative of the Byzantine government, as well as a leader in the Christian Church. Although numerous Muslim armies under the command of Khalid ibn al-Walid and Amr ibn al-'As began to surround the city, Sophronius refused to surrender the city unless Umar came to accept the surrender himself.

Having heard of such a condition, Umar ibn al-Khattab left Madinah, travelling alone with one donkey and one servant. When he arrived in Jerusalem, he was greeted by Sophronius, who undoubtedly must have been amazed that the caliph of the Muslims, one of the most influential people in the world at that point, was dressed in no more than simple robes and was indistinguishable from his servant.

Umar was given a tour of the city, including the Church of the Holy Sepulchre. When the time for prayer came, Sophronius invited Umar to pray inside the Church, but Umar refused. He insisted that if he prayed there, later Muslims would use it as an excuse to convert it into a mosque – thereby depriving Christendom of one of its holiest sites. Instead, Umar prayed outside the Church, where a mosque (called Masjid Umar – the Mosque of Umar) was later built.

Capture of Jerusalem

Jerusalem is a city holy to the three largest monotheistic faiths – Islam, Judaism, and Christianity. Because of its history that spans thousands of years, it goes by many names: Jerusalem, al-Quds, Yerushaláyim, Aelia, and more, all reflecting its diverse heritage. It is a city that numerous Muslim prophets called home, from Sulayman and Dawood to Isa (Jesus). May Allah be pleased with them.

During the Prophet Muhammad's life, he made a miraculous journey in one night from Makkah to Jerusalem and then from Jerusalem to Heaven – the Isra' and Mi'raj. During his life, however, Jerusalem never came under Muslim political control. That would change during the caliphate of Umar ibn al-Khattab, the second caliph of Islam.

The Treaty of Umar

As they did with all other cities they conquered, the Muslims had to write up a treaty detailing the rights and privileges of the conquered people and the Muslims in Jerusalem. This treaty was signed by Umar and Patriarch Sophronius, along with some of the generals of the Muslim armies. The text of the treaty read:

The divine pledge we take to God in these words:;' In the name of God, the Merciful, the Compassionate. ; is the assurance of safety which the servant of God, Umar, the Commander of the Faithful, has given to the people of Jerusalem. He has assured them of safety for themselves, their property, their churches, their crosses, the sick and healthy of the city, and all the rituals that belong to their religion. Muslims will not inhabit their churches and will not be destroyed. Neither they, nor the land on which they stand, nor their cross, nor their property will be damaged or reconverted. No Jew will live with them in Jerusalem.

The people of Jerusalem must pay taxes like the people of other cities and must expel the Byzantines and the robbers. Those of the people of Jerusalem who want to leave with the Byzantines, take their property and abandon their churches and crosses will be safe until they reach their place of refuge. The villagers may remain in the city if they wish but must pay taxes like the citizens. Those who wish may go with the Byzantines, and those who wish may return to their families. Nothing is to be taken from them before their harvest is reaped.

If they pay their taxes according to their obligations, then the conditions laid out in this letter are under the covenant of God and are the responsibility of His Prophet, the caliphs and the faithful.

– Quoted in *The Great Arab Conquests,* from *Tarikh Tabari*

At the time, this was by far one of the most progressive treaties in history. For comparison, just 23 years earlier, when Jerusalem was surrendered by the Persians from the Byzantines, a general massacre was ordered. Another massacre ensued when Jerusalem was conquered by the Crusaders from the Muslims in 1099.

The Treaty of Umar allowed the Christians of Jerusalem religious freedom, as dictated in the Qur'an and the sayings of Muhammad ﷺ. This was one of the first and most significant guarantees of religious freedom in history. While there is a clause in the treaty regarding the banning of Jews from Jerusalem, its authenticity is debated. One of Umar's guides in Jerusalem was a Jew named Kaab al-Ahbar. Umar further allowed Jews to worship on the Temple Mount and the Wailing Wall, while the Byzantines banned them from such activities. Thus, the authenticity of the clause regarding Jews is in question.

What is not in question, however, is the significance of such a progressive and equitable surrender treaty, which protected minority rights. The treaty became the standard for Muslim-Christian relations throughout the former Byzantine Empire, with the rights of conquered people being protected in all situations and forced conversions never being a sanctioned act.

Revitalization of the City

Umar immediately set about making the city a critical Muslim landmark. He cleared the area of the Temple Mount, where Muhammad ﷺ ascended to heaven. The Christians had used the area as a garbage dump to offend the Jews, and Umar and his army (along with some Jews) personally cleaned it and built a mosque – Masjid al-Aqsa – there.

Throughout the remainder of Umar's caliphate and into the Umayyad Empire's reign over the city, Jerusalem became a major centre of religious pilgrimage and trade. The Dome of the Rock was supplemented to complement Masjid al-Aqsa in 691. Several mosques and public institutions were soon established throughout the city.

The Muslim conquest of Jerusalem under the caliph Umar in 637 was clearly an essential moment in the city's history. For the next 462 years, it would be ruled by Muslims, with religious freedom for minorities protected according to the Treaty of Umar. Even now, as fighting continues over the future status of the city, many Muslims, Christians, and Jews insist that the Treaty maintains legal standing and look to it to help solve Jerusalem's current problems.

Umar's Edict on the Dhimma (protected communities)

Umar also set out conditions or regulations relating to the treatment of those people who entered into protective pacts with the Muslims, the *all-adh-dhimma,* which allowed 'peoples of the book' (*ahl-al-kitab*) to retain their non-Muslim faith under certain conditions, six of which were necessary, six desirable. The essential conditions were: the *dhimmi* should not revile the Qur'an, nor Muhammad, nor Islam; they should not marry a Muslim woman; they should not attempt to convert a Muslim or injure him in life or goods; they should not assist the enemy nor harbour spies. For the *dhimmi* committing any of these offences, the protection of the Muslims was withdrawn; that is, he became an outlaw, and his life was forfeited. The six "desirable" conditions were that they should wear distinctive clothing, the *guitar,* a yellow patch on their dress, and the girdle (*zander*); that they should not build houses higher than those of the Muslims; nor ring their wooden bells (*Marcus*), nor read their scriptures in a loud voice; nor drink wine in public, nor let their crosses or swine be seen, that their dead should be wept and buried in silence; and that they should not mount a horse, only mules and asses. The breach of these regulations was visited with penalties, although several of these, such as the wearing of distinctive dress, were often not enforced. (**Muir** 1924:137)

Umar and non-muslims

Umar took a very lenient attitude towards non-Muslims in the Islamic nation. He gave protection to *Dhimmis* (non-Muslim subjects in an Islamic country) and punished the Muslims who attacked them. The governor of Hims, Umair ibn Saad, rebuked a non-Muslim and later repented. Subsequently, he resigned from the post for that reason. When the resignation letter was submitted to the Caliph, he found the decision to be correct. Once, a Christian lady complained to the Caliph regarding the sale of her house for the expansion of a mosque suggested by the governor. Even though the governor offered the cost of the property many times, she was not willing to sell it. Umar cancelled the deal. Once, the Caliph wrote to Abu Ubaidah, the governor of Syria, "Do not allow any Muslim to attack non-Muslims and acquire their wealth. Obey all conditions are laid down in the agreement with them. Christians of Jerusalem greeted Umar with joy when he went there to take charge of Palestine.;

Crime and punishment

Caliph Umar earned the title *Al-Farooq* due to his ability to distinguish between right and wrong. One day, the Caliph saw a healthy person beating a weak person. The healthy person was Jabl, the ruler of Ghassan. Umar told him to undergo punishment for the crime. However, he escaped to Rome, fearing retribution. Umar declared, "Law is equal for all."

Caliph Umar punished the guilty in such a way as to correct them and not to take any revenge. Once, a person was produced before the Caliph for an act of prostitution. Umar questioned four persons who accompanied the accused person for witnesses. But, only three persons stood witness, and the fourth said he was informed of the incident. Thereby, the accused was acquitted, and the three witnesses were punished. Umar directed Amr ibn Aaas to behave impartially with all criminals when he heard that his son Abdur Rahman was punished at a hidden place. In contrast, his partner was punished publically for the same crime.

Caliph Umar was not a blind follower of the law. Once, a woman involved in a sexual offence was brought before Umar. On her admittance of the crime, Umar was ordered to execute the punishment (death punishment). However, Umar re-examined Ali ibn Abi Talib's suggestion that the motivator should also be punished. He found that she was compelled to do the crime in an inevitable situation. Umar set her free. Those against whom charges were levelled were sentenced, and punishment was given if they were found guilty. The newly introduced jail system was an outstanding achievement of Umar's reign. Jails were set up in all major cities.

Caliph Umar was very keen and stubborn in implementing the Divine law (Shari'ah). He used to weep, saying, "If a lamb happens to die out of hunger on the banks of the Tigris, Umar will have to answer to Allah on the Day of Judgment."

A tourist's travel in Umar's kingdom

in the very early history of Islam, Umar unified his people with swords and laws. The guide showed a party of tourists around the Old City of Jerusalem and ushered the visitors up a flight of steps, under a row of stone arches, and into a vast rectangular courtyard. Beyond the courtyard sprawled the timeless city, the houses crowded together in the impressive confusion of the centuries, separated by a maze of narrow streets and back alleys alive with humanity.

The ambience was quite different inside the courtyard. Here, there was no confusion. The surface paved with stones extended on every side of the big building in the centre so that it stood isolated in solitary splendour and all the more impressive for sharing the space with no rival.

The guide showing a party of tourists around the Old City of Jerusalem ushers them up a flight of steps, under a row of stone arches, and into a vast rectangular courtyard. Beyond the courtyard sprawls the timeless city, the houses crowded together in the impressive confusion of the centuries, separated by a maze of narrow streets and back alleys alive with humanity."The Mosque of Umar," the tourist guide would exclaim with a sweep of his hand. All eyes followed the vaulting lines of the architecture up past columns, arches and cornices to the soaring dome above.

The voice of the tourist guide reverberated with the drones. "You will notice that the Mosque of Umar has eight symmetrical sides—an octagon within a square courtyard. The arches are semicircular, preserving the geometrical proportions and at the same time breaking the monotony of the straight lines."

The guide pointed up at the dominating feature. "The dome completes the pattern of unity and variety, a semi-sphere on a level base. Unlike the walls, which were made out of solid stone, the dome was made of wood. The builders put a coating of lead on the outside and, as we shall see when we enter, a coating of plaster on the inside. The decorations beneath the dome are typically Islamic, especially in the use of intricate mosaics. However, they are not uniform in style; they show a succession of styles over a long period."

He paused for effect. "This is, after all, an old building. Few examples of Islamic architecture are older than the Mosque of Umar."

Who," exclaimed one tourist, "was Umar?"

The question was a strange one. It was like asking who Alexander was, or Caesar, or Justinian. Umar the Great ranks with them as a world figure. However, he was not reasonably known even in the West except to historians. Among Islamic peoples, his greatness was also obscured by the greater fame of Haroun al-Rashid and Saladin — to whom he bequeathed the imperial basis of their power.

Before Umar, the Arabs lived mainly within the confines of the Arabian Peninsula. After Umar, they ruled the Middle East from Egypt to Syria and north through Syria to the frontier of the Byzantine Empire. Umar the Great reigned over more provinces than any man since Alexander the Great. That alone places him in the forefront of the makers of history.

Why is his reputation not commensurate with the grandeur of his achievement?

For one thing, he was not a flamboyant personality. He clung to the simple ways of the Bedouin even after he had become the most powerful man in the world. His generals of the conquest quickly adopted the luxurious manners of the Syrians and the Persians. Their caliph never owned more than one shirt and one mantle at a time, and his meals at home were as frugal as those he ate on the battlefield.

When Umar first entered Jerusalem after the surrender of the city, he found his military men already dressed in gorgeous robes and glittering jewels, the spoils of plunder. He, they told one another privately, looked less like a caliph than like a beggar on a broken-down camel. He summoned them to a conference at which he criticized their departure from the old ways of the desert and declared emphatically: "It is not fitting that we, to whom so much has been given, should be so eager to take so much."

Umar never took anything for himself. He died as poor as he lived.

Again, he never tried to snatch the military laurels from his fighting men. He was a statesman and a strategist of empire-building. Still, he allowed his generals to give complete freedom of action during their campaigns, and he willingly conceded the limelight to them when they returned as victors. He meditated in his tent while they paraded through the streets to the cheers of the crowd.

When he cashiered his foremost tactician, Khalid, this was not out of jealousy for a brilliant subordinate but because he found Khalid guilty of extortion during his Syrian command. "Oh, Khalid," the Caliph lamented, "I would forgive you if you had stolen from me."

Simplicity, poverty, and justice—these are three qualities of the brave and energetic man who led the Arabs out of the confines of the Arabian Desert and into the lush lands of the age-old Fertile Crescent.

Umar arrived on the scene at the moment best suited to his genius. Two things needed fast action. It was necessary to unite the Arabs under a new system that would replace the anarchy of nomadic life in the desert. Umar solved this problem by establishing the Caliphate in its historical form. The attitude of the Arabs to their enemies had to be determined. Umar solved this problem with his sword.

The true meaning of the Caliphate did not permeate under the first Caliph, for Abu Bakr reigned for only two years and was mainly concerned with his religious duties. The second Caliph saw that Islam would be under constant attack without a strong right arm. He added military responsibilities to the Caliphate so that the Islamic peoples might know to whom to look for defence against their enemies.

Umar adopted a title to go with this specific function, a title that rings through history from his time to the present: Commander of the Faithful.

With domestic affairs straightened out, the Caliph turned to foreign affairs. Once more, he brought order into events that began before his Caliphate. The Arabs were already fighting around their perimeter. This border skirmishing revealed the startling fact that the glorious Byzantine and Persian Empires were far weaker than anyone had suspected. There would be nothing impractical about the desert warriors mounting a full-scale drive against these once-mighty neighbours.

Umar resolved to invade the imperial provinces that faced Islam along the arc of the Fertile Crescent.

Syria came first. Umar sent an army under Khalid toward Damascus. The Byzantine Emperor Heraclius hastened down from Constantinople with a more significant force. Khalid out-manoeuvred him, lured him into a trap in a canyon of the Jordan Valley, and overwhelmed him in the decisive Battle of Yarmuk (636). Heraclius fled back to Constantinople. Syria fell to the Arabs.

The Patriarch of Jerusalem, Sophronius, realizing the futility of attempting to hold the city, surrendered to the Caliph himself. This was the occasion of Umar's criticism of the luxury of his generals. A more famous anecdote tells of the Patriarch escorting the Caliph around Jerusalem and inviting him to say a prayer in the Church of the Resurrection. "No," the Caliph replied, "for if I do, my people may appropriate the Church when I am no longer here to protect your rights."

Iraq came next. The Persian Emperor sent the legendary Rustam down the Euphrates to deal with these upstarts from the desert. Instead, they dealt with him at the crushing Battle of Qadisiya (637). The Persians fled back to Persia. Iraq fell to the Arabs.

The Patriarch of Jerusalem, Sophronius, realizing the futility of attempting to hold the city, surrendered to the Caliph himself.

This was the occasion of Omar's criticism of the luxury of his generals. A more famous anecdote tells of the Patriarch escorting the Caliph around Jerusalem and inviting him to say a prayer in the Church of the Resurrection. "No," the Caliph replied, "for if I do, my people may appropriate the Church when I am no longer here to protect your rights."

Iraq came next. The Persian Emperor sent the legendary Rustam down the Euphrates to deal with these upstarts from the desert. Instead, they dealt with him at the crushing Battle of Qadisiya (637). The Persians fled back to Persia. Iraq fell to the Arabs.

A family's yearning for a dose of holiness in Jerusalem b

The Patriarch of Jerusalem, Sophronius, realizing the futility of attempting to hold the city, surrendered to the Caliph himself. This was the occasion of Omar's criticism of the luxury of his generals. A more famous anecdote tells of the Patriarch escorting the Caliph around Jerusalem and inviting him to say a prayer in the Church of the Resurrection. "No," the Caliph replied, "for if I do, my people may appropriate the Church when I am no longer here to protect your rights."

Iraq came next. The Persian Emperor sent the legendary Rustam down the Euphrates to deal with these upstarts from the desert. Instead, they dealt with him at the crushing Battle of Qadisiya (637). The Persians fled back to Persia. Iraq fell to the Arabs.

Egypt was more accessible because the death of Heraclius left the province in turmoil. The Arabs were in control of the Land of the Nile by the end of 641. That same year, they occupied the headwaters of the Tigris and Euphrates and penetrated Persia after winning the Battle of Nihawand.

Omar had, within the space of some five years, transformed the Fertile Crescent from a threat into a bulwark. This incredible feat was distinctly his since he had, with a consummate understanding of the epoch in which he lived, chosen where and when to strike on each campaign. His people, reacting spontaneously to the success of his grand strategy, called him Omar the Great.

History endorsed his statesmanship. His death at the hands of an assassin in 644 did not cause his work to crumble. He had given Islamic power the momentum to expand in subsequent centuries as far as Spain and India and, in 1453, into Constantinople itself. A Western historian offers this summation of his career: "Omar the Great he was to his contemporaries, and Omar the Great he remains to us, the first and foremost Commander of the Faithful."

Much of the history of Islam is his monument. So is the Mosque of Omar in Jerusalem—built fifty years after his death, named in his honour by his grateful people, carefully preserved to this day, thirteen centuries after he moulded the wanderers of the desert into a force that brought unity to much of the Middle East.

Jerusalem, the city at the heart of all three Abrahamic faiths, is undergoing one of the most disturbing episodes in its long history. As the scion of its oldest Arab family, I find the developments of the past few weeks – the bloodshed, yes, but more fundamentally, the wave of intolerance – deeply troubling, breaking longstanding pacts between the faiths to share the city and its religious treasures.

Our family arrived in Jerusalem in the 7th century with the Arab Muslim army led by caliph Umar bin al-Khattab, a companion of the Prophet Mohammed. The city was ruled by the Roman Empire, which had barred Jews from entering for centuries. The covenant of Umar – the truce between Umar and Sophronius, patriarch of Jerusalem – included a promise by the city's new Muslim rulers to protect the Christian inhabitants. There was only one clause that the Christians insisted on, which the Muslims did not implement: the condition that Jews would not be allowed back into Jerusalem.

Instead, the Muslim conquest opened the city up to Jewish residents once more. One of our forefathers was a signatory to Umar's covenant. We are proud to say the Muslim decision to allow Jews to resettle in Jerusalem was a moment of significance in the city's history. Exclusion and discrimination gave way to tolerance and respect.

Our family was responsible for the custodianship and the key to the Church of the Holy Sepulchre, Christendom's holiest site, more than 1,400 years ago. Since then, and to this day, we have performed this role – with the only interruption occurring during the Crusades in the 11th century. The Christian and Muslim leaders of the day, Richard the Lionheart and Saladin, agreed to restore the Nuseibeh custodianship of the church to keep peace between the Christian denominations after intra-Christian fighting and bloodshed, often within the holy building itself.

What we are seeing today is not the worst Jerusalem has seen. But it threatens to turn into a global conflict. When the city was affected by religious strife, the suffering was reflected elsewhere in the region and beyond. Rhetoric and mutual intolerance are spreading, with every incident ratcheting up the sense of gloom and mistrust. A vicious cycle of incitement is creating an unholy race back towards the Dark Ages.

The murders at the Jerusalem synagogue were a highly condemnable part of savagery. So, too, was the brutal killing of the Arab youth, Mohammed Abu Khdeir – as well as the murders of the Jewish youths for which this was seen as a vendetta, and dozens of deaths, including those of Arabs, followed. For many, the city was becoming a place of exclusion, each group attempting to assert control at the expense of the other. This not only went against our Abrahamic culture, the root of Western civilisation, but also the notion of one God and the equal status of His children – Jews, Christians and Muslims.

The great kabbalist Yehuda Ashlag taught us that the means for correcting the problems in the world are mercy, truth, righteousness and peace. None of these qualities are evident in today's disputes over possessionUmar's hatred of Islam.

Umar's relationship with the Dome of the Rock

Islam is the third great monotheistic religion in the world. Its followers, about a billion people, constitute the majority of the population in some 50 countries. Like Judaism and Christianity, Islam has rich and deep associations with the city of Jerusalem.

Islam is an Arabic word that means "submission"; in its religious context, it means submission to the will of God alone. Prophet Muhammad was born in Makkah, in present-day Saudi Arabia, in the year 570 and died in 632, delivering the message of Islam. Such was the power of the divine message he preached that, within 100 years of his death in Madinah, Islam had spread across North Africa, into Spain across the borders of France in the West, and to the borders of India and China in the East.

Very early in this period—in 637—the forces of Islam won Jerusalem from the Byzantine Empire, whose capital was in Constantinople, signing a treaty by which the holy city came to the custody of 'Umar ibn al-Khattab, the second caliph, or successor, of Muhammad. For the following 1280 years, except for the period between 1109 and 1187, during the Crusades, Jerusalem remained in Muslim hands. In 1917, during World War I, the British took control of the city Muslims call al-Quds, "The Holy."

Umar's relationship understands Jerusalem's position in Islam. We need to look at how Islam sees itself in relation to Judaism and Christianity, to which, of course, Jerusalem is also sacred.

Islamic doctrine states that God has, since creation, revealed His teachings repeatedly to humankind through a succession of prophets and scriptures. The first of this line was the prophet Noah, according to many Muslim scholars; others believe Adam must be considered the first. But in this line of succession, Muhammad is the last, or "seal" of the prophets, and the teachings revealed to him are the culmination of all the previous messages. Muslims believe that the Qur'an, the literal word of God revealed to Muhammad, follows the Torah and the Gospels as God's final revelation. Thus, the Qur'an accords excellent reverence to the Hebrew prophets, patriarchs and kings who received revelations from God and are associated with Jerusalem. Similarly, Jesus Christ is revered as one of God's most dedicated messengers, and Jerusalem, as the locus of much of his teaching, is further blessed by that association.

To Islam, then, Jerusalem is sacred for many of the reasons it is holy to Judaism and Christianity, but in addition, it is sacred for specifically Muslim reasons. The most important of these is the Prophet Muhammad's miraculous nocturnal journey, or *is,* to *Bayt al-Maqdis,* "the house of holiness," in Jerusalem and his ascent from there to heaven—the *Mi'raj.* These events are mentioned in a number of verses of the Qur'an, most clearly in the first verse of Chapter 17, titled *Al-Isra'.* Accounts of the Prophet's life supply the details. Led by the angel Gabriel, Muhammad travelled in one night from Makkah to the site of *al-masjid al-Aqsa,* "the furthest mosque," on Mount Moriah, called the Temple Mount, in Jerusalem. The site derives its name from the temples and houses of worship built there over the millennia, including the temple of the prophet Solomon, the temple of Jupiter, the Herodian temple and the al-Aqsa Mosque.

There, Muhammad led Abraham, Moses, Jesus and other prophets in prayer. Then, from a rock on the Temple Mount, Muhammad was taken by Gabriel to heaven itself, to "within two bow-lengths" of the very throne of God.

The spot from which the Prophet's ascent began was sanctified in the eyes of Muslims by the *misery. T*he Qur'an refers to the prayer site as *al-masjid al-aqsa.* From Muhammad's journey evolved a vast body of Muslim devotional literature, some authentic and some uncanonical, that places Jerusalem at the centre of Muslim beliefs concerning life beyond the grave. This literature is in circulation in all the diverse languages spoken by the world's one billion Muslims, most of whom, to this day, celebrate the anniversary of the *Mi'raj*.

Jerusalem is also uniquely linked to one of the "pillars" of the Muslim faith, the five daily prayers. The earliest Muslims, for a time, turned toward Jerusalem to pray. A later revelation transferred the *qibla,* the direction of worship, to Makkah, but to this day, Jerusalem is known as "the first of the two *qiblas.*" According to Prophet Muhammad's teachings, it was during the *Mi'raj* that God ordered Muslims to pray, and the number of daily prayers was fixed at five.

The centre of Muslim power shifted, through the centuries, from one significant capital to the next: from Madinah to Umayyad Damascus to Abbasid Baghdad to Mamluk Cairo and Ottoman Constantinople. But after Jerusalem became part of the Muslim state in 637, whichever dynasty was in control of the city lavished it with care and attention in the form of public monuments: mosques, colleges for the study of the Qur'an and the traditions of the Prophet, hospitals, hospices, fountains, orphanages, caravansarais, baths, convents for mystics, pools and mausolea. This is why Jerusalem's Old City, within the 16th-century walls built by the Ottoman sultan Süleyman, strikes the modern-day visitor with its predominantly Muslim character.

Caliph 'Umar personally came to Jerusalem to accept the city's surrender from the Byzantines and visited the site of *al-masjid al-Aqsa,* known to some Muslims today as *al-Haram al-Maqdisi al-Sharif,* "the Noble Sanctuary of Jerusalem," or simply *al-Haram al-Sharif.* The site lay vacant and in ruins. Umar ordered it to be cleaned, and he took part in the ritual. When the site had been cleansed and sprinkled with scent, 'Umar and his followers prayed at the rough rock from which Prophet Muhammad had ascended to heaven.

Two generations later, about 691, the Umayyad caliph 'Abd al-Malik ibn Marwan's Syrian craftsmen built in the exact location the earliest masterpiece of Islamic architecture, the Dome of the Rock *(Qubbat al-Sakhra)*—the octagonal sanctuary, centred on the rock, whose golden dome still dominates the skyline of Old Jerusalem. 'Abd al-Malik's son al-Walid, who ruled from 705 to 715, built the second significant monument, the al-Aqsa Mosque, also on the Temple Mount.

The octagonal plan of the Dome of the Rock may not have been accidental. Cyril Glassé, in his *Concise Encyclopedia of Islam,* points out that "the octagon is a step in the mathematical series going from a square, symbolizing the fixity of earthly manifestation, to circle, the natural symbol for the perfection of heaven in traditional Islamic architecture, this configuration symbolizes the link between earth and heaven. Nor is it a coincidence that the elegant calligraphy that encircles the structure inside and out—240 meters, or 785 feet, of it—includes all the Qur'anic verses about the prophet Jesus. "The calligraphic inscriptions," writes Glasse, "recall the relationship between Jerusalem and Jesus...; and the architecture, above all the octagonal form supporting a dome, is symbolic of the...ascent to heaven by the Prophet, and thus by man." Mount Moriah, with the Dome of the Rock at its centre, is thus "the place where man, as man, is joined once more to God...."History, tradition and symbolism intersect in this building, whose presence permeates Jerusalem.

History Of Masjid Al-Aqsa And The Dome Of The Rock

Al-Masjid al-Aqsa is the name of the place of worship built by Sulaymaan (peace be upon him). Some people started to give the name al-Aqsa to the prayer place which was built by Umar ibn al-Khattab in front of it.

Praying in this prayer place, which Umar built for the Muslims, is better than praying in the rest of the mosque because when Umar conquered Jerusalem, there was a massive garbage dump on the rock since the Christians wanted to show their scorn for the place towards which the Jews used to pray. Umar issued orders that the filth be removed. He said to Ka'b [al-Ahbar]: "Where do you think we should build a place of prayer for the Muslims?" Ka'b replied, "Behind the rock." Umar said, "O you son of a Jewish woman! Are influenced by your Jewish ideas! Rather, I will build it in front of it."

Hence, when the imams of this ummah entered the mosque, they would go and pray in the prayer place that Umar built. With regard to the Rock, neither Umar nor any of the Sahabah prayed there. There was no dome over it during the time of the Rightly-Guided Caliphs. It was open to the sky during the caliphate of Umar, Uthman, Ali, Mu'awiyah, Yazeed and Marwaan… The scholars among the Sahabah and those who followed them in truth did not venerate the rock because it was an abrogated qiblah… instead, it was revered by the Jews and some of the Christians."

(Majmoo'at al-Rasaa'il al-Kubra, 2/61)

[Umar denounced Ka'b al-Ahbar and called him the son of a Jewish woman because Ka'b had been a Jewish scholar and rabbi. When he suggested to Umar that he should build the mosque behind the rock, it was out of respect for the rock so that the Muslims would face it when praying, and awe of the rock was part of the religion of the Jews, not the religion of the Muslims.

Umar's welcome to Jerusalem

In Jerusalem, there are holy areas such as the Church of the Holy Sepulchre. Muslims are free to move around and to pray the five daily prayers in Al-Aqsa Mosque. Walking down the streets that connect several houses of worship, a Muslim runs into a Jew and then a Christian; he nods respectfully and extends greetings of peace each time, wishing his neighbour a good day. None of the people hates those of other faiths;

there is no oppression, violence, checkpoints, demolitions, barbed wire, arrogance, or forced conversions. Jerusalem is a hub of knowledge, worship, and trade; it demonstrates peaceful coexistence and mutual respect and understanding across the three religious faiths.

It may sound like a fantasy or a picture from utopia, but it's not. That is precisely what Umar ibn Al-Khattab's Jerusalem was like. That was a reality in Jerusalem for 400 years under Muslim rule, from the time Umar ibn Al-Khattab entered Jerusalem around the year 637 till it was captured by the Crusaders in 1099.

Going further back in history, we see that Jerusalem was a common warring ground between the two mighty empires: the Byzantines and the Persians. Jerusalem had been an essential Byzantine city, but it fell to the Persians in the year 614 during the Byzantine-Sassanid Wars. The Persians looted the town, destroyed the Church of the Holy Sepulchre, and are said to have massacred its 90,000 Christian inhabitants. The Jews, who underwent persecution in their Roman- homeland, had aided the Persians.

The Byzantines regained control of Jerusalem in 628 after Emperor Heraclius led a final battle against the Persians; Heraclius was victorious. When they were in power again, they made repairs to the city, and the Byzantines banned the Jews from worshipping on the Temple Mount and the Wailing Wall.

After the death of Prophet Muhammad (peace be upon him) in the year 632, his companion, Abu Bakr, became the Caliph (ruler). During Abu Bakr's lifetime, he secured the Arabian Peninsula under his sovereignty and initiated a conquest in the east towards Iraq.

In 634, Abu Bakr died, and Umar ibn Al-Khattab succeeded him. Umar expanded the Muslim empire north, south, east, and west. He sent armies led by the brilliant military commanders Khalid ibn Al-Waleed and Amr ibn Al-As to Syria, which was still under Byzantine control.

The decisive Battle of Yarmuk in 636 was a massive blow to Byzantine power in the region, leading to the fall of numerous cities throughout Syria, such as Damascus.

Once Syria had fallen into the hands of the Muslims, Umar ibn Al-Khattab ordered the Muslim armies to march towards Jerusalem, and they received reinforcements from another military commander, Abu Ubaida ibn Al-Jarrah, from northern Syria. The Muslims arrived at Jerusalem around early November, and the Byzantine forces withdrew into the well-fortified city. Rather than instigating violent assaults on Jerusalem, the Muslim troops surrounded the fort and laid siege to the town.

At the time of the siege, Patriarch Sophronius, a representative of the Byzantine government and a leader of the Christian Church, was in charge of Jerusalem. Realizing that resistance was pointless and after a siege of approximately four months, Bishop Sophronius and the Christians in Jerusalem decided to surrender. The Muslim conquest of Jerusalem was bloodless.

However, Sophronius had one condition: he would surrender the keys to the city only if the Caliph Umar ibn Al-Khattab came to Jerusalem himself to receive the keys, accept the surrender, and sign a peace pact.

The ee was c; conflicts among Muslims about the approach to handling the concurrence of Byzantine'. Since Muslims had defeated the Byzantine forces, and the vanquished were not in a position to make demands, should the Caliph accept them, even though? In Medina, Umar ibn Al-Khattab consulted his council. Ali bin Abi Talib, who had been one of the closest aides of the and was known for his wisdom, believed that Jerusalem was as much sacred to the Muslims as the Jews or the Christians and that in view of the sanctity of the place, the sanctity demanded its surrender should be honoured by the Caliph personally. Umar accepted Ali's advice.

Umar ibn Al-Khattab, the ruler of the Muslim Empire, travelled to Jerusalem, not with a royal entourage of servants and guards but with a single servant and one riding camel. During the journey, Umar and his servant took alternating turns, riding the camel and walking. Umar wore simple, coarse clothes; none could have distinguished between the ruler and the servant.

As he approached Jerusalem, it so happened that the servant was on the camel, and the Caliph was walking alongside. The servant had pleaded with Umar to ride instead, but he refused. When someone had advised Umar ibn Al-Khattab to wear luxurious robes befitting of a Caliph, he replied that he derived his strength and status from his faith in Islam and not from any dress.

Umar ibn Al-Khattab was greeted at the gates of Jerusalem by Sophronius. The people of Jerusalem were in awe of the Caliph; he was dressed simply like an average person, and he was walking on foot while his servant was riding.

The Bishop of Jerusalem handed over the keys of the city of Jerusalem to Umar ibn Al-Khattab. Muslims carried out no killing or destruction. It was a peaceful transition, and all the holy sites of Christians were left untouched. Caliph Umar signed a treaty with Sophronius, and as a result, Christians were allowed to live in the city but had to pay jizya or tax. The treaty Umar signed was as follows:

"In the name of God, the Merciful, the Compassionate. This is the assurance of safety which the servant of God, Umar, the Commander of the Faithful, has given to the people of Jerusalem. He has assured them of safety for themselves, their property, their churches, their crosses, the sick and healthy of the city and all the rituals which belong to their religion. Muslims will not inhabit their churches and will not be destroyed. Neither they, nor the land which they inhabit, nor their cross, nor their property will be damaged. The dwelling people will also not be forced to undergo conversion."

Alkhateeb wrote, "Umar was given a tour of the city, including the Church of the Holy Sepulchre. When the time for prayer came, Sophronius invited Umar to pray inside the Church, but Umar refused. He insisted that if he prayed there, later Muslims would use it as an excuse to convert it into a mosque – thereby depriving Christendom of one of its holiest sites. Instead, Umar prayed outside the Church, where a mosque called Masjid Umar was later built."

Umar ibn Al-Khattab sought to visit the rock from which Prophet Muhammad (ascended to Heaven on his night journey of Israa and Miraj. Umar ibn Al-Khattab cleared the area of the Temple Mount, cleaned it up, and built a mosque, Al-Aqsa Mosque. After staying for ten days in Jerusalem, the Caliph returned to Medina.

Umar ibn Al-Khattab protected the rights not only of the Christians but also of the Jews. For the first time, after almost 500 years of oppressive Roman rule, Jews were once again allowed to live and worship inside Jerusalem. Caliph Umar and the Muslim rulers after him understood the significance of Jerusalem in the hearts of Jews, Christians, and Muslims. The three religions flourished in Jerusalem.

Over time, many scholars from the three religions came and settled in Jerusalem. For Muslims, Jerusalem, especially the Al-Aqsa Mosque, became a centre of learning. It also became common for Muslims to start mentioning in their wills the desire to be buried in Jerusalem. There are now thousands of Muslim graves in Jerusalem. The Muslim rulers also built many schools, religious centres, and hospitals in Jerusalem.

That is the Jerusalem that we yearn for, Umar's Jerusalem. Jerusalem remained under Muslim rule until it was captured by Crusaders in 1099, during the First Crusade. Umar travelled north on one camel with a single attendant, taking turns with him for the ride. As he approached Jerusalem, it so happened that the attendant was on the camel, and the Caliph was walking alongside him. The potentates of Jerusalem thought that the rider was the Caliph and the man on foot, in his patched clothes, was the servant. They offered abeyance to the rider. When the Muslim commanders greeted the real Caliph, the potentates of Jerusalem were astonished and bowed down in awe. Umar treated the conquered people with unsurpassed magnanimity. The capitulation document signed with the Christians upon the fall of Jerusalem provides an example,

5. THE ARAB CONQUESTS, THE SPREAD OF ISLAM AND THE FIRST CALIPHATES

When the British formed the basis of their empire in the 1600s by acquiring territories in India and North America, they already had many centuries of experience of foreign involvement. One of the most remarkable aspects of the force that reshaped Eurasia 1,000 years earlier is that there was no prelude: the Arab conquests and the Islamic empire that they created came out of nowhere. By the time of the death of the Prophet Mohammed in 632, most of the tribes of the Arabian peninsula had united under the banner of Islam, some out of faith, others from expediency. But few people outside Arabia knew who Muslims were or worried about the threat they might pose.

There were two because of the Prophet's miraculous night journey; it was towards Jerusalem, not Mecca, that early Muslims prayed. In the spring of 637, the Patriarch Sophronius, whose home city of Damascus had already fallen to Arab arms, attempted to stall the inevitable by insisting he would only hand over the keys of Jerusalem to the Caliph. More surprise then came when the caliph Umar duly arrived on a camel dressed. Even more when he refused to pray in the Church of the Holy Sepulchre — in spite of Jesus being a prophet in Islam — because he knew that if he did so, his followers would turn the church into a mosque. Instead, he and his successors built the Dome of the Rock and the Al Aqsa mosque, the scene of the current conflict. There were yet more surprises to come. If Muslim fighters fell in battle, they got rapturous honour similar to martyrs in heaven.

The Arab armies that moved out of their harsh homelands and into the Fertile Crescent had two advantages over their adversaries, and these, as Justin Marozzi makes clear in his lively narrative, were the keys to their success. Unlike their Byzantine, Persian or Egyptian adversaries, Muslim fighters were driven by more than the desire to do battle, to loot, to win glory or save their necks. Theirs was a holy fight, a jihad, and if they fell in battle, the Prophet had assured them, they would find a rapturous welcome as martyrs in heaven.

Historians generally view Umar to be one of the most powerful and influential Muslim caliphs in history.[1] He is revered in the Sunni Islamic tradition as a great, just ruler and paragon of Islamic virtues,

Under Umar, the caliphate expanded at an unprecedented rate, conquering the Sasanian Empire and more than two-thirds of the Byzantine Empire.[3] His attacks against the Sasanian Empire resulted in the conquest of Persia in less than two years (642–644). According to Jewish tradition, Umar set aside the Christian ban on Jews and allowed them into Jerusalem to worship. An enslaved Persian assassinated Umar, Abu Lu'lu'a Firuz, in 644.

With the sudden death of Abu Bakr after only two years of rule in 634, Umar was a unanimous replacement. There were no disputes about his ascension to power, and he had the endorsement of Muhammad's relative and future caliph, Ali.

As the military exploits of Umar Ibn Khattab were a crucial part of his period as caliph, let's look at some of the critical empires and regions that defined this period.

Byzantine Empire	The continuation of the Roman Empire that spanned much of Eastern Europe, the Mediterranean and North Africa.
Sassanid Empire	Sometimes referred to as the Persian Empire, the Sassanids originated in Iran. Their empire spanned much of Mesopotamia and approached the Arabian Peninsula.

Mesopotamia	An area of Western Asia that spanned modern-day Iraq, Kuwait, Syria, Iran and Turkey.
The Levant	An area to the east of the Mediterranean Sea of critical strategic significance for Umar. It provided a gateway into Mesopotamia and North Africa.
The Maghreb	The area of North Africa that borders the Mediterranean Sea.

Umar quickly set about continuing the expansion of the Islamic State. Now that the Muslims controlled the Arabian Peninsula, they were on the doorstep of the **Byzantine** and **Sassanid** empires.

Abu Bakr, who sent war veteran **Khalid ibn al-Walid** to attack and defeat the Sassanid army in **Firaz**, pre-empted an invasion from one of the two empires. Umar streamlined his plans, winning control of the countryside and then the crucial Byzantine stronghold of **Damascus** in 634.

The Byzantine Emperor **Heraclius** did not expect an attack from the south. His army had just beaten the Sassanid Empire in the east in 628 in a gruelling conflict that lasted more than two and a half decades. Moreover, seizing the **Levant** was of great strategic importance to the Muslims, as it was a gateway into **Mesopotamia** and the **Maghreb**.

What was the Islamic justification for war?

Although the **Qu'ran** did not endorse violence, the caliphs justified their military campaigns through the concept of **'jihad'** or 'struggle'. As they believed there was only one God, there could only be one community or **'ummah'** to worship him. The **'Dar al-Islam'** was the name that they coined for this community, meaning 'Realm of Submission to God and Peace'. As a result, anything outside of their ummah was labelled the **'Dar al-Harb'** or 'Realm of War'.

For Umar, the Byzantines and Sassanids were non-believers who needed to be converted into the Dar al-Islam.

The outstanding leadership of Araba

The Arabs also had history on their side, for they emerged just as the two old eyes of the world had exhausted each other in a protracted war for dominion over the Fertile Crescent. Arab fighters might have been unskilled in warfare, but they were fresh. They were inspired by religious fervour, and some competent generals led them. Among the leaders were Khalid ibn Walid, whom the Prophet had called the Sword of Islam, and Uqba ibn Nafi al Fihri, who brought the Prophet's message to North Africa with such missionary zeal that he stopped only after he had ridden his horse into the Atlantic surf somewhere beyond Tangier.

By the time of Prophet Muhammad's death, it was the 730s. By then, the caliph's armies had dominion over the former Persian empire as far as what is now Kyrgyzstan in Central Asia and across North Africa from Egypt to Morocco and up through Spain and Portugal, where Al Andalus, the Muslim kingdom in Iberia, would become a cultural beacon.

The end also comes as something of a surprise — halfway up through France, in 732, where Charles, duke and prince of the Franks, ended Arab ambitions in the north and earned himself the title of Martel, or Hammer. Eighteen years later, at Talas, on what is now the Kazakh–Kyrgyz border, a Tang Chinese army marked the easternmost limit of Arab achievements.

The inevitability of war

When war became inevitable for Arabs, Rustam made a tactical blunder. The Persian soldiers wore heavy armour, unsuitable for warfare in the desert. The Arabs, on the other hand, had no armour and were used to mobile desert warfare. Against his own better judgment, Rustam chose the plain of Qadasia in the desert, about forty miles from the Euphrates, for the upcoming confrontation. The desert heat sapped the strength of the Persian soldiers in their heavy armour. In the initial combat, the elephants in the Persian army created enormous difficulty for the Muslim warriors. For two days, the battle went on and was indecisive. On the third day, the wheels of fortune turned as the Arab soldiers, seeking to neutralize the elephants, shot sharp arrows at their eyes. The injured elephants turned around and dispersed, trampling their troops. Rustam fought bravely but was slain in the battle.

The Battle of Qadasia (637) was one of the turning points in world history. It marked the end of the Persian Empire and the beginning of the Islamic Empire. Persia became a part of the Islamic world and, for fourteen hundred years, has been a pivotal region in Muslim affairs.

From Qadasia, Sa'ad ibn Waqqas advanced to the old Biblical city of Babylon, which offered only feeble resistance. The towns of Kosi and Babrasheer followed suit. Madayen, the capital of the Persian Empire, was now within striking distance. The bulk of the Persian army had been lost in the Battle of Qadasia. Yazdgard tried to slow down the advance of Arab troops by destroying the bridge that linked the western shores of the Tigris River to Madayen. These strategies and lies, however, proved futile. The Arabs put their horses into the river and rode across to the other shore, and Madayen fell in 637. The treasures of the Persian capital were now in Muslim hands. Incredible quantities of gold, silver, jewels, carpets and artefacts were seized and transported to Medina. Included in the war booty was an elephant that aroused a great deal of curiosity among the ladies in Medina.

Yazdgard fled Madayen towards Merv in northeastern Persia. Realizing that the war with the Muslims was not just a skirmish but a full-scale invasion, he called on all Persians and their allies to defend Persia. A vast army of 1,50,000 warriors was assembled and put under the command of Mardan Shah, who had already seen action against the Arabs at the Battle of the Euphrates. To inspire the Persians, Mardan

Shah was vested with the *draft*, the national emblem of Persia. The f of Kufa, Ammar ibn Yassir, sent this information to the Caliph and asked for additional troops. Umar (r) sent a corps of 30,000 under the command of Numan ibn MuQur'an. Peace talks proved futile, and the two armies met at the Battle of Nahawand. In the initial engagements, Numan ibn MuQur'an was seriously wounded, but the Muslim commanders kept this fact hidden from his companions. Towards the end of the first day, the enemy lines broke, and the Muslims were victorious. Numan did not survive his wounds and died that evening.

Persian resistance continued from its eastern provinces. Yazdgard set himself up in Merv and took personal command of his forces. Realizing that an injured enemy is a dangerous enemy, Caliph Umar (r) resolved to put an end to all Persian resistance. From Nahawand, the Arab armies split up and mounted a multi-pronged drive against Persian strongholds. Abi al Aas captured Persepolis. Aasim ibn Amr took Sistan. Hakam ibn Umair conquered Makran and Baluchistan. Azerbaijan fell to Othba ibn Farqad. Buqair ibn Abdulla subdued Armenia. A contingent under Ahnaf ibn Qais marched on Khorasan. By the year 650, the Persian Empire was entirely under the control of Arab armies. Yazdgard fled Persia and died in exile.

Within a decade after the election of Umar ibn al Khattab (r) as the Caliph, the map of West Asia and North Africa had changed. Medina was now the capital of the largest empire in the world, extending from Tripoli in North Africa to Samarqand in Central Asia. This empire was ruled not by a king or a general but by a revolutionary creed: "There is no deity but God, and Muhammed is His Messenger". The Caliph was no more than a servant of God and the keeper of Divine Laws.

The victory over Persia

When Caliph Umar came to know of the victories over Persia, he went to the mosque in Medina and addressed the people: " O believers! The

Persians have lost their kingdom. They cannot harm us any more. God has made you inherit their country, their properties and their riches so that He may test you. Therefore, you should not change your ways. Otherwise, God will bring forth another nation in place of you. I feel anxiety for our community from our people".These were prophetic words. As we shall see in other articles, the riches of Persia did change the ways of some in Medina and led to the civil wars that tore the Islamic community apart.

Umar wept when the following verse in the Qur'an was revealed to the Prophet: "We offered the trust to the mountains, heavens and the earth, but they declined, being afraid thereof, but humankind accepted it. Indeed, humankind was unjust and foolish"(Qur'an, 33:72-73). Umar (r) understood that the trust referred to here is human free will. Humankind, drunk with the love of God, accepted this trust, while all other creation declined it. When the will of man is exercised in a manner that befits human nobility, it elevates him to a position higher than that of the angels. Humankind has a tryst with destiny to realize its sublime nature in the matrix of human affairs. When free will is abused, it reduces humans to the most wretched of creatures. No man understood this better than Umar (r), and few since the Prophet carried this trust with as much wisdom, humility, determination, sensitivity, persistence and courage. Measured by any yardstick, Umar (r) was one of the most significant figures in human history.

Umar laid the foundation of Islamic civilization. He was the historical figure who institutionalized Islam and determined the manner in which Muslims and non-Muslims would relate to each other and strive to fulfil the mission of *Tawhid* on earth. Ironically, this man of justice was assassinated for a verdict he had given in a civil case brought before him. One of the Companions, Mugheera bin Sho'ba, rented a house to a Persian carpenter named Abu Lulu Feroze. The rent was two dirhams a day, a sum Abu Lulu felt was too high. He complained to the Caliph Umar (r), who gathered all the facts, listened to both sides and made the judgment that the rent was fair. This seemingly minor incident caused one of the most significant upheavals in Islamic history. Abu Lulu was so distraught at the verdict that he resolved to take the life of the Caliph. The following day, as Umar (r) appeared at the mosque to lead the prayer, Abu Lulu hid in a corner, his double-edged sword concealed under his long robes. As the Caliph stood at the head of the congregation reciting the Qur'an, Abu Lulu jumped at him and thrust his double-edged sword into the Caliph's stomach. The internal wound bled profusely, and Umar passed away the following day. The year was 645.

Umar presided over the first significant wave of Arab conquests, which were the work of great captains such as Khalid ibn al-Walid. Hostile at first to Muhammad, he became an ardent convert. The bond was reinforced by Prophet Muhammad's marriage to Umar's daughter, Hafsa. His genius was administrative rather than military, and his achievements included systematizing the rule of his vast territories, establishing the Islamic calendar, organizing state pensions, and upholding justice. Here are glimpses of the biography of Umar that shaped his destiny as well as that of Islam.

As a man of knowledge and education, Caliph Umar organised a prolific system for the propagation of learning in all regions during his period of administration. The learned Caliph started educational centres in Kufa and Basra in the Iraq region. He selected Hims and Damascus as centres of knowledge in the Syrian region. In the Palestine region, Jerusalem became the centre of knowledge and learning under Umar bin Khattab.

Tented scholars and teachers were recruited to train students at professional centres in different regions of the Arabian subcontinent. The state well-paid the scholars. The educational centre at Kufa handed t;o th;e custody of Ibn Masud, a great scholar. Kufa has remained the centre of learning for a long time. The Caliph appreciated the group of Kufaites during Caliph Ali ibn Abu Talib's time for their high standard of learning. Two great scholars of Umar's time, Ibn Abbas and Abu Hurairah, who were great authorities of Hadith literature, headed the centre at Basrah. Abu Musa al Ashaari was another great scholar at Basra during Umar's time. The egalitarian views of authorities under the Islamic state invited students from different parts of the world, and Kufa, Damascus, Basra, and Flem became cosmopolitan cities.

Distribution of Zakat during the reign of Umar

Zakat is an essential pillar in Islam that has a dimension of worship but an economic value that benefits the Muslim community. In the current management of zakat, in addition to gathering problems, there is also the distribution of zakat. In Islamic history, the successful example of the management of zakat was exemplified by the prophet, who followed the caliph al-residue. One of the pros and cons of zakat. Therefore, this study tried to analyze the zakat distribution policy in the time of Umar because it is a successful example of the management of zakat. The results of the study explained that the distribution system of zakat conducted by caliph Umar ibn Khattab used the decentralization of zakat. This is chosen because it is more direct to the community in which the region is collected by zakat by the government-appointed zakat agency. Also, it is more effective and efficient to do than zakat centralization. Furthermore, the priority distribution of zakat target is permissible according to the condition and state of mustahik zakat in a region. Not to be imposed with the distribution of zakat for the eight ashraf or, in part, adjusted to the state of mustahik.

Educational syllabus

Caliph Umar selected a group of three teachers, Maadh bin Jabal, Ubadah ibn Samat and Abu al-Darda, from the Ansars for the propagation of knowledge in Syria and Palestine. Those scholars were assigned the task of training scholars, who, in turn, trained teacher trainees. In fact, the system started by Umar Khattab was the forerunner of teacher training schools of modern times. Hims was the centre of training school, and trained teachers were sent to Damascus and Jerusalem. Abu Darda spent his later years at Damascus, where he trained teacher trainees. Maadh was sent to Palestine later, while Ubadah remained at Hims till the end.

With the intention of spreading the tradition of the Prophet, Umar sent a group of Ansars, who were well-versed in tradition, to Kufa. As the traditions of the Prophet contained essential elements of knowledge, they promoted further research, which led to inventions and discoveries by great scientists like Ibn Haitham, Al Farabi, Al Khawarasmi, Ibn Sina, Jabir ibn Hayyan, Ibn Khaldun, and so many others.

Law and order

Caliph Umar was the first Islamic administrator to establish a highly organised police department. The police force under its head, 'Sahibul Ahdath', maintained law and order in various provinces so that even animals got justice from the Caliph. As liquor is the mother of all evils and thus prohibited as per Islamic law, those who were liquor addicts were exiled to remote areas after prescribed lashes. Those who consumed liquor were also made bald.

Caliph Umar was a man of prudence and rationalism. He never misused the law. Once, a man was produced before him for theft. Even though, as per Islamic law, he had done a crime which prescribed a 'hand cut', he was forgiven and acquitted due to the fact that he had done the crime under an inevitable situation – to satisfy hunger. At another time, a group of people were produced before the Caliph for killing a camel for food. The Caliph found that they were not paid or given food by their master, Ibn Hatim, for several days. They were acquitted, and Umar commented, "If law had permitted, I would have punished the master for the crime they committed."

Administrative measures

Caliph Umar was the architect of a stable Islamic government of Muslim regions. Appointing a governor in the Basra province, Umar wrote to him, "Listen, you are not appointed to rule over the necks of the people but to guide them on the right path, which you know from the Qur'ān and the Sunnah of the Prophet (peace and blessings of Allah be to him). While the governor was the head of provincial administration, the Collector (*Amil*) was the head of the finance and revenue department.

Caliph was the Chief Judge of the Empire. There were also Qazis in the provinces assisted by a team of judicial experts in Shari'ah. Apart from Qur'ānic injections and Sunnah in judicial matters, *Ijma* (collective opinion) was also allowed.

Caliph Umar's role in making an Islamic Empire was significant. He played a vital role in the victories of Muslims against enemies during the Prophet's time and the later period till the end of his regime. He added many regions to the Islamic nation; Palestine came under the Islamic Empire during his time.

Criteria for appointing governors

Caliph Umar divided the Empire into eight provinces: Medinah, Makkah, Kufa, Basra, Egypt, Palestine, Syria, and Jazriah. A governor was the head of each region, and a well-coordinated team of administrators worked under the governor. Any person could approach the governor for a solution to grievances.

In order to maintain the integrity of administration, Umar laid down challenging criteria for the selection of candidates for appointment as Governors. Some accounts have come down to us, which show how scrupulous Umar was in choosing his Governors.

It is related to the time Umar decided to appoint a governor. The governor-designate came to Umar to get his appointment orders. Umar asked his Secretary to draft the order. As the order was being drafted, Umar's younger son came and sat in his lap. Umar caressed the child. Thereupon, the Companion said, "Amir ul Muminin, your children come to you freely, but my children do not dare to come near me". Thereupon, Umar said, "If your children are afraid of you, the people will be still more afraid of you. The oppressed will hesitate to bring forward their complaints to you. As such, you are not fit to be a governor, and the orders about your appointment as governor have been cancelled."

Once, Umar thought of appointing a Companion as Governor. Before the orders of appointment were issued, that Companion called on Umar and solicited appointment as a Governor. Umar said:

"I was going to appoint you as a governor on my account, but now that you have asked for this appointment yourself, I think you are not fit for the office. As you have asked for the office, I fear you will use it as an office of profit, and I cannot allow that. I would appoint only such men who regard such office as a burden to those whom he entrusted to them in the name of Allah."

The appointment of Governor for Kufa became an excellent headache for Umar. If he appointed a man who was harsh and stern, the people would complain against him. If he appointed a soft-hearted man, the people would take advantage of his leniency. Umar wanted his comrades to advise him regarding the selection of the right man for the office of the Governor of Kufa. One man rose to say that he could suggest a man who would be the fittest person for the job. Umar enquired who he was, and the man said," Abdullah bin Umar" Umar said, "May God curse you. You want me to expose myself to the criticism that I have appointed my son to a high office. That can never be".

Around Umar, prominent people such as Usman Ali, Zubair, Talha, and others were present. Umar did not offer them any office. Someone asked Umar why he had not appointed such prominent persons as governors. Umar said, "These notables occupy a high status because of their virtues and other qualities. I do not appoint them as Governors lest for any lapse they may lose the prominence they enjoy at present."

Once, the post of the Governor of Hems fell vacant, and Umar thought of offering it to Ibn Abbas. Umar called Ibn Abbas and said, "I want to appoint you as the Governor of Hems, but I have one misgiving." "What is that?" asked Ibn Abhas. Umar said, "I fear that sometimes you would be apt to think that you are related to the Holy Prophet and would come to regard yourself above the law." Ibn Abbas said, "When you have such a misgiving, I would not accept the job." Umar then said, "Please advise me what sort of man I should appoint." Ibn Abbas said, "Appoint a man who is good and about whom you have no misgiving".

Someone asked Umar, "What is your criterion for selecting a man for appointment as a Governor?" Umar said, "I want a man who, when he is among men, should look like a chief although he is not a chief, and when he is a chief, he should look as if he is one of them."

Military administration

Like civil administration, military administration was very systematic and rooted in justice and discipline. There was no excess misbehaviour or maladministration as we see today in Egypt or Israel. Every soldier obeyed the command of the officer who was trained in Islamic principles set up by the Prophet (peace and blessings of Allah be to him) on matters concerning military actions.

The Caliph was the supreme commander of the army. There was a commander-in-chief (Ameer) who represented the Caliph, and he was also the Imam of the military. There were separate commanders for each province. Umar was a military genius, and he divided the empire into nine military districts: Kufa, Medinah, Basra, Mawsil, Misr, Fustat, Damascus, Hims, and Palestine, and military stations were established at strategic points. He reformed the military and enlarged the number of soldiers. His army consisted of people of different races and tribes.

The army had two divisions: Infantry and Cavalry. The army men were highly trained in military lessons as well as in Islamic principles.

Personal merits

Caliph Umar faithfully followed Prophet Muhammad (peace and blessings of Allah be to him) in all aspects of administration and was very sincere in safeguarding public property. He was a man of simple life and claimed no advantage as a ruler. He mostly wore patched clothes. Once, people saw him wearing clothes made out of ration share of cloth and found it to be more than his share. When objected, Umar explained to them that it was also the share of his son, viz., two shares. He was a true successor to Abu Bakr and continued the impartial rule set up by the first Caliph. He was free from nepotism and red-tapism. Recruitment and selection were based strictly on merit on merit, and those who exercised unnecessary power were punished, as in the case of Amr ibn Aas, the governor of Egypt, for favouring his son over his rival, a Christian, in a race. Caliph Umar used to serve as a messenger (or a postman) and a servant to low-income families. Umar became significant on the basis of his faith and pious deeds and not due to his physical power.

Once, when Umar suggested that there should be a limit to *Mehr* (a compulsory gift given by the bridegroom to the bride), an old lady corrected Umar, saying there is no limit to *Mehr* according to Islamic principles. Once Umar heard a pregnant woman crying due to delivery pain, he took his wife along with him to the house and helped the woman in delivery. Umar prepared food for the family and provided financial assistance. Another time, the Caliph saw an old lady with a heavy load. He helped her carry the bag, and she commented, "You are best suited for Caliphate (*Khilafat*). One day, a man complained that his hair was cut and punished unnecessarily by Abu Musa Ashaari. Realising the incident to be accurate, the Caliph ordered Abu Musa Ashaari to undergo punishment.

Once, a man came to the Caliph and started saying, 'curse on you'. When the Caliph enquired about the reason for it, the man replied that the governor of Egypt, Eyalu ibn Ghanam, was doing injustice and maladministration. After enquiry, the governor was dismissed from his post.

Umar's simple lifestyle influenced many contemporaries, including Umair ibn Saad, the governor of Hims, Abu Ubaidah, the governor of Syria and Salman Farsi. Umar always preferred faith and virtue to wealth and power. That is why he directed his son to marry a poor girl who denied adding water to milk at her mother's suggestion. Umar never allowed *shirk*, even at any micro level.

Umar's devotion to Islamic principles was so firm that he could not admit the demise of the Prophet (peace and blessings of Allah be to him). He shouted with a sword in his hand that if anyone said the Prophet was dead, he would cut his head. Then Abu Bakr read Qur'ānic *ayaats*, which read, 'Muhammad is a human being, and Messengers also have to leave this world'.

Umar was very keen on keeping the officials humble and God-fearing. During his meeting with the Christian Patriarch at Jerusalem, it was time for prayer. The Patriarch told the Caliph to perform prayer in the Church, on which Umar commented, "If I do it, later Muslims would raise a claim for that reason." Umar ordered to cut a tree under which the Prophet had once sat, fearing it would become a place of pilgrimage.

Umar was a good orator as well as a wise man. His quest for knowledge motivated him to establish many educational institutions. He was an expert wrestler and a horse rider.

Umar was a research scholar and spent most of his time in the pursuit of knowledge. He had a deep understanding of the Holy Qur'ān and the Prophet's tradition (*hadith*). It is said that Umar reported 537 hadiths. He was a talented person and an exponent in the branches of jurisprudence. He could suggest solutions to any complicated problems on the basis of the Holy Qur'ān and Hadith. He conducted discourses on various topics, and his study classes were attended by famous scholars like Ubayy ibn Kaab, Saeed ibn Thabith, Abdullah ibn Abbas, Abdur Rahman ibn Auf and Abdullah ibn Masud.

Criminals were punished harshly. He systematically organised various Islamic activities, and it was Umar who regularly regularised Taraweeh (during the month of Ramadhan).

Many books on the history of the early Islamic period were written in Arabic. Urdu book Al-Farooq by Allama Shibli Nuamani is an authentic book about Caliph Umar. The book *Khulafau Rashid* by Prof. Muhammad Aslam Jayrajpuri is also beneficial in understanding Caliph Umar.

Into Syria

During Muhammad's life, the Byzantine Empire made clear its desire to eliminate the new Muslim religion growing on its southern borders. The Expedition of Tabuk thus commenced in October 630, with Muhammad leading an army of 30,000 people to the border with the Byzantine Empire. While no Byzantine army met the Muslims for a battle, the expedition marked the beginning of the Muslim-Byzantine Wars that would continue for decades.

The students of Byzantine also had access. It was during the caliphate of Umar ibn al-Khattab that Muslims would begin to expand northwards into the Byzantine realm seriously. He sent some of the ablest Muslim generals, including Khalid ibn al-Walid and Amr ibn al-'As, to fight the Byzantines. The decisive Battle of Yarmuk in 636 was a massive blow to Byzantine power in the region, leading to the fall of numerous cities throughout Syria, such as Damascus.

In many cases, Muslim armies received a warm welcome. By the local population – both Jews and Christians. The majority of the Christians of the region were Monophysites, who had a more monotheistic view of God that was similar to what the new Muslims were preaching. They welcomed Muslim rule over the area instead of the Byzantines, with whom they had many theological differences.

Economic policies of Umar

The Bayt al-Maal is the place to which the income of the state is brought and the place from which all the outgoings of the state come, such as the stipends paid to the caliphs, armies, judges and agents and the expenses of public facilities and other things that belong to the state.1

Official records (*Dawaween, sing. Diwan*) refer to the documents in which the affairs of the state were recorded. The word *diwan* was given by the Persians to the place where the scribes and employees in charge of these records gathered.2 Initially, the Islamic state did not have a B*ayt al-Maal* in the sense that it was known later on because the policy of the Messenger (Sallahu Alaihi Wasalaam) was not to delay in dividing or spending wealth. Abu Bakr followed the same method as the Prophet (sallahu Alaihi Wasalaam), and 'Umar followed the same way as his two companions at the beginning of his caliphate until the authority of the Islamic state spread east and west.

Then he started to think of a way to manage the wealth and booty, as well as the income from *jizyah, kharraj,* and zakah that the caliph was accumulating as the result of the conquests. Moreover, the army had expanded and needed a way to manage its needs and record the names of its men, lest some of them miss out on payments and others be paid more than once.

The conquests and victories continued, and wealth continued to increase in a way that the Muslims had never known before. 'Umar decided that it was beyond the capability of the caliph and his governors to keep track of everything and that it was economically unwise to leave control of financial affairs in the hands of the agents and governors without regulating it or maintaining accounts. The result of that thinking was the establishment of rules to control the way in which this wealth was handled. Thus, the *diwan* was set up. 'Umar was the first one to establish the *diwan* (official records) in the Islamic state?.[3]

How that happened was narrated by the historians: "Abu Hurayrah said that he came from al-Bahrayn with five hundred thousand *dirhams,* and I went to 'Umar ibn al-Khattab (Razi Allahu Anhu), who asked me about the people, and I told him. Then he asked me, 'What have you brought?' I said, 'I have brought five hundred thousand *dirhams.'* He said, 'Woe to you! Do you know what you are saying?' I said, 'Yes, a hundred thousand, and a hundred thousand, and a hundred thousand, and a hundred thousand, and a hundred thousand, and a hundred thousand, and a hundred thousand, and a hundred thousand. He said, 'You must be tired. Go back to your family and sleep, and come to me in the morning.' The next morning, I went to him, and he again asked, 'What have you brought?' I said, 'I have brought five hundred thousand *dirhams.'* He said, 'Woe to you! Do you know what you are saying?' I said, 'Yes, a hundred thousand ...' and I counted it five times on my fingers. He said, 'Are you sure?' I said, 'I do not know anything other than that.' He ascended the *minbar* and praised and glorified Allah, then he said, '0' people, a mat deal of wealth has come to us. If you wish, we will give it to you by measure, or if you wish, we will count it out for you.' A man stood up and said, '0' *Ameer al-Mu 'mineen, I* think that these Persians keep records for themselves.[4] 'Umar liked the ideal[5], so he consulted the Muslims about keeping records. Some of them gave their suggestions, except for al-Waleed ibn Hisham ibn al-Mugheerah, who said, 'I went to Syria, and I saw that their kings kept records and organized the army. So keep records and organize the army.' According to some reports, the one who said that was Khalid ibn al-Waleed."

Some historians state that there was one of the Persian satraps in Madeenah, and when he saw that 'Umar was not sure what to do, he said to him: " *Am- al-Mu'mineen,* the rulers of Persia have something that they call *diwan*. Whatever income they get and whatever they spend is all controlled, and nothing is left unrecorded.

The people who are entitled to stipends are all written down under different categories with no room for error." 'Umar liked this idea and said, "Describe it for me." So the satrap described it for him, and then he compiled the official records of those who were entitled to stipends.[7]

'Uthman liked the idea of keeping official records, and he suggested: "I think that there is enough wealth for everybody, but if no records; or mony something and should far if money is uncleaned and will become defunct.-.

These are some of the reports which indicate that 'Umar consulted those who were with him numerous times. There is a difference of opinion among historians as to the year in which the official records were set up. Some say that it was in 15 A.H., such as at-Tabari, who Ibn al-Atheer and others followed. Other historians say that it was in Muharram 20 A.H., such as al-Baladhuri, al-Waqidi, al-Mawirdi, Ibn Khaldoon9, and others. It is more likely to have happened in 20 A.H. because in 15 A.H., the battle of al-Qadisiyah took place, and the conquests of Iraq, Syria, and Egypt were not completed until after that.

'Umar divided the wealth in a manner different from that employed by Abu Bakr. Abu Bakr had divided the wealth among the people equally, whereas 'Umar divided it on the basis of seniority in Islam (who had come to Islam first), participation in jihad and support for the Messenger of Allah (Allahu Alaihi Wasalaam). f

'Umar thought that this was what should be done during the time of Abu Bakr, and when he saw Abu Bakr dividing the wealth equally among the people, he said to him: "Are you giving equal shares to those who migrated twice and prayed to face both *qiblahs* and to those who became Muslim during the year of the Conquest out of fear of the sword?" Abu Bakr said to him: "What they did was for the sake of

Allah, and their reward is with Allah. In this world, all that you need is what a traveller needs." 'Umar said to him: "Do not make one who fought against the Messenger of Allah (Allahu Alaihi Wasalaam) like one who fought alongside him.12

Hence 'Umar divided the people into different categories when he allocated wealth, as follows: Those who had come to Islam first and strove hard, by means of whose jihad this wealth had become possible.

Those who brought benefits to the Muslims, such as governors and scholars who brought both worldly and spiritual benefits

Those who strove to ward off harm to the Muslims, such as the *Mujahideen* who were fighting for the sake of Allah, soldiers, spies, advisors, and so on

Those who were in need

This policy of dividing wealth is what 'Umar referred to when he said: 'No one has more right to this wealth than anyone else, but a man is paid according to his seniority, or according to how much benefit he brings to the Muslims, or according to how much he strives to ward off harm, or according to his needs.14

'Umar called 'Aqeel ibn Abi Talib, Makhramah ibn Nawfal and Jubayr ibn Mut 'im - who were young men of Quraysh – and said: 'Write down the people's names according to their status." They started with Banu Hashim and wrote down their names, then they wrote down Abu Bakr and his people, then 'Umar and his people, and they wrote down all the tribes and gave that to 'Umar. When he looked at it, he said: "No, this is not how I wanted it to be. Start with those who are closest to the Prophet (sallahu Alaihi Wasalaam), then the next closest and the next closest, and put 'Umar where Allah put him."

Banu 'Adiyy came to the caliph 'Umar (Razi Allahu Anhu) and said: "You are the successor *(khalifa)* of the Messenger of Allah (sallahu Alaihi Wasalaam), the successor of Abu Bakr (Razi Allahu

Anhu), and Abu Bakr was the successor of the Messenger of Allah (Sallahu Alaihi Wasalaam). Why don't you put yourself in the category where these people who wrote it down suggested you should be?" He said, 'No, no, *O'*Banu 'Adiyy. Do you want to take advantage of me? Do you want me to give my *hasanat* to you? You are to be placed in the proper position, even if it is at the bottom of the list. I have two companions who follow a path, and if I follow a different route, I will end up in a different place. By Allah, we have not reached such a high position in this world, and we do not hope for reward from Allah except by virtue of Muhammad (sallahu Alaihi Wasalaam). He is our leader, and his people are the noblest of the Arabs, followed by the next closest.15

'Umar began to record in his official records the names of those who were entitled to stipends and how much they were entitled to. This was called *diwan al-Jund* (the record of the troops) on the basis that all the Muslim Arabs were soldiers in jihad for the sake of Allah. In his record of the forces, he started with Banu Hashim, those who were closest to the Messenger of Allah (Allahu Alaihi Wasalaam), then those who were next nearest, and then those who came after them in different categories. He gave each of the Muslims a certain amount. He allocated stipends to the wives and concubines of the Prophet (Sallahu Alaihi Wasalaam) and all the Muslims, men, women, and children at birth, and enslaved people, in varying amounts.

By devising the record, 'Umar demonstrated his concern for jihad for the sake of Allah. He paid a great deal of attention to the *Mujahideen* and the protection of their rights. The records of troops were kept in Arabic in Madeenah at the hands of a number of brilliant men of Quraysh and those who knew their lineages. He then ordered that similar records be retained in other parts of the Muslim world. These records were kept in the languages of the conquered lands and were not translated into Arabic until the caliphate of 'Abdul-Malik ibn Marwan and his son al-Waleed.

After compiling these records, 'Umar began to collect the wealth for a year, and then he divided it among the people because he thought that collecting it would bring a more incredible blessing. Collecting the wealth needed trustworthy people. Zayd ibn Arqam was in charge of the *Bayt al-Maal* at the time of Umar. "' Abu 'Ubayd narrated with his isnad from 'Abdul-Qari - from the tribe of al-Qarah that he said: "I was in charge of the *Bayt al-Maal* at the time of 'Umar ibn *al-* Khattab (Razi Allahu Anhu)

Reference

1. *'Asr Al-Khalifah ar-Rashidah, P. 189.*

2. *Ibid.*

3. *Siyasat Al-Mal fee Al-Islam, P. 155.*

4. *Muqaddamat Ibn Khaldoon, 243; Siyasat al-Mal fee al-Islam, P.155.*

5. *Siyasat al-Mal fee al-Islam, P. 157.*

6. *At-Tabaqat by Ibn aSaad, 3/300, 302, a Saheeh Report.*

7. *Muqaddimar Ibn Khaldoon, P. 244; Al-Kharaj by Abu Yoouf, Pp. 48, 49.*

8. *Al-Ahkam as-Sultaniyah, Pp. 226, 227; Futooh al-Buldaan, p. 436.*

9. *Al-Ahkam as Sultaniyah, P. 226; Tareekh al-Islami as-Siyasi, 1/456.*

10. *Al-Ahkam as-Sultaniyah, P. 226; Siyasat al-Mal, P. 158.*

11. *Muqaddimat Ibn Khaldoon, P. 244; Siyasat al-Mal, P. 159.*

12. *Siyasat al-Mal fee al-Islam, P. 159.*

13. *Ibid.*

14. *Al-Ahkam as-Sultaniyah by al-Mawirdi, P. 201.*

15. *As-Siyasah ash-Shar'iyyah by Ibn Taymiyah, P. 48; Awlawiyat al-Farooq, P. 358.*

16. *Jami' al-Usool, 2/71; Akhbar 'Umar, P. 94.*

17. *Futooh al Buldan, P. 436; al-Ahkam as-Sultaniyah, P. 227.*

18. *Siyasat al-Mal fee al-Islam, P. 160.*

19. *Subh al-A'sha fee Qawaneen al-Insha, by al-Qalqashandi, 1/89.*
   Fiqh az-Zakah, 1/318;

Economic measures

Islamic economic system was strictly followed, and the Prophet set up the system of public treasury for the welfare of the people, which Umar maintained. The taxation system was favourable to all sections of people.

Zakat was collected according to Islamic law. The state also raised money and other wealth in the form of *Sadaqua* (gift or contribution). Jizia was a form of taxation for non-Muslims, who were safe under the administration and exempted from Zakat and other forms of taxation collected from Muslims. *Kharaj* was the tax levied on Jews for the ownership of the state land they retained. The revenue collected from land property owned directly by the state came to be known as *Al-Faj*. One-fifth share of the spoils of the war belonged to the state known as *Ghanimah* or *Khams*.

Money Supply and Currency

In the Middle Ages, Arab Muslims inherited the massive coin stocks struck by Byzantium and Iran to support their war efforts in the sixth and early seventh centuries. Up to the late seventh century, solidi and drachms continued to circulate, and Arab Muslims made use of the available stocks. The situation changed during the reign of 'Abd al-Malik (685–705) and the second *fitna*. With the rise of the 'counter-caliph' Ibn al-Zubayr, 'Abd al-Malik felt the need to assert the Umayyad's imperial authority to keep the unity of the *Umma*. His famous reform in coinage was to impose the Umayyads' ideology through the use of new Islamic currencies. This chapter examines how Caliph 'Abd al-Malik's monetary reforms in the late seventh century played a fundamental role in triggering exchange and increasing the velocity of money circulation. It also explores how, in the late eighth, ninth, and tenth centuries, influxes of precious metal from the release of antique treasuries, the intensified exploitation of existing mines, and the discovery of ore veins and deposits in the Near East, Central Asia, and Africa, helped to sustain a developing culture of consumption.

Management of Zakat

Zakat is an essential pillar in Islam that has a dimension of worship but an economic value that gives benefit to the Muslim community. In the current management of zakat, in addition to gathering problems, there is also the distribution of zakat. In Islamic history, the successful example of the management of zakat was exemplified by the prophet, who followed the caliph al-residue. There are advantages and disadvantages to the centralization and decentralized problems of zakat. Therefore, this study tried to analyze the zakat distribution policy in the time of Umar because it is a successful example of the management of zakat. The results of the study explained that the distribution system of zakat conducted by caliph Umar ibn Khattab used the decentralization of zakat. This is chosen because it is more direct to the community in which the region is collected by zakat by the government-appointed zakat agency. Also, it is more effective and efficient to do than zakat centralization.

Furthermore, the priority distribution of zakat target is permissible according to the condition and state of mustahik zakat in a region. Not to be imposed with the distribution of zakat for the eight ashraf or, in part, adjusted to the state of mustahik

An estimate of Umar

We came across some great personalities in ancient human history, such as Alexander, Julius Caesar, Hammurabi, Ashoka, Samudragupta, and so on. Among such great personalities, Umar Khattab's place is summarised by Irwin I T Rosenthal, a famous historian, in these words: "Many scholars acquainted with the spiritual thought linked Plato's Ideal Republic with the reign of Caliph Umar. Some also claimed that the ideal Islamic state as that envisaged and demanded by the Shari'ah was superior to all the other forms of state, including Plato's Republic." (Some aspects of Islamic culture, quoted by M A Karandhikar in *Islam in India's Transition to Modernity*, p. 65).

Caliph Umar was not merely a great soldier but an equally great administrator as well. He reorganised the regions he had added to the Islamic Empire left by the Prophet (peace and blessings of Allah be to him) for administrative convenience. He was a genius administrator as well as a staunch follower of Islam. He followed the Prophet (peace and blessings of Allah be to him) in all walks of life inch by inch and foot by foot. In fact, it was Umar who spread the Islamic form of administration. Even though the Caliph was the head of administration, it was really 'by the people'.

Philip K Hitti writes: "Simple and frugal in manner, his (Abu Bakr) energetic and talented successor, Umar (C.E. 634-44) who was of towering height and strong physique continued at least for some time after becoming Caliph to support himself by trade and lived throughout his life in a style as that of a Bedouin sheikh. His impeccable character became an exemplar for all conscientious successors to follow. He owned, we are told, one shirt and one mantle only, both conspicuous for their patchwork, alert on a bed of palm leaves and had no concern other than the maintenance of the purity of the faith, the upholding of justice and the ascendancy and security of Islam and the Arabians. Arabic literature is replete with anecdotes extolling Umar's stern character." (*History of the Arabs*, p. 175)

According to *Cambridge History of Islam*, "Physically Umar was a giant with a long beard. His very appearance inspired respect.... He was fond of walking the streets of Medinah afoot with a hidden whip in his hand, which he did not hesitate to apply to the shoulders of those who infringed the law". (Ed. by P M Holt and others, p. 66)

6. THE GREATNESS OF CALIPH UMAR

The romance of history is not only fascinating but also genuinely inspiring. Every age has been a model for the succeeding one, and thus, the history of the kingdoms and the human race has evolved from cave dwellers to visitors to the moon. Burin this vast penumbra, history remains studded with only a few individuals whose lives shine in luminescence and whose ideals are living models of shimmering meteors of wisdom. These great men have been the pathfinders and torchbearers of plans that shaped glorious civilizations.

Men of genius are meteors intended to burn to light their century. In history, some men were exquisite kings, philosophers, scholars, rulers, and generals who could grasp the true purpose of life quite early and harnessed it into great societies and did not have to share the disgrace of many others who could not catch the luminescence of this truth and had to remain content with leaving a poor legacy.

Those noble souls whose teachings survived the driftwood of history and whose names continue to burnish with greatness were men driven by a constant urge to change society by liberating segments of the population that were fenced from each other by prejudice. All great men - social reformers, thinkers, politicians, sages, or patriots - differ from ordinary men in one respect. They dare to dream and also work to transmute that dream into reality. They give life meaning and purpose and devote themselves to achieving it.

Caliph Umar Al-Farooq, the second caliph of Islam, stands as a monumental figure in history whose unwavering resolve and visionary leadership reshaped the Islamic world. Umar (ruled 634–644) had not so much to stimulate conquest as to organize and channel it.

He chose as leaders skilful managers experienced in trade and commerce as well as warfare and imbued with an ideology that provided their activities with a cosmic significance. The total numbers involved in the initial conquests may have been relatively small, perhaps less than 50,000, divided into numerous shifting groups. Yet few actions took place without any sanction from the Medinan government or one of its appointed commanders. The fighters, or *muqātilah*, could generally accomplish much more with Medina's support than without. 'Umar, one of Muhammad's earliest and staunchest supporters, had quickly developed an administrative system of manifestly superior effectiveness. He defined the *ummah* as a continually expansive polity managed by a new ruling elite, which included successful military commanders like Khālid ibn al-Walīd. Even after the conquests ended, this sense of expansiveness continued in the way Muslims divided the world into their zone, the Dār al-Islām, and the zone into which they could and should expand, the Dār al-Ḥarb, the abode of war. Islam supplied the norms of 'Umar's new elite. Taken together, Muhammad's revelations from God and his Sunnah (precedent-setting example) defined the cultic and personal practices that distinguished Muslims from others: prayer, fasting, pilgrimage, charity, avoidance of pork and intoxicants, membership in one community centred at Mecca, and activism (jihad) on the community's behalf.

Forging the link of activism with faithfulness

'Umar symbolized this conception of the *ummah* in two ways. He assumed an additional title, *amīr al-mu'minīn* ("commander of the faithful"), which linked organized activism with faithfulness (*īmān*), the earliest defining feature of the Muslim. He also adopted a lunar calendar that began with the emigration (Hijrah), the moment at which a group of individual followers of Muhammad had become an active social presence. Because booty was the *ummah*'s primary resource, 'Umar concentrated on ways to distribute and sustain it. He established a *dīwān*, or register, to pay all members of the ruling elite and the conquering forces, from Muhammad's family on down, in order to enter the *ummah*. The immovable booty was retained for the state. After the government's fifth share of the movable booty was reserved, the rest was distributed according to the *dīwān*. The *muqātilah* he stationed as an occupying army in garrisons (*amṣār*) constructed in locations strategic to further conquest: al-Fusṭāṭ in Egypt, Damascus in Syria, Kūfah and Basra in Iraq. The garrisons attracted the indigenous population and initiated significant demographic changes, such as a population shift from northern to southern Iraq. They also inaugurated the rudiments of an "Islamic" daily life; each garrison by a caliph\s representative with several responsibilities, such as, responsible for setting aside an area for prayer, a mosque (*masjid*) named for the prostrations (*sujūd*) that had become a characteristic element in the five daily worship sessions (*ṣalāt*s). There, the fighters would hear God's revelations to Prophet Muhammad, which were being recited in ecstatic intonations by men who had developed and perfected a niche in the artistry. The most pious might commit the whole to memory. There, too, the Friday midday *ṣalāt* could be performed communally, accompanied by a critical educational device, the sermon (*khuṭbah*), through which they honed their principles of faith. The mosque fused the practical and the spiritual uniquely. Because the Friday prayer included an expression of loyalty to the ruler, it could also provide an opportunity to declare rebellion.

His reign from 634 to 644 CE marked a transformative period characterized by rapid expansion and profound administrative reforms. Umar was not just a conqueror; he was a master strategist who led the Muslim armies to significant victories against the Byzantine and Sasanian empires, greatly extending the realm of Islam.

A commitment to justice and equity marked his governance. Umar established a comprehensive legal system that emphasized the rights of all individuals, regardless of their social status. He was renowned for his humility and piety, often prioritizing the welfare of his people over personal gain. His innovative initiatives included the establishment of welfare programs, the creation of a postal system, and the introduction of a census to manage resources better.

Moreover, Umar's architectural contributions, such as the construction of roads, mosques, and administrative buildings, laid the groundwork for future Islamic civilization. His legacy as a just ruler, wise administrator, and devout believer continues to inspire generations, illustrating the profound impact of steadfast leadership on the course of history. Umar Al-Farooq's life exemplifies how dedication to faith and justice can indeed bend history to one's will.

The most notable military figure of Abu Bakr's era was Khalid ibn al-Walid (l. 585-642 CE). Abu Bakr had cherished him (despite his flaws) for his unique talent in warfare. Khalid's skills proved to be a clinching doctor in the Ridda Wars and the subsequent invasion of Iraq as well; from Iraq, he moved to the Syrian front to confront a significant Byzantine counterattack on the orders of Abu Bakr at the Battle of Ajnadayn (634 CE). That day proved to be a decisive Muslim victory, but Abu Bakr did not live long enough to enjoy success, and the advance of the Muslim army was paused in the absence of Khalid. At his deathbed, Abu Bakr nominated Umar as his successor, who then became the Caliph in 634 CE (he added the phrase "commander of the faithful" after his title) and ruled for ten years until 644 CE. Umar's priority was to consolidate his hold over the empire and get a grip on the administration. He then turned his attention to the ongoing campaigns in Iraq and Syria.

Umar stripped Khalid of his command of the Syrian division for uncertain and highly debated reasons. He instead entrusted the command to his favourite person: Abu Ubaidah (l. 583-639 CE), a humane leader and a true gentleman; he had also been one of Muhammad's favourite companions (there were ten in total, four of whom were the four Rashidun Caliphs). The Caliph also reinforced the Muslim forces in Iraq with fresh troops under a new leader: Saad ibn Abi Waqqas (1. 595-674 CE).

Khālid ibn al-Walīd (died 642)

Today, Muslim leadership is confronted with a moral dilemma: how to find the delicate balance between the two poles on the spectrum: inclusivity at one end, martial activism at the other."

Alexander the Great, Genghis Khan, and Napoleon Bonaparte – if people in a random exercise were asked to name the greatest military commanders in world history, chances are they would name one of these three, if not all of them. Of course, there are also other famous military commanders in different times and cultural zones.

However, few would name perhaps the most significant military commander of them all, Khalid Bin Walid. No doubt Muslims would name him, and there are many Muslims named after him, but non-Muslim history books and commentary tend to ignore Khalid. He was one of the two generals (with ʿAmr ibn al-ʿĀṣ) of the enormously successful Islamic expansion under the Prophet Muhammad and his immediate successors, Abū Bakr and ʿUmar.

In his acts of personal boldness and physical courage in the heat of battle, he reminds us of Alexander the Great. In the coordination of his battalions and the speed and accuracy with which they met at distant designated places, he was like Genghis Khan and his swift horse riders. In his ability to move his battalions strategically and with lightning speed, he was like Napoleon in his early military career.

Besides, Alexander's conquests disintegrated upon his death, and Genghis' empire split into separate kingdoms after he died. Napoleon's career ended ignominiously after his disastrous invasion of Russia and defeat at Waterloo.

In contrast, Khalid bin Walid, who was either in command or participated in some 100 military engagements, emerged triumphant in every battle, and the impact of his victories can still be seen in the regions where he fought and triumphed. Some of his battles were so fierce that, as he famously observed after one of them, he broke seven swords. He was one of the two generals (with ʿAmr ibn al-ʿĀṣ) of the enormously successful Islamic expansion under the Prophet Muhammad and his immediate successors, Abū Bakr and ʿUmar.

Although he fought against ProphetMuhammad at Uḥud (625), Khālid was later converted (627/629) and joined Muhammad in the conquest of Mecca in 629; after that, he commanded a number of conquests and missions in the Arabian Peninsula. After the death of Muhammad, Khālid recaptured a number of provinces that were breaking away from Islam. He was sent northeastward by the caliph Abū Bakr to invade Iraq, where he conquered Al-Ḥīrah. Crossing the desert, he aided in the conquest of Syria. Though the new caliph, ʿUmar, formally relieved him of high command (for unknown reasons), Khālid remained the effective leader of the forces facing the Byzantine armies in Syria and Palestine.

Routing the Byzantine armies, he surrounded Damascus, which surrendered on Sept. 4, 635, and pushed northward. Early in 636, he withdrew south of the Yarmūk River before a powerful Byzantine force that advanced from the north and the coast of Palestine. The Byzantine armies were composed mainly of Christian Arab, Armenian, and other auxiliaries; when many of these deserted the Byzantines, Khālid, reinforced from Medina and possibly from the Syrian Arab tribes, attacked and destroyed the remaining Byzantine forces along the ravines of the Yarmūk valley (Aug. 20, 636). Almost 50,000 Byzantine troops were slaughtered, which opened the way for many other Islamic conquests.

Battles of Yarmouk & Al-Qadisiyya

In 636 CE, the Byzantine Empire struck back at the Muslims. Although Khalid was no longer officially in command, he was highly respected by the soldiers owing to his expertise in warfare and, taking his advice, the Muslim forces retreated to the Yarmouk River. It was here that the battle that would determine the fate of the region for centuries to come took place. The elite Byzantine troops outnumbered their foes, but Khalid was no stranger to fighting against odds. The Byzantines suffered a crushing defeat; the army was routed with slaughter, and many perished due to drowning in the river. Not only did the Muslim position in Syria become uncontested, but they also took hold of the Levant soon after; later in the same year, they were at the gates of Jerusalem – the third holiest Islamic city, also blessed for the Jews and Christians.

The same year, on the other side of the Syrian Desert, the Saracen forces (as European history refers to Arabs and Muslims) under Sa'ad met the mighty Sassanian Empire under their legendary leader, Rustam Farrokhzad – a man with a similar reputation to that of Khalid. The Battle of al-Qadisiyya (636 CE) proved to be hopeless for the Arabs at first, but the fateful death of Rustam demoralized his forces, who were then utterly defeated. The Rashidun forces had emerged triumphant against staggering odds once again, and this victory had immediately brought the whole of Iraq and the Sassanian capital of Ctesiphon under their control. Umar ordered the forces not to proceed into the unfamiliar territory of Iran lest they be defeated and their gains reversed. The importance of these two victories cannot be overstated. The defences of the opposing forces were crushed, and they could not field effective counterattacks at similar levels anymore.

After the success at Yarmouk, Umar arrived in Syria and the Levant primarily to receive the surrender of Jerusalem (which was under siege) and also to manage domestic affairs in the region. Umar removed Khalid from command for good; sources argue whether Umar had personal problems with him or if it was due to Khalid's harsh nature. The vast majority of Muslim historians suggest that Umar might have done so to show that it was God who gave them their victories and that no matter who led them, God's help was the only determining factor; at least, this was what he announced in public. Umar might have actually thought his actual reason remains shrouded in mystery.

Khalid, despite some controversies against him, was very popular among the Muslim troops who would follow him into any battle, no matter how bad the odds were. Before his dismissal, Khalid had led successful expeditions into Anatolia and Armenia in 638 CE. Though he was encouraged to rebel against the Caliph, he refused to do so and retired peacefully. Umar appointed Abu Ubaidah as the governor of Syria, and he also wished to nominate him as his successor. Still, the latter died in 639 CE in the wake of the plague that devastated the area.

Surrender of Jerusalem

Jerusalem is a holy city for Muslims, just as it is for Christians and Jews. According to Islamic tradition, Prophet Muhammad is said to have journeyed in 621 CE to the city overnight and ascended to heaven from there; Muslims debate the exact nature of this travel: some claim it to be a dream, others suggest that the journey was heavenly, and still, others say that it was a physical journey. In either case, Jerusalem acquired unprecedented importance in Islam after that.

In 637 CE, when the Muslim forces were at the doors of the holy city, the Patriarch of Jerusalem, Sophronius (l. c. 560-638 CE), seeing that no Byzantine force was to come for their relief, sued for a peaceful surrender, personally to Umar. As noted earlier, this prompted the Caliph to depart his capital without any entourage and in an entirely unceremonious manner; he reached Syria, where he offered lenient terms to the newly conquered **cities** (as Khalid had done as well), and then he went to Jerusalem, where he was given a guided tour of the town by Sophronius, who then surrendered it to him. More than five centuries earlier, in 70 CE, the Romans had ousted the Jews.

Further Imperial Gains

After strengthening his hold over Syria and the Levant, in 640 CE, Umar was convinced by Amr ibn al-Aas (l. c. 573-664 CE, one of the military commanders who had been sent to Syria in Abu Bakr's reign) to invade Egypt on the pretext of cutting off Byzantine naval assaults on the Levant. Umar, a man of cautious nature, was reluctant at first to risk such a grand undertaking, but he eventually bent to Amr's will. Reinforced by the Caliph's forces under Zubayr ibn al-Awamm (l. 594-656 CE), Amr faced the Byzantine army, which was decisively defeated in the Battle of Heliopolis (640 CE) and by 642 CE and Egypt had been taken.

The time of Umar Farooq was an exceptional and groundbreaking period in the development of Islam. Umar's administration and justice phase are unavoidable for historians and scholars. As a brilliant monarch, he established offices for all departments, expanded Haram and Masjid-e-Nabawi, and improved Bait-ul-Mal. Umar's justice was straightforward. Justice is straightforward. Bribery, perjury, favouritism, and dishonesty were unknown. The caliph himself had to testify. Due to his personality, he spread Islam well. He exemplified justice and fairness as Khilafah. He established postal police and others. He is an outstanding figure of Islam whose insightful contributions to Islam, fortitude and bravery, judgments based on justice, victories, and extraordinary actions have enlivened Islam. Human history cannot demonstrate them.

Administration

Umar was a superb administrator. He established a *Shura* (consultative) council and sought advice on matters of state. He divided the far-flung empire into the provinces of Mecca, Medina, Syria, Jazira (the fertile region between the Rivers Tigris and the Euphrates in Iraq), Basra, Khorasan, Azerbaijan, Persia and Egypt. A governor, answerable to the Caliph, was appointed for each province. The responsibilities of each governor's authority were clearly defined. The Governors who used their office to get rich were severely punished. The executive and the judiciary were separated, and Qadis were appointed to administer justice.

Caliph Umar (r) was open-minded and accepted and adopted what was good in other civilizations. Where applicable, he learned from and adopted the technologies and administrative practices of the conquered people. Windmills were in extensive use in Persia at the time, and Umar (r) ordered the construction of windmills in several Arab cities, including Medina. When Abu Huraira returned with a large booty from Bahrain, there were differences among the Midianites as to how to divide it up. Khalid bin Walid, observing the divisions, suggested to the Caliph that a department of documentation be set up in Medina similar to the ones he had seen in Persia. Caliph Umar (r) inquired about the Persian practices and, after satisfying himself that they were indeed applicable to the Caliphate, ordered that a department of documentation be set up. As most Arabs were illiterate, he hired Persian scribes to man this new department. The scribes documented each item of booty and the claims on each so that the Caliph could equitably divide it among the claimants. Later, the department was expanded to report all transactions of the treasury and the army. Following the example of Umar ibn al Khattab (r), the preparation and maintenance of documentation became an honoured profession among Muslims, and Caliphs and sultans alike, down to the Ottomans in modern times, kept this tradition alive.

It was during the Caliphate of Umar that Islamic jurisprudence and its methodologies based on the Qur'an, *Sunnah*, *ijma* and *qiyas* were fully established. The mandates of Umar (r), reflecting the consensus of the Companions, provided the foundation for the Maliki School of *Fiqh* that emerged a hundred years later.

- The military was organized professionally. Soldiers were paid, and defensive cantonments were established in Medina, Kufa, Basra, Mosul, Fustat (Cairo), Damascus, Edesa, and Jordan. Finance, accounting, taxation and treasury departments were organized with full accountability. Police, prisons and postal units were established.

- The land was surveyed, and agriculture was encouraged. Old canals were excavated, and new ones were built. Large areas of land were brought under cultivation. Roads were laid out and were regularly patrolled. A traveller could safely move all the way from Egypt to Khorasan in Central Asia.

- The vast territories of West Asia and North Africa were welded into a free trade zone. Trade fostered prosperity. Education was encouraged, and teachers paid. The study of the Qur'an, *Hadith*, language, literature, writing and calligraphy received patronage. Umar (r) was himself a poet of repute and a noted orator. Over 4,000 mosques were built during the Caliphate of Umar (r).

- Technology, such as the construction of windmills, was encouraged. Old bridges and roads were repaired, and new ones were built. A population census was taken after the example of the Chinese in the Tang dynasty. And it was Umar (r) who started the Islamic calendar based on the Hijra of the Prophet.

- The military successes of Umar's reign tend to remain the focal point of most histories written about him, but his administrative skills easily overshadow the achievements on the field; some of the most essential features of Umar's policy are as follows:

- Lenient terms were offered to newly conquered people, including religious freedom, although they were to pay a special tax called *jizya*.

- The purchase of land in newly acquired territories was prohibited.

- Troops were housed separately from local populations in garrison cities.

- Pensions, police force, courts, and allowances were introduced to facilitate people.

- A permanent state treasury called *f al-Mal* (house of fortune) was established.

- An uncompromising judicial system based upon supreme standards of justice was established.

To the people who had come under his rule through conquest, he offered lenient terms, low taxes, complete protection from abusive governors or troops and religious independence. Since non-Muslims were exempt from the payment of alms (*zakat*) or from military duty (which was obligatory on all non-disabled Muslims), they were subject to a separate tax – *jizya*, and they were referred to as *dhimmis* (protected people). Umar also kept tribal feuds of the hothead Arabs from surfacing through his strict rule – his successors would not be as successful as him in doing so.

Instead of distributing conquered lands among troops, as must have been expected from a desert sheikh, Umar introduced pensions for his men (to be paid by a bureaucratic office named the *diwan*) and allowed landowners to retain their properties. He also safeguarded the newly conquered people from molestation by rogue soldiers by building garrison cities to house the armies – separate from the locals: examples of such cities include Fustat in Egypt and Kufa and Basra in Iraq.

He tackled several dire issues, such as the devastation brought about by the plague in Syria, after which Muawiya (l. 602-680 CE) was sent as the new governor after Abu Ubaidah had passed away. He also distributed food among the local population during a famine in

Arabia (638 CE), saving the lives of countless people. Not only did he introduce judges and juries to handle local cases, but he also introduced special courts to hold officials accountable for misuse of power. A police force was introduced to maintain discipline in cities instead of handing over such a delicate duty to the armies. To finance such institutions and to provide for the people, a permanent state treasury, the *Bayt al-Mal* (house of fortune), was established.

Umar's love for justice surpasses all of his other traits, both in determining the effectiveness of his rule and his posthumous fame (at least in the eyes of the Sunnis and even some Shias as well). Owing to his just nature, he had earned the title of *Farooq,* the one who distinguishes between right and wrong. In Islamic tradition, a story often associated with him dictates that he flogged his son on charges of adultery and the poor lad died. The charges were proven false after his death, but the grieve-stricken father did not avenge his beloved son.

Although this incident (and many more like it) may not be more than just a fable, one can still see the impact of his character that might have inspired such odes in his favour centuries after his death. Scholar Syed Ameer Ali also makes mention of one such incidence:

When the spoils of Jalula and Madain (from Iraq; Madain refers to Ctesiphon) arrived at Medina, the Caliph was found weeping. Asked his reason, he replied that he saw in those spoils the future ruin of his people, and he was not wrong (29-30)

In the seventh century, the envoy of the Roman Emperor set out for Medinah, accompanied by a large entourage, flaunting the pageantry of adornments that the Roman Empire was famous for. On arrival in the metropolis of Islam, he enquired from a passer-by: "Tell me please, where is the palace of the Caliph?"

The Arab looked around. He was amused when told that it was the palace of Umar, the Caliph of Islam," When the visitor expressed a desire to meet Unar, the envoy willingly agreed. "Oh! You want to see Umar. Come on, I will take you in his presence," replied the Arab.

The envoy was escorted to the Mosque of the Prophet, and, to his utter astonishment, a man who was lying on the bare floor of the mosque was Indcited to him as Caliph Umar, the greatest ruler of his time, whose armies held sway over the three known continents of the world. The envoy was taken aback at such a strange sight. The report of what he observed in Medinah was enough to impress the Roman Emperor with the invincible might of Islam.

Umar's chronology is embedded in this epitaph: Umar, in full **'Umar ibn al-Khaṭṭāb** (born *c.* 586, Mecca, Arabia [now in Saudi Arabia] - died November 3, 644, Medina, Arabia), the second Muslim caliph (from 634). He was the second successor, or Caliph, to Muhammad, but he was also Muhammad's father-in-law. Umar is sometimes referred to as the "St. Paul" of Islam, first because of his success in spreading Islam and second because he was initially opposed to Islam but underwent a conversion experience that caused him to reverse course and support Prophet Muhammad. It was under him that Arab armies conquered much of the world, which became the Arabia of his day.

He is a significant figure in the development of Muslim civilization. He supervised the installation of Abu Bakr as the first Caliph and masterminded the victories over the Byzantine and Persian empires. Simplicity, poverty, and justice - these are three qualities of the brave and energetic man who led the Arabs out of the confines of the Arabian Desert into the lush lands of the age-old Fertile Crescent.

Umar was part of the first emigration to Medina and became an essential companion of Muhammad. He participated in all of the Muslim battles against the Quraish. Umar was an implacable Puritan and the architect of the whole political geography of the Islamic empire. A member of the clan of 'Adī of the Meccan tribe of Quraysh, 'Umar at first opposed Muhammad but, in about 615, became a Muslim. By

622, when he went to Medina with Muhammad and the other Meccan Muslims, he had become one of Muhammad's chief advisers, closely associated with Abū Bakr. His position in the state got a boost by Prophet Muhammad's marriage to his daughter Ḥafṣah in 625. On Muhammad's death in 632, ʿUmar was primarily responsible for reconciling the Medinan Muslims to the acceptance of a Meccan, Abū Bakr, as head of state (caliph). Abū Bakr (reigned 632–634) relied extensively on ʿUmar and nominated him to succeed him. As caliph, ʿUmar was the first to call himself "commander of the faithful" (*amīr al-muʾminīn*). His reign saw the transformation of the Islamic state from an Arabian principality to a world power.

Umar was a member of the Umayyah clan of the Makkan Quraysh tribe – thus, the name of the empire he founded was the Umayyad Empire. After the death of Muhammad, Umar made sure that the community leadership went to Abu Bakr. This effort helped ensure that the group maintained solidarity despite differing loyalties between those from Makkah and those from Medinah. Abu Bakr designated Umar as his successor when he was on his deathbed.

The great expansion

Throughout this remarkable expansion, ʿUmar closely controlled general policy and laid down the principles for administering the conquered lands. The structure of the later Islamic empire, including legal practice, is primarily due to him. ʿUmar established the *dīwān* (a register of warriors' pensions that, over time, evolved into a powerful governmental body), inaugurated the Islamic Hijrī calendar, and created the office of the qadi (judge). He also established the garrison cities of Al-Fusṭāṭ in Egypt and Basra and Kūfah in Iraq.

Converting to Islam in the 6th year after Muhammad's first revelation, Umar spent 18 years in the companionship of Muhammad. He succeeded Caliph Abu Bakr on 23 August 634 and transformed his inherited empire. His reign saw the evolution of the Islamic state from an Arabian principality to a world power, controlling the whole territory of the former Sassanid Persian Empire and more than two-thirds of the Eastern Roman Empire.

A bold strategist

Umar's legislative abilities, his firm political and administrative control over a rapidly expanding empire and his brilliantly coordinated attacks against the Sassanid Persian Empire that resulted in the conquest of the Persian Empire in less than two years marked his reputation as an astute political and military strategist. Throughout this remarkable expansion, Umar closely controlled general policy and laid down the principles for administering the conquered lands. The structure of the later Islamic empire, including legal and administrative systems and financial architecture, is primarily a result of his farsightedness and wisdom. A strong ruler, stern toward offenders, and ascetic to the point of harshness, He commanded enormous respect for his justice and authority.

Umar personified what the Arabs called *muruwwa*, the virtue of being a man. It connotes a cluster of virtues: bravery, generosity, practical wisdom, and honour, all of which are highly valued and praised in the Arab tribal culture. Umar had extraordinary practical knowledge. Practical learning - the Greeks called *phronesis*–is essentially the art of knowing the right thing to do at the right time and in the right way. It encompasses the ability to see ahead, predict how things will unfold, and forecast the consequences of a given course of action.

Throughout his reign, Umar remained a legendary Puritan, a stern, austere man who came down hard on any public display of vulgarity, gambling, improper dress, the misuse of state property, or abuse of delegated powers. He expected those entrusted with the high office to have a morality that matches their exalted responsibilities.

In 644, 'Umar was slained by a Persian Christian named Abū Lu'lu'ah and died from his wounds three days later. While he lay dying, 'Umar appointed a six-man council that eventually selected 'Uthmān ibn 'Affān as his successor.

A strong ruler, stern toward offenders, and ascetic to the point of harshness, 'Umar commanded great respect for his justice and authority. His role in decisively shaping the early Islamic community is widely acknowledged.

When the Roman emperor heard about his death, he said: "A virtuous person has passed away... I am hardly surprised to see an ascetic who renounced the world and gave himself to the prayers of Allah. But I am certainly surprised at a person who had all the world's pleasures at his feet and yet shut his eyes against them and lived a life of purity and renunciation."

Umar focused on pleasing God; he feared God's punishment and hoped for Paradise. Umar could distinguish between truth and falsehood; he was pained when the *ummah* or any member of it was hurt, and he felt joy when those under his care were content and happy worshipping their Lord.

Many regard Umar as one of the greatest political geniuses in history. He was the architect of the Islamic Empire. Under his leadership, the empire expanded at an unbelievable pace, and several administrative reforms dominated several. As a jurist, he began to codify Islamic law. He decreed that the Islamic calendar should be counted from the year of the *Hijra* of Muhammad from Makkah to Medinah.

The achievements of Umar are all the more remarkable, considering that he lacked the advantage of birth, nobility, or wealth that some of the other Companions enjoyed. He was born into the tribe of Bani 'Adi, a poorer cousin among the Quraysh. In his own words, before he accepted Islam, he was at various times a petty merchant and a shepherd who would often lose his sheep. From such humble beginnings, he rose to weld together an empire more significant in size than Rome or Persia, governed it with the Wisdom of Solomon, and administered it with the sagacity of Joseph.

The Prophet had great pride in Umar's knowledge and impeccable faith. He bore witness to the superiority of Umar in his faith and understanding, saying: 'While I was sleeping, I saw the people we gave an audience to me. Each of them was wearing a shirt. Some reached to their breast, and some reached farther than that. Then Umar was shown to me with his shirt reaching to the ground.' They asked: 'How do you interpret it, Allah's Messenger?' He said: 'Faith' [Al-Bukhari]. About his knowledge, the Prophet said, 'While sleeping, I drank until I saw springs coming from my fingernails. Then, I gave Umar some to drink.' They exclaimed, 'How do you interpret it, Allah's Messenger?' He said: 'Knowledge.' Prophet Muhammad said, "If there were to be a Prophet after me, then he would be Umar ibn Al-Khattab." *(Sahih Bukhari Volume 5, Book 57, Number 38)*.

Umar was one of the 'chosen ten' Companions of the Prophet of Islam, assured of a place in Paradise. However, this did not stop him from tirelessly working all his life to please God. He was a man of knowledge, known for his generosity and tireless devotion to the worship of God and, perhaps, above all, his devotion to the *ummah* of Muhammad. Prophet Muhammad would repeatedly counsel the *ummah*, "A man is not a true believer until he loves for his brother what he loves for himself."

As long as he lived, Umar's moral authority was undisputed. Al Tabari records: 'Umar said to Selman: 'Am I a king or a Caliph?' and Selman answered: 'If you have levied from the lands of the Muslims one dirham, or more, or less, and applied it unlawfully, you are a king, not a Caliph.' And 'Umar wept. Umar owned one shirt and one mantle, both of which had stitches of patchwork.

The glory of Islam was Umar's sole concern, and so were his achievements. After Prophet Muhammad himself, he was the principal figure in the expansion of the Arab kingdom. Simplicity, poverty, and justice are three qualities of the brave and energetic man who led the Arabs out of the confines of the Arabian Desert into the lush lands of the age-old Fertile Crescent. Without his rapid conquests, it is doubtful if Islam would have been so expansive.

Furthermore, most of the territory conquered during his reign remained Arab. Of course, it was Muhammad who was the prime mover. But it would be a grave mistake to ignore Umar's contribution. Umar capitalized on the momentum built in Prophet's time and harnessed it into a well-crafted and marvellously executed strategy.

7. A PARAGON OF NOBILITY

Prophet Muhammad planted the seed of *tawhid*. At its most elemental level, *tawhid* means belief in one God. In its historical sense, it connotes a God-focused civilization, where the focus of the entire human effort is on seeking Divine pleasure. Abu Bakr, with his wise intercession at a historic moment, ensured that the seed did not perish with the death of the Prophet. During the caliphate of Umar, the seed grew into a full-blown tree and bore fruit. Umar shaped the historical edifice of Islam, and whatever Islam became or did not become in subsequent centuries is due primarily to the work of this great soldier.

Indeed, Umar was the architect of Islamic civilization. Umar wept when the following verse in the Qur'an was revealed: "We offered the trust to the mountains, heavens and the earth, but they declined, being afraid thereof, but humankind accepted it. Indeed humankind was unjust and foolish" (Qur'an, 33:72-73). Umar understood that the trust referred to here is human free will. Humankind accepted this trust, while all other creations declined it. When the will of man is determined to benefit human nobility, it elevates him to a position higher than that of the angels. When free will is misused, it reduces humans to the most wretched creatures. No man understood this better than Umar and few since the Prophet carried this trust with as much wisdom, humility, determination, sensitivity, persistence, and courage. Measured by any yardstick, Umar was one of the most significant figures in human history.

A simple and pious ruler

The most delicate pearls in the world come from the Arabian Gulf. Pearls were m graded in five categories. The pearl of the highest quality, the perfect pearl, is called *al-Jiwan*. Among all leadership qualities, great and small, integrity is *al-Jiwan*. Integrity implies such rectitude that one is incorruptible or incapable of being false to a trust or a responsibility or one's standards. As the Latin proverb says, integrity is the noblest possession. In the case of Umar, his impeccable integrity was his most treasured asset.

Umar despised the trappings of kingship and wealth. Foreign visitors were always amazed that there was no protocol for gatekeepers, court chancellors, or bodyguards. Umar was extraordinarily pious and averse to worldly luxuries. He preferred simplicity to extravagance. He deposited all assets and wealth meant for the ruling caliph into the Bait Al Maal. He even abandoned the royal palace and lived in a modest house. He wore rough clothes instead of royal robes and often went unrecognized in public like his great-grandfather, Caliph Umar ibn Al Khattab.

Umar led an austere life that had been transfused in him by his revered Master—Prophet Muhammad. He would preside over the advisory council meetings in the mosque, where he would receive ambassadors from the Persian and Roman empires. He was a firm believer in the efficacy of prayer and disdained superstitious beliefs. The Christian Copts of Egypt became anxious when the flow of the Nile was delayed. According to an old custom, the local people decided to cast into the river an effigy of a beautiful woman, The Bride of the Nile. They sought permission from the Caliph. Umar sent the following reply to them:

"From Commander of the Faithful to river Nile. Greetings, If in times you have risen on your own will, then stay your flood; if by the will of Almighty Allah, then to Him we pray that your waters may rise and overspread the land." Umar instructed that this document was to be flowed in the river. The result was that the tide began to rise in large quantities.

Umar's honesty

On one occasion, Umar said from the pulpit, "O people, in case you ever find me tilting towards worldliness, what will you do then?" A man rose from the gathering, drew his sword and said, "You will be beheaded with it." To further test him, Umar said, "You, daring to say so to me." The man remained resolved and said, "Yes, it will be like this for you." Umar remarked, "Thank God. I have men like you who dare to straighten me out if ever I choose to deviate from the right path".

On several occasions, foreign envoys and messengers deputed to Umar by their rulers and generals found him resting under a palm tree or praying in the mosque with ordinary people. It was impossible to distinguish the Caliph from the general crowd. Such was the simplicity and earthiness of Umar. He slept on a bed of palm leaves. His diet was dates or coarse barley bread dipped in salt; his drink was water; sometimes, he would eat bread without salt by penance. He preached in a tattered cotton gown, patched in 12 places.

Once, the Governor of Kufa visited him while he was eating barley bread and olive oil. The Governor said, *Ameerul Mu'mineen* (Muslim Head of State), enough wheat is produced in your dominions, why don't you take wheat bread? Feeling somewhat offended, the Caliph asked him in a melancholy tone, "Do you think what is available to every person inhabiting my vast dominions?" "No," replied the Governor. "Then how can I take wheat bread unless it is available to all my people

The Qur'an condemns those who overindulge in worldliness and, yet, says that monasticism is not something God prescribes (Q57:27). The problem, though, is that too often, the "balance" tilts more towards materialism than simplicity. Therefore, one of our time's spiritual and ethical responsibilities is to rediscover an appreciation for living a simple life.

Prophet Muhammad said, "Every religion has a chief characteristic, and the chief characteristic of Islam is modesty." During his travels,

Umar would take no tent but throw his gown over a low bush and lie down in the shade. He performed the pilgrimage nine times during his caliphate. Piety, abstinence, and downright simplicity were the hallmarks of his character. "His walking stick," wrote one Muslim historian," struck more terror in those who were present than another man's sword." He would spend several nights visiting townships and going about the streets of Medinah to find out if anyone needed help or assistance. The general social and moral tone of Muslim society is well-illustrated by the words of an Egyptian who was spying on the Muslims during their Egyptian campaign. He reported: "I have seen a people, every one of whom loves death more than he loves life. They cultivate humility rather than pride. None is given to material ambitions. Their mode of living is simple. Their commander is their equal. They make no distinction between superior and inferior, between an enslaved individual and an enslaved person. When the time of prayer approaches, none remains behind...."

Al-Awza'i once narrated: "Umar came out in the depths of the night and was sighted by Talha, a renowned Companion of the Prophet. 'Umar went and entered a house and then entered another one. The following morning, Talha went to this house, where he saw a blind, disabled old lady. He said to her, 'Why does this man come to you?' She said, 'he has taken care of me since such and such. He comes, helps me with what is good for me, and takes away the harm.' Talha said, 'O Talha, may your mother be bereft. Are you following the slips of 'Umar?'" (*The Virtues of 'Umar ibn Al-Khattab*, by Ibn al-Jawzi, p. 68)

Treatment of conquered

Umar designed and controlled the general policy for administering the newly conquered territories and their people. Accordingly, the conquered masses were undisturbed so;uut t; heirs fi;h, community life, and properties, provided they paid the protection money (*jizyah*). However, this tax was levied on non-disabled men only. The weaker sections who lived on alms were exempted. This tax was assessed on a sliding scale: four gold coins (the golden denarius or dinar then weighed around 4 grams) for a wealthy merchant, two for a shopkeeper, and one for a poor labourer. Local notables were included in the new administration, and old taxes were collected./ Greek, Persian, or Copt remained the official language in these territories for fifty years. Conversion of the subjects to Islam was not encouraged. Non-Muslims took part in consultations on matters of national interest. Local Zoroastrians and Marian chiefs in Iraq were consulted, and a Copt from Egypt was invited to Medina for consultation. The head of the revenue department in Medina was Greek. In 13 AH (635), 4000 prisoners arrived in Medina after the capture of Kaisariyah (Caesarea). Some of them were employed as clerks, and some as manual labourers for the Muslims. Abu Musa Ashari had a Christian secretary.

Compassion and justice

Umar instructed Muslim armies to be humane and not to destroy any crops of enemies. The landowners who lost their crops on account of the movement of the troops were given appropriate compensation. Once, he gave 10,000 dirhams to a farmer whose harvest had been destroyed by the Muslim army.

On his way back from Syria, Umar passed by some men who had been standing in the sun with oil poured over their heads (to attract the flies). On inquiry, he was informed that they were liable for a levy but had not been paid it and were punished, so they relied on the rule. When Umar came to know that they were too impoverished to pay the penalty, Umar waived the fees and allowed them t;o;g;o.

Umar inferred from a verse of the Holy Qur'an that *sadaqa* money should be expended on two groups, *fuqara* and *masakin*. By the former is meant the helpless Muslims, and by the latter, needy Jews and Christians. Accordingly, non-Muslims were also helped with such funds. Once Umar saw an old Christian begging, he asked why he was begging. " I have to pay *Jizyah*, and I am unable to do that due to my age," was his reply. Umar regretted that we enjoy the fruits of their labour when they are young and should be neglectful when they are old. He brought the older man home, provided assistance, and directed the supervisor of *Bait al-Mal* (state treasury) to give him a subsistence allowance. The man was also exempted from paying *Jizyah*.

When Umar was passing through al-Jabiyah in the province of Damascus, he saw some Christians smitten with elephantiasis, and he ordered that they be given something out of the *sadaqah. F*ood stipends are assigned to them.

Old age pensions were given to older people, whether they were Muslims or non-Muslims; similarly, poor houses were open to all. When Jews of Khaybar and Christians of Najran were ordered to settle elsewhere, they were paid the total value of their lands and properties. Likewise, when the people of Araboos, a town situated on the border between Syria and Asia Minor, were exiled because of their espionage for the Romans, they were given double the value of their properties, land, and cattle.

Writes Ameer Ali, the noted historian, "(He was) stern but just, far-sighted thoroughly versed in the character of his people, he was specially fitted for the leadership of the unruly Arabs. He had held the helm with a strong hand. He was a man of towering height, austere and frugal, always accessible to his subjects."

He never denied the military laurels to his fighting men. He was a statesman and an acknowledged and acclaimed strategist of empire-building. Still, He allowed his generals complete freedom of action during their campaigns and willingly conceded the glory they deserved when they returned as victors.

Stern ruler

A strong ruler, stern towards offenders, and ascetic to the point of harshness, Umar was universally respected for his justice and stentorian authority. He warned his deputies, whether governors of vast provinces or generals in command of tens of thousands of warriors, not to be seduced into basking in pomp and splendour or to be ever found closing the house doorways to people with low incomes. He despised extravagance and displays of opulence. Once, a Christian complained to Umar in the Harem in Makkah that he had been doubly taxed on his horse. He submitted this complaint when Umar was delivering the sermon there. Later, when he returned to the capital, the same Christian who had complained came to him to remind him of it. Umar told him, "I'm the *Hanifi* who took care of your complaint there and then."

The rule of democracy

True democracy, as preached and practised during the caliphate of the first four Caliphs, has hardly any parallel in history. The Qur'an explicitly states that since Islam is a democratic religion, the state must conduct its affairs through democratic consultation. The Prophet himself did not make any significant decision without consultation. The seedling of democracy planted by the Prophet and nourished by Abu Bakr blossomed in the caliphate of Umar. Two consultative bodies functioned during his reign; one was a general assembly that was convened when the state was confronted with critical matters. The other was a unique body comprising unquestionable integrity persons consulted on routine and urgent matters. Even issues relating to the appointments and dismissals of public servants were brought before this particular committee, and its decisions were carefully adhered to. Non-Muslims were also invited to participate in such consultations. The native Parsi chiefs were frequently consulted regarding the administration of Iraq (Mesopotamia).

Similarly, Muqauqis were consulted in Egyptian matters, and a Copt had been invited to Medinah as the representative of Egypt. The provincial governors were appointed on the advice of the people and the local inhabitants. At times, the various posts in the provinces were filled by election. When the appointment of the Tax Officers was to be made for Kufa, Basra, and Syria, Umar permitted the inhabitants of those provinces to select suitable and honest officers of their own choice. The Caliph later endorsed the selection of the people. Umar strongly believed that the people must have a say in the administration of the caliphate. He strongly espoused and practised participatory approaches. Even a poor older woman could publicly question the great Caliph for his various activities, and he had to explain his conduct on the spot.

All the governors were required to assemble at Makkah on the occasion of the *hajj*, and any person could complain against any officer. Umar believed their function was not to rule the people; they had to serve them by building a welfare society. Umar's guiding principle of administration was: "By God, he that is weakest among you shall be in my eyes the strongest until I have vindicated for him his right. He is the strongest, and I will treat him as the weakest until he complies with the law."

Umar was ruthless with his commanders and governors because he believed passionately in public honesty, the accessibility of rulers, and the dignity of the people. The Caliph himself practised what he preached. Never in the annals of history has one found public service that could match the one practised in the early caliphate of Islam. Umar lived like an ordinary man, and every man was free to question his actions. Once, he said, "I have no more authority over the *Baitul Mal* (State Treasury) than a custodian has over the orphan's property. If I were well-to-do, I would not accept any honorarium; if not, I would draw a little to meet the ordinary necessities of life. Brothers, I am your servant; you should control and question my actions. One is that public money should neither be unnecessarily hoarded nor wasted. I must work for the welfare and prosperity of our people." Once, a person shouted in a public meeting, "O, Umar! Fear God." The audience wanted to silence him, but the Caliph prevented them from saying, "If the people do not exhibit such frankness, they are good for nothing, and if we do not listen to them, we will be like them." Such encouragement to the expression of the public ensured the efficiency and honesty of public service and state administration. The people realised the actual worth of public opinion.

Leadership

Umar watched the people like a shepherd does over his herd. He would spend the nights in worship, often waking his family in the last part of the night to join him. One of Prophet Muhammad's companions narrates that Umar once distributed 22,000 dirhams to people in need and had a habit of giving away bags of sugar. When asked for clarification, Umar was asked why he spread the sugar, he said, "Because I love it, and God said in the Qur'an, 'By no means shall you attain piety unless you spend (in God's Cause) of that which you love; and whatever of good you spend, God knows it well." (Qur'an 3:92).

He believed in dispensing prompt and timely justice through his earthly wisdom, and he epitomized the great juristic principles of later modern and sophisticated societies. He demonstrated that uncommon commonsense could even trump learning and erudition. Much jurisprudential rhetoric has crystallized from age-old commonsense principles towards half-fangled clichés and jargon.

To Umar, justice was a goddess whose symbols were a throne that tempests could not shake, a pulse that passion could not stir, eyes that were blind to any feeling of favour or ill will, and the sword that fell on all offenders with equal certainty and with impartial strength. If there was somebody in the flesh with these physical features, it was Umar.

His one burning desire was to do natural justice. In achieving that aim, he brushed aside the conservatism, which fails to conserve, and nurtured the form at the expense of the substance. He won great laurels in every field, but he always remained the gentle, modest, affectionate man. There are few persons other than Umar with whom the following lines of James Russell Lowell fit better:

His magic was not far to seek,

He was so human! Whether strong or weak

Far from his kind, he neither sank nor soared,

But sat an equal guest at every board.

No beggar ever felt him condescend,

No prince presume, for still himself, he bore

At manhood's superficial level, and where'er

He met a stranger, and he left a friend there.

The demotion of Khalid

Khalid bin Walid was an exemplary military commander of Islamic armed forces since the tenure of Abu Bakr. He was also known as *Sayf Allāh al-Maslūl* (Drawn Sword of God). He occupied a unique position on account of his courage and bravery. He was known to be a gritty and tenacious soldier who inspired awe in the opponents' camps. Umar always held him in high esteem and admired his chivalry.

In a weird development, Umar stripped Khalid of his command of the Syrian division for uncertain and highly debated reasons. He instead entrusted the power to his favourite person: Abu Ubaidah (l. 583-639 CE), a humane leader and a true gentleman; he had also been one of Muhammad's favourite companions (there were ten in total, four of whom were the four Rashidun Caliphs). The Caliph also reinforced the Muslim forces in Iraq with fresh troops under a new leader: SA'd ibn Abi Waqqas (l. 595-674 CE).

In 636 CE, the Byzantine Empire struck back at the Muslims. Although Khalid was no longer officially in command, he was highly respected by the soldiers owing to his expertise in warfare. Taking his advice, the Muslim forces retreated to the Yarmouk River. It was here that the battle that would determine the region's fate for centuries to come took place. The elite Byzantine troops outnumbered their foes, but Khalid was no stranger to fighting against odds. The Byzantines suffered a crushing defeat; the army was routed with slaughter, and many perished due to drowning in the river. Not only did the Muslim position in Syria become uncontested, but they also took hold of the Levant soon after; later in the same year, they were at the gates of Jerusalem – the third holiest Islamic city, also blessed for the Jews and Christians.

The same year, on the other side of the Syrian Desert, the Saracen forces (as European history refers to Arabs and Muslims) under Sa'ad met the mighty Sassanian Empire under their legendary leader, Rustam Farrokhzad – a man with a similar reputation to that of Khalid. The Battle of al-Qadisiyya (636 CE) proved hopeless for the Arabs at first, but the fateful death of Rustam demoralized his forces, who were utterly defeated. The Rashidun forces had emerged triumphant against staggering odds once again, and this victory had immediately brought the whole of Iraq and the Sassanian capital of Ctesiphon under control. Umar ordered the forces not to proceed into the unfamiliar territory of Iran lest they be defeated, and their gains reversed. The importance of these two victories cannot be overstated; the defences of the opposing forces were crushed, and they could not field effective counterattacks at similar levels anymore.

After the success at Yarmouk, Umar arrived in Syria and the Levant primarily to receive the surrender of Jerusalem (which was under siege) and to manage domestic affairs in the region. Meanwhile, it became known that Umar had removed Khalid from command for good; sources argue whether Umar had personal problems with him or if it was due to

Khalid's harsh nature. The vast majority of Muslim historians suggest that Umar might have done so to show that God gave them their victories and that no matter who led them, God's help was the only determining factor; at least, this was what he announced in public.

Despite some controversies against him, Khalid was very popular among the Muslim troops who would follow him into any battle, no matter how bad the odds were. Before his dismissal, Khalid had led successful expeditions into Anatolia and Armenia in 638 CE. Though he was encouraged to rebel against the Caliph, he refused and retired peacefully. Umar appointed Abu Ubaidah as the governor of Syria, and he also wished to nominate him as his successor. Still, the latter died in 639 CE in the wake of the plague that devastated the area.

Khalid's fame worried Umar, who saw it as a possible threat to his authority. Umar needed the pretext to take punitive action against Khalid. He found one such excuse when Khalid, during his stay at Emesa, had a unique bath with a particular substance prepared with an alcoholic mixture. Umar's spies informed him of the incident. Since alcohol was forbidden, a firm ground arose for punishment, and Umar took notice of it, asking Khalid to explain the misconduct. Khalid felt that this was carrying the Muslim ban on alcohol a bit too far since it dealt only with the drinking of it and not its external applications. The excuse was enough for Umar and the senate at Medinah to be satisfied. Incidentally, another more potent opportunity came Umar's way when, shortly after Khalid's capture of Marash (Kahramanmaraş) in the autumn of 638, he came to know of Ash'as, a famous poet and warrior on the Persian front, reciting a poem in praise of Khalid and receiving a gift of 10,000 dirhams from him, apparently from the state treasury.

Umar and his senate identified this act as a misuse of state treasure, though not as punishing as losing one's office. In the case of Khalid, this was the excuse that Umar needed. He immediately wrote a letter to Abu Ubaida asking him to bring Khalid in front of them and take off his cap.

Umar wanted Abu Ubaida to ask Khalid what funds were used: from his pocket or the state treasury. If he confessed to using the spoils, he was guilty of misappropriation. He was guilty of extravagance if he claimed that he gave from his pocket. In either case, he would be dismissed, and Abu Ubaida would take charge of his duties. Umar was known for his punctiliousness with rules and never compromised while dispensing justice. He immediately relieved him from his position when he was in the midst of the battle of Yarmouk. The manner of Khalid's deposition is worth mentioning. In a public assembly, the messenger entrusted with the writ of testimony questioned Khalid about the source from which he had met the grant. Umar's orders were that Khalid should be forgiven if he only admitted his offence, but Khalid was unwilling to confess. The messenger was, therefore, compelled, as a mark of deposition, to remove Khalid's turban from his head, and, as a punishment for his defiant attitude, his neck was with the same turban. Khalid's humble acceptance of his new position, a mere warrior among the thousands of other Arab horse riders, was the stoic action that would complete his identity among the pantheon of Arab heroes. It was surprising to find that a mighty general who had no equal in the whole of the Islamic world and whose redoubtable sword had sealed the fate of Iraq and Syria was thus made to drink the cup of humiliation to the dregs but suffered not a murmur to escape his lips. The event, however, shows Khalid's sincerity and love of truth on the one hand and Umar's might and grandeur on the other.

On reaching Amasia, Khalid made a speech regarding his deposition, in which he observed that Umar, the Commander of the Faithful, appointed him Chief of Syria but dismissed him when he had conquered the whole of that country.

On this, a soldier got up and said: "Hold thy tongue, O Chief! Such words might engender sedition."

"Yes," rejoined Khalid, "but sedition cannot grow while Umar lives."

Khalid came to Medinah and waited on Umar.

"O Umar!" said he "by Allah, you do me an injustice."

"How did you manage to amass so much wealth?" asked Umar.

"From the spoils of war," replied Khalid.

He then added that he was willing to make any sum over and above sixty thousand dirhams that might be found. A surplus was found and was remitted to the public treasury.

"Khalid!" said Umar to the ex-Commander-in- Chief, "By Allah, I love you and honour you at the same time." Thus, he wrote to all the provincial governors to the effect that he did not dismiss Khalid not because of being offended or because he deemed him guilty of breach of trust but because people grew more and more attached to him and that he accordingly considered it advisable to depose Khalid so that his admirers might realize that God does not dispose of everything.

The wife of Khalidwas pained at the episode and exclaimed to Khalid: "You were given the title of 'Saifullah' meaning, 'The Sword of Allah' and, the sword of Allah is not meant to be broken, and hence, it is not your destiny to be a 'martyr' but to die like a conqueror."

When he cashiered his foremost tactician, Khalid, this was not because of a fit of brilliant subordinate jealousy but because he found Khalid guilty of certain charges. Still, Umar continued to respect the great soldier for his valour. Some versions say the soldier was not happy as it was his dream to die a martyr, which couldn't be achieved.

8. A PIONEERING REFORMER

Umar was one of Prophet Muhammad's earliest and staunchest supporters and quickly developed an administrative system of superior effectiveness. s known for his economic policies

He defined the *ummah* as a continually expansive polity managed by the new ruling elite, which included successful military commanders like Khālid ibn al-Walīd. Even after the conquests ended, this sense of expansiveness continued in the way Muslims divided the world into their zone, the Dār al-Islām, and the zone into which they could and should expand, the Dār al-Ḥarb, the abode of war. Islam supplied the norms of Umar's new elite.

Umar was a great reformer and a path-builder. The message we must take from his life and work is that if we have to move from one century to another successfully, we must be able to meet the manifold challenges that await us creatively. Islam is a living faith, a dynamic religion with firm principles and sufficient flexibility to adapt to all times and conditions. We must continuously reinterpret and rethink the tradition of Islam in terms of contemporary challenges.

The Journey of a Visionary Leader

Umar ibn al-Khattab's story begins in the heart of the Arabian Peninsula amidst the harsh deserts and thriving trade routes. Born into the Quraysh tribe, renowned for their leadership in Mecca, Umar's early life was shaped by the tribal customs and idolatrous practices prevalent before the advent of Islam. A man of muscular physique, sharp intellect, and formidable determination, he initially perceived Islam as a threat to the social fabric of Quraysh society.

Despite his early resistance, the transformative journey of Umar from a staunch adversary to a devoted follower of Islam stands as a testament to the profound impact of faith and conviction. It was during a moment of intended violence, when Umar set out to harm the Prophet Muhammad that the verses of the Qur'an touched his heart. Overwhelmed by the beauty and truth of the words he heard, Umar's hostility transformed into submission to the divine, marking a pivotal turn not only in his life but also in the history of Islam. This moment of conversion is a compelling narrative of change, highlighting the power of guidance and the potential within every individual for profound transformation.

As a new adherent to Islam, Umar's influence and zeal became a cornerstone in the young Muslim community. His conversion brought strength, legitimacy, and protection to the Muslims, who were facing persecution and hardship. The same vigour he once directed against Islam, he now channelled into its service, becoming a staunch defender of the faith and the Prophet's trusted companion. Umar's story from this point onward is a remarkable chronicle of faith, leadership, and unwavering dedication to justice and the principles of Islam.

From Foe to Faithful

Umar ibn al-Khattab's early scepticism towards Islam is well-documented, marking a period of internal conflict and societal tension. Yet, his heart-changing encounter with the Qur'an's verses showcases the profound impact of divine words on a seeking soul. Umar's dramatic shift from a formidable opponent to a staunch believer highlights the transformative power of guidance and the importance of keeping an open heart. This pivotal moment in Umar's life not only altered his destiny but also fortified the growing Muslim community with a leader of unmatched vigour and conviction.

Leadership and Expansion

As a Caliph, Umar's governance was revolutionary. Significant expansions marked his tenure, yet it's his just and compassionate rule that stands out. Umar was a pioneer in establishing welfare states, ensuring justice and provision for all, regardless of status or faith. His strategic insight was matched by a profound commitment to the ethical principles of leadership, setting standards that remain influential.

A Compassionate Conqueror

Umar's approach to leadership and conquest was unique. His respect for life, dedication to justice, and emphasis on the welfare of citizens, regardless of their religion, set a precedent in governance. The story of Umar sparing Jerusalem's inhabitants and preserving its holy sites during its capture exemplifies his visionary approach to leadership and respect for diverse cultures and religions.

Legacy of Humility

Despite his power, Umar lived a life of simplicity, remaining accessible and accountable to the people. His legacy teaches us the importance of humility, service, and the transformative impact of living by one's values. Umar's life is a powerful reminder of the strength found in compassion and humility, guiding principles for leaders in any era.

Lessons of Leadership

Umar ibn al-Khattab's journey from a sceptical observer to a revered leader in Islamic history is a narrative of transformation, leadership, and enduring legacy. His life offers invaluable lessons on the impact of visionary leadership and the power of faith to effect change.

Discover More

Did Umar's story inspire them? Dive deeper into the rich history of Islamic leaders who shaped our world. Sign up for our history program to explore the lives of influential figures like Umar ibn al-Khattab and their lasting legacies.

Transparency in administration

The success of Umar's administration was mainly due to his strict vigilance with the officials. When a Governor was appointed, his appointment letter detailed his duties and privileges. This letter was publicly read out to make people aware of the appointment's terms and hold him accountable for any abuse of power.

Addressing a group of Governors, he once said, "Remember, I have not appointed you to rule over your people, but to serve them. You should set an example with your good conduct so that people may follow you."

Umar took particular care to emphasize that there should not be much distinction between the ruler and the ruled, and the people should have easy and free access to the state's highest authority. He insisted that Governors live simple lives, keep no guard at their doors and be accessible to the people at all times. Umar himself set the example for them. Whenever he was appointed governor, he used to draw up a certificate of inauguration in writing, which he would get witnessed by some of the emigrants or helpers. It contained the following directions: "He must not ride on horseback, eat white bread, nor wear fine clothes, nor set up a door between himself and those who ought to ask of him." He kept strict vigil over the assets of governors who used to record the possessions at the time of their appointment, and whatever was later acquired by them was partly or wholly confiscated.

Ahmad Ibn Yahya al-Baladhuri, the author of the *Kitab Futuh al-Buldan* ("Book of the Conquests of the Lands"), an inventory of movable and immovable assets of the crucial officials was prepared at the time of his appointment, which was updated from time to time. Any unusual increase in assets had to be adequately accounted for and explained. All the high officials had to report to the Caliph every year at the time of *Hajj*. According to Abu Yusuf, the author of *Kitabul Khiraj*, a treatise on taxation and fiscal problems of the state, any unsatisfied individual could complain to the errant official irrespective of his rank. The complaints had to be disposed of in a fixed timeframe. Even the highest officials of the state were not spared if the complaints were found to be genuine. Once, a person complained that a certain governor had flogged him for no fault. The matter was enquired into, and the Governor was publicly flogged with the same number of stripes for his errancy.

Muhammad bin Muslamah Ansari, a person of unquestionable integrity, was appointed as the roving investigator, who visited different countries and enquired into public complaints. Once, some disgruntled citizens filed a complaint with the Caliph, saying that Saad bin Waqas, Governor of Kufa, had constructed a palace at once. Umar dispatched Muhammad Ansari, who pulled down a portion of the palace that hindered the easy entry of the public. On another complaint, Saad was deposed. The Caliph received a report that Ayaz bin Ganam, the *Amil* (Governor) of Egypt, had kept a gatekeeper for his house. Muhammad Ansari, who was immediately sent to Egypt, found the report to be correct and brought the Governor to Medinah. The Caliph humiliated him publicly.

Amr ibn al-Asi had his possessions confiscated by the Caliph when he was Governor of Egypt. Similarly, the Caliph seized 12000 dirhams from Abu Hurairah, who was once Governor of al-Bahrain.

At times, a commission was appointed by the Caliph to enquire into various charges. Such strict measures adopted by Umar ensured an efficient and transparent administration in his vast state. Even the officials working thousands of miles away from Medinah could not dare to do anything against the interests of the people and the state. None could ever contemplate incurring the displeasure of the iron Caliph.

Innovations in agriculture

Water scarcity converted the barren Arabian Peninsula into a vast desert that has never yielded substantial agricultural produce. Her scattered population always had to fall back on a foreign supply of food grains to supplement the dates and the little corn grown in their lands. Agriculture in Arabia, which has had the distinction of being the cradle of the world's great prophets, has been very primitive and was confined to those tracts where water was available in the form of springs. Taif, a hilly place, is known as the garden of Hejaz, where wheat is also cultivated, besides grapes, apples, figs, pomegranates, and dates. With its springs and wells, Medina is a green spot in a vast desert, and dates, wheat and barley are grown there.

The great Prophet of Islam had left behind him a group of selfless people whose sagacity and generosity, faith and unity, the spirit of sacrifice and service won for them laurels not only on the battlefields but in almost all branches of human activity. Agriculture was no exception, and as early as the reign of the second Caliph of Islam, Arabs made considerable progress in agriculture and introduced many beneficial measures for its advancement in their dominions, including Egypt, Syria, Iraq, and Hejaz.

During the reign of the second Caliph, the Arab conquest was extended over Asia and Africa. Arabs were confronted with new problems that the administration of such a vast empire had brought to its wake. The Arabs adapted native techniques used for handling such issues in their dominions.

Umar had fixed the land revenue rates according to the land type. He charged four dirhams on one jar of sown wheat, while he charged 2 dirhams for a similar plot of barley. Nothing was set for pastures and uncultivated land. In this way, he systematized revenues that, before his time, were charged haphazardly. There were several rules for the revenues of Egypt, whose agricultural output depended on the floods of the Nile River. According to reliable historical sources, Iraq's annual revenues amounted to 860 million dirhams, an amount that was never exceeded even after the death of the great Caliph. However, he was very lenient in levying them. The main reason behind the easy realisation of revenue was that the people had become prosperous.

He introduced many far-reaching reforms. One of these was the abolition of landlords or zamindari and the subsequent disappearance of the evils being wrought on the poor tenants by the vested landed interests. When the Romans conquered Syria and Egypt, they confiscated the land from the soil tillers and allotted it to the nobles, churches, members of the royal family, and the armed forces.

In general, Umar's solution was to leave the conquered peoples in possession of their lands and their religion in exchange for the payment of tribute, which was to be disbursed by the Muslim government to its armies and citizens. To institutionalize this policy, a divan, or register, was drawn up, which regularized the stipends that Muslims were to be paid according to religious and tribal principles. Relations between Muslims and non-Muslims were further stabilized by exempting the latter from military service and guaranteeing them protection in return for the taxes they paid.

After the conquest of these countries, Umar returned the land to those local inhabitants who were the rightful owners. The just and benevolent Caliph was exceptionally generous to the tillers of the soil, and he even issued strict orders that non-natives and Arab soldiers who had intruded into these countries should be granted land for cultivation purposes. Such steps by the second caliph of Islam restored confidence among the local inhabitants, gave a great impetus to the advancement of agriculture in those countries, and contributed to the enormous increase in agricultural production. The tenants became prosperous, and their standard of living was raised, which led to the easy realization of land revenues by the custodians of the State.

It was those generous and liberal tax policies of the second Caliph that the Christian Qibtis of Egypt, who were farmers, always sided with Muslim Arabs in preference to Roman Christians. He designed schemes for the advancement of agriculture and constructed irrigation canals, wells and tanks in his vast dominions. He established a public welfare department that monitored and expanded these works. The famous historian Allama Maqrizi says that more than one lac and twenty thousand labourers were employed in such works throughout the year in Egypt alone. Several canals were constructed in Khuzistan and Ahwaz during this period.

Sound governance

- To meet the needs of the public and to govern well, Umar also introduced the following reformation:

- Institution of *hisbah*. This is an institution to maintain law and order in the marketplace. It is headed by an officer known as *Muhtasib*.

- There was an exclusive office for investigating complaints addressed to the Caliph. A very reliable and trustworthy person was appointed for the post.

- A *bait al-mal* or Treasury House.

Umar separated the judicial and executive duties to specialize in the effective management of both. Special judges (*Qadi*) were appointed to perform the function of the judiciary, who were distinct and separate from the role of the Governor of the province and territories, and *Qadi*'s were placed under the supervision of the Caliph. Separation of power can give the judicial benefit management and enable the administration of the court to run efficiently. The ideological system suggested by Umar was among the best, with the separation of power encouraging leaders and the people to use power and authority correctly.

Further, strategic planning in economic systems was also introduced, providing the most benefit to the people and state and, in due respect, to his responsibility and accountability to Allah. Caliph Umar inspired the best economic systems. He introduced a variety of revenue systems for countries, which formed the foundation of the land tenure system.

The different systems of land tenure that were prevalent in the Muslim Empire during the caliphate of 'Umar Ibn al-Khattab were:

- *Iqta* or Individual ownership system. The grant conferred proprietary rights on the beneficiaries such that an *iqta* became *iqta talk*, where the owners were free to use the land in any way they liked.

- *Hima* or collective land-ownership system. Hima was a vital institution that was prevalent at the time of Umar. It means that one or more tribes own the land.

- With the conquest of different countries' Crown lands and state landlordism., state landlordism also flourished. Under this system, land belonged to the state, and cultivators were the state's tenants. The tenant did not enjoy proprietary rights, and the occupants could not transfer or sell the land.

- Private landlordism was first practised by the Prophet, who agreed with the Jews and Khaybar.

- Peasant-proprietorship. In this system, the owner tilled the land. This system was standard in Arabia, especially in those parts that were arable and fertile.

Umar also introduced land reform following the conquest of agricultural countries like Iraq, Iran and Egypt. Umar took a bold step in abolishing absentee landlordism and changing the Islamic Empire's whole pattern of land ownership.

Moreover, Umar's principle of *al-shura* best explains the efficacy of collective governance. *Al-shura* is an Arabic term that means mutual consultation. This principle demonstrates many vital values for governance, including transparency, accountability, respect, empowerment, freedom of expression, the dignity of the human individual and cooperation all together in one practice. In addition, it proves that Islamic governance appreciates and welcomes other parties and entities in its decision-making system. These entities kept on expanding and growing, with their members consisting of leaders from various tribes who were proven to be qualified, including 'Ali Ibn 'Abi Talib, 'Uthman Ibn al-'Affan, Talhah, 'Ubaydillah, al-Zubayr 'Awwam, Saad'Abi Waqqas, and 'Abdul Rahman Ibn 'Auf. They were the meeting members, especially when deciding on important matters. Caliph Umar gave a message to them, saying, "I find out that all of you are the leaders of your community, and all matters that need to be decided must stop upon all of you."

This principle and practice also stipulate 'rida al awam', which is popular consent; 'ijtihad jama'i', which is collective deliberation; and 'mas'uliyah jama'iyyah', which is a collective responsibility, as a prerequisite to the establishment of Islamic effective governance.

Umar's initiatives in the professionalization of the administration

Umar was an excellent administrator. He established a *Shura* (consultative council) and sought advice on matters of state. He divided the far-flung empire into the provinces of Makkah, Medinah, Syria, Jazira (the fertile region between the rivers Tigris and Euphrates in Iraq), Basra, Khorasan, Azerbaijan, Persia and Egypt. A Governor, answerable to the Caliph, was appointed for each province. The responsibilities and the limits of each Governor's authority were clearly defined. Governors who misused their office were severely punished. The executive and the judiciary were separated, and Qadis were appointed to administer justice.

Appointing a Governor in the Basra province, Umar wrote to him, "Listen, you are not appointed to rule over the necks of the people but to guide them on the right path, which you know from the Qur'ān and the *sunnah* of the Prophet." While the governor was the head of provincial administration, the Collector (*Amil*) was the head of the finance and revenue department.

The Caliph was the Chief Judge of the Empire. There were also Qadis in the provinces assisted by a team of judicial experts in Shari'ah. Besides Qur'ānic injections and *sunnah* in judicial matters, *ijma* (collective opinion) was also allowed.

Umar was open-minded, accepted, and adopted what was good in other civilizations. Where applicable, he learned to embrace the conquered people's technologies and administrative practices. His achievements are codified into the *Await – i-Umar*, the forty-one initiatives of Umar. Windmills were extensively used in Persia at the time, and Umar ordered the construction of windmills in several Arab cities, including Medinah.

When Abu Hurairah returned with a large booty from Bahrain, there were differences among the Midianites as to how it was to be divided. Khalid bin Walid, observing the divisions, suggested to the Caliph that a documentation department be set up in Medinah similar to the ones he had seen in Persia. Caliph Umar enquired about the Persian practices and ordered a documentation department after being satisfied that they could indeed be applied to the Caliphate. As most Arabs were illiterate, he hired Persian scribes to man this new department. The writers documented each item of booty and the claims on each so that the Caliph could equitably divide it among the claimants. Later, the department was expanded to document all treasury and army transactions. Following the example of Umar, the compilation and maintenance of documentation became an honoured profession among Muslims, Caliphs and Sultans alike, down to the Ottomans in modern times, keeping this tradition alive.

During the caliphate of Umar, Islamic jurisprudence and its methodologies based on the Qur'an, *sunnah, ijma* and *qiyas* were fully established. The mandates of Umar reflecting the consensus of the Companions provided the foundation for the Maliki School of *Fiqh (jurisprudence)* that emerged a hundred years later.

Streamlining the armed forces

The conquest of such a vast area in such a relatively short time soon created challenging administrative problems for Umar. Since the Arabs had no experience as rulers of an empire, they were forced to rely significantly on the bureaucracies created by the Byzantine and Sassanian governments. Nevertheless, Umar is credited with introducing several new administrative practices and institutions which, in conjunction with the customary practice of the conquered lands, gave stability to the Arab occupation and allowed the conquests to maintain their momentum.

Umar established garrison cities, first in Iraq and later in Egypt, to administer the newly conquered territory and to serve as bases for the invasion of Persia. In this way, Basra and Kufa were founded by Umar in 635, both of which became important centres of Islamic civilization.

At the same time that Umar's armies were achieving victory in Persia, another army was still invading Egypt. Between 639 and 642, the Arabs succeeded in driving the Byzantines from Egypt and establishing a Muslim government there. Again, Umar's policy of establishing new garrison cities was followed by the founding of al-Fustât, later to become Cairo.

With astonishing speed, Umar spread Arab Muslim rule from Persia to Egypt. He forged a remarkable unity in the empire by appointing provincial officials loyal to him and his principles and setting a stern example of piety and morality in the capital. He is celebrated in Arabic historiography for his unaffected, rough manner and devotion to his religion - the prototype of the unspoiled Arab ruler.

A model revenue system

Umar paid great attention to improving the state finances, which were placed on a sound footing. He had established the "Diwan", or the finance department to which the revenue administration was entrusted. The land was surveyed, and agriculture was encouraged. Old canals were excavated, and new ones were built. Large areas of land were brought under cultivation. Roads were laid out and regularly patrolled. A traveller could move safely from Egypt to Khorasan in Central Asia.

The vast territories of West Asia and North Africa were welded into a free trade zone. Trade fostered prosperity. Education was encouraged, and teachers paid. The study of the Qur'an, *hadith*, language, literature, writing and calligraphy received patronage. Umar was himself a poet of repute and a noted orator. Over 4,000 mosques were built during the caliphate of Umar.

The revenue of the commonwealth was derived from three sources: (1) *Zakat,* or the tax levied on a gradual scale on all Muslims possessing means; (2) *Kharaj,* or the land tax levied on *dhimmis*, and (3) *jizyah* or capitation tax. The last two taxes, for which Western historians have condemned Muslims, were realised in the Roman and Sasanid (Persian) Empires. The Muslims only followed the old precedents in this respect. The taxes realised by the non-Muslims were far less burdensome than those realised by the Muslims. Islam, which preached a socialist type of state, laid greater emphasis on the equitable and fair distribution of wealth. The hoarding of wealth was against the teachings of Islam. The second Caliph scrupulously followed these tenets. He founded a *Baitul Mal* (Public treasury) whose primary function was the distribution rather than wealth accumulation.

The Caliph himself took very little from the *Baitul Mal*. His ancestral occupation was business. Naturally, he had to be paid some honorarium for his holy office. The matter was referred to the special committee, in which Ali's opinion was accepted that the Caliph should get as much honorarium from the *Baitul Mal* as would suffice for the necessities of an ordinary citizen.

The Caliph fixed land revenue rates according to the land type. While he charged four dirhams for one *jar* of wheat, he charged two dirhams for a similar plot of barley. Nothing was set for the pastures and uncultivated lands. The jerib or jib is a traditional unit of land measurement in the Middle East and southwestern Asia. It is a unit of area used to measure landholdings. In this way, he systematised the fixation of revenues, which, before his time, was charged haphazardly. Different rules were framed for the revenues of Egypt, whose agricultural output depended on the flood of the Nile.

According to reliable historical sources, the annual revenue of Iraq amounted to 860 million dirhams, an amount which never exceeded after the death of the great Caliph. However, he was very lenient in his realisation. The main reason behind this easy realisation of the state money was that his people had become very prosperous.

Umar introduced far-reaching reforms in the agricultural sector, which we do not find even in the most civilized countries in modern times. One of these was the abolition of *zamindari* (landlordism), which brought freedom for tenants from exploitation. When the Romans conquered Syria and Egypt, they confiscated the lands of the tillers of the soil and allotted these to the army, nobles, churches and the members of the royal family. During the conquest of these countries, Umar returned these properties to the local inhabitants, who were the rightful owners of the land. The just and benevolent Caliph was exceptionally generous to the local tillers of the soil and even issued strict orders that no other persons, including the Muslim soldiers who were spread all over these countries, should be granted any piece of land for cultivation purposes. Such steps by the Caliph restored confidence among the local population and gave great impetus to agriculture in these countries. This resulted in an enormous increase in agricultural output. The tenancy became prosperous, and their standard of living was much raised. It led to the easy realisation of land revenues by the custodians of the state.

The liberal policy followed by the Arabs in the fixation on revenues and their land reforms immensely helped their military conquests. Due to this liberal policy of the second Caliph, the Christian Copts of Egypt, who were farmers, always sided with the Muslim Arabs in preference to Roman Christians. The Caliph was not content with just these reforms. He worked out beneficial schemes for the advancement of agriculture and constructed irrigation canals, wells and tanks in his vast dominions. He established a public welfare department that looked after such construction works and furthered these beneficial schemes. The celebrated historian Allama Maqrizi says that more than one lac and twenty thousand labourers were continually employed in such works throughout the year in Egypt alone. Several canals were constructed in Khuzistan and Ahwaz during this period. A canal called "Nahr-Amirul Momineen" connected the Nile with the Red Sea and was built to ensure quick grain transport from Egypt to the holy land.

Expeditions were undertaken according to seasons. Expeditions in cold countries were undertaken during the summer and in hot countries in winter. In spring, the troops were generally sent to lands with a salubrious climate and a good pasture.

Much thought was given to sanitation in the layout of cantonments and the construction of barracks. Special provisions were made for roads and streets in cantonments, and Umar issued instructions prescribing the width of roads and highways.

Justice in handling conquered territories

Umar ruled more than 14 hundred years ago. The total area of his caliphate was around 23 lakh square miles, continuously expanding its frontiers. To rule over such a big caliphate stretched from Libya to Makran and from Yemen to Armenia, Umar had to establish an entirely new administrative system. For the Arabs, it was the first time that such a central government was established.

Umar believed in Shura and what we call the devolution of power today. He would not have decided without consulting the assembly of great companions. Familiar people were also consulted on matters of particular significance.

He used to say: "There is no concept of a caliphate without consultation". The roots of modern democracy can be seen in the administration of Umar at a time when despotic kings and emperors ruled the whole world.

Supervision of Governors

Umar divided the whole country into provinces and smaller units. He followed a stringent standard for the appointment of governors and took particular care in appointing men of approved integrity to high offices under the state.

He kept a watch over them like a hawk, and as soon as any lapse on their part came to his notice, immediate action was taken. Before assuming his responsibility, a Governor was required to declare his assets and a complete inventory of his possessions was prepared and kept in record.

If an unusual increase was reported in the assets of a Governor, he was immediately called to account, and the state confiscated the unlawful property. At the time of appointment, a Governor was required to pledge: (1) that he would not ride a Turkish horse; (2) that he would not wear fine clothes; (3) that he would not eat sifted flour; (4) that he would not keep a porter at his door; and (5) that he would always keep his door open to the public. This is how it was ensured that Governors and Principal Officers would behave like ordinary people and not like extraordinary or heavenly creatures.

The Governors were required to come to Makkah on the occasion of the Hajj. In public assembly, Hazrat Umar would invite all those who had any grievance against any office to present the complaint. In the event of complaints, inquiries were made immediately, and grievances were redressed.

The caliph also established a particular office to investigate complaints against the Governors. The department was under the charge of Muhammad bin Maslamah Ansari, a man of undisputed integrity. In critical cases, Muhammad bin Maslamah was deputed by the caliph to proceed to the spot, investigate the charge and take action. Sometimes, an inquiry commission was constituted to investigate the charge. On occasions, the officers against whom complaints were received were summoned to Medinah and put to explanation by the caliph himself.

9. THE GREAT CONQUEROR

Umar's caliphate is notable for its vast conquest. With the aid of brilliant field commanders, Umar could incorporate present-day Iraq, Iran, Azerbaijan, much of Armenia, Georgia, Syria, Jordan, Palestine, Lebanon, Egypt, Byzantine and part of Afghanistan, Turkmenistan and southwestern Pakistan into the caliphate. During his reign, the Byzantines lost more than three-fourths of their territory, and in Persia, the Sassanid Empire ceased to exist. Islam was a powerful link in the smooth flow of Western civilization from its Graeco-Roman origins to its more recent European and American manifestations. Instead, at its zenith, the 'Abbasid caliphate stretched over the entire Middle East and part of North Africa and influenced Islamic regimes as far west as Spain. Bennison's examination of the politics, society, and culture of the 'Abbasid period presents a picture of a society that nurtured many of the "civilized" values that Western civilization claims to represent, albeit in different premodern forms - from urban planning and international trade networks to religious pluralism and academic research.

Umar's reign is also acclaimed for his administrative reforms, which began the process of turning Muhammad's band of followers into a functioning political entity that could govern a vast empire. Less than a hundred years after the death of Muhammad in A.D. 632, his followers had burst out of the Arabian Desert to conquer and create an empire whose glory was to shine for a thousand years.

Braving themselves like a cavalry of God, the Muslims spread the faith through their new converts from vanquished territories. Devout Arab traders later carried their faith to Malaysia, Indonesia, Singapore and the Philippines. Other traders introduced the Qur'an to black tribes of Africa that lived south of the Sahara Desert.

Umar had not so much to stimulate conquest as to organize and channel it. He chose leaders who were skilful managers experienced in trade and commerce as well as warfare and imbued with an ideology that provided their activities with a cosmic significance. The total numbers involved in the initial conquests may have been relatively small, perhaps less than 50,000, divided into numerous shifting groups. Yet few actions took place without any sanction from the Medinan government or one of its appointed commanders. The fighters, or *muqātilah*, could accomplish much more with Medina's support than without.

The Renaissance in early Islam was very swift and riven by very high ethical standards. The extraordinary nobility of Prophet Muhammad and the early Caliphs captivated the world, and the new religion drew adherents at a phenomenal rate. By Muhammad's death in 632, Islam was well-established as the faith of Arabia. Within a century, its sway extended from Spain to India.

The Islamic civilization produced unparalleled literature, science, philosophy, theological discourse, architecture, and cultural influences globally - influences so strong that they made European nobles want to dress like Muslims. Unlike the Byzantines, with their suspicion of classical science and philosophy, the Muslims were actively enjoined by the traditions - the *proclamations* of the Prophet - to "seek learning, though it is in China." Another well-known rule states: "The search for knowledge is obligatory for every Muslim"; another, "The ink of scholars is worth more than the blood of martyrs."

Just as important as the extent of Umar's conquests is their permanence. Although its population converted to Islam, Iran regained its independence from Arab rule. But Syria, Iraq and Egypt never did. Those countries became thoroughly Arabized and remained so to this day. Umar had to devise policies for the proper administration of the great empire, which was very diverse politically, culturally and socially. He decided that the Arabs were to be a privileged military caste in the conquered regions and that they should live in garrison cities, apart from the natives. The subject peoples were to pay tribute to their Muslim (predominantly Arab) conquerors but were otherwise left in peace. In particular, they were not forcibly converted to Islam.

More than 1,400 years after his reign, Umar is recalled as a man of compassion, righteousness and justice. Drawing on these principles, Umar treated all under his care equally, regardless of whether rich or poor, black or white, powerful or weak. He feared that God would question him about his actions. He was constantly worried that there might be sick or poor people among the believers that he may have neglected. Despite the high office he held, Umar was so deeply concerned about his responsibility towards his subjects that once, when a bridge was being built across a river, Umar wanted the construction to be defect-free lest he might have to answer for even the slightest injury to any living being on account of any snag during the process of building. Umar's rule is replete with his righteousness and commitment to justice.

During Umar's rule as Caliph, building on the precepts of Abu Bakr, the Islamic empire expanded to occupy lands of the Persian and Byzantine empires, as well as the Sassanid dynasty. The caliphate was organised under a unified sovereign authority, formed by different provinces ruled by provincial Governors selected by the Caliph.

On his election as Caliph, Umar faced the geopolitical situation in West Asia, which required immediate attention. The Arabian Peninsula is a vast desert, except for its southwestern tip near Najran and Yemen, where the monsoons bring in the rain from the Indian Ocean and make the area fertile. To the north, the extent of the desert is marked by the Jordan River, which separates it from the hills of Palestine and Lebanon. To the east, its boundaries are marked by the Euphrates. The area between Euphrates and Tigris is called the *Jazira* (island). This area, known in ancient times as Mesopotamia, was named *Iraq e Arab* in the early Islamic period. The waters of the two rivers irrigate this area and have made it the cradle of civilizations. In the east of the river Tigris, the land gradually rises into the Persian Plateau, leading into the heartland of ancient Fars. The Arabs called this area *Iraq e Ajam* and included the Farsi (Persian) speaking areas of Khuzistan, Hamadan, Fars, Persepolis, Isfahan, Azerbaijan, Khorasan, Makran and Baluchistan.

A study of the military operation would reveal the factors which spurred the sweeping victories of Muslims in such a short period. During the reign of the second Caliph, Muslims ruled over an area of 22530 square miles, including Syria, Egypt, Iraq, Persia, Kurdistan, Armenia, Azerbaijan, Kirman, Khorasan, Mekran and part of Baluchistan. A handful of ill-equipped and unskilled Arabs had overthrown two of the world's mightiest empires. The teachings of the Prophet of Islam had infused a new spirit in the adherents of the new faith, who fought simply for the sake of God. The wise policy followed by the second Caliph of Islam in the selection of his generals and the liberal terms offered to the conquered races were instrumental in the lightning victories scored by Muslims. Umar was a great military strategist; he issued detailed instructions on the conduct of operations. A perusal of the history of Tabari would reveal that Umar, sitting thousands of miles away, guided his armies on the battlefronts and monitored and directed their movements. The rigid hand he kept upon his most popular generals indicates his extraordinary capacity to rule and govern a vast, sprawling empire. Through his letters to his generals, he endeavoured incessantly to goad his warriors towards excellence and merit. He believed it would enhance the morale of the armed forces.

The Persian and Byzantine empires held the balance of power in the region, with the Euphrates River as the historical divide between their respective areas of influence. Persia also controlled Yemen and the territories along the Red Sea, north of Makkah and Medinah. The emergence of Islam and the unification of the Arabs altered this balance of power. It was a situation that neither the Byzantinians nor the Persians could ignore. Khosroe, the emperor of Persia, was on record as having ordered an assault on Medinah. The Byzantinians had attacked the northern frontier and killed the Muslim general Zaid bin Haris (632). Border clashes began during Abu Bakr's caliphate between the newborn Islamic state and the two superpowers. The triumph of Umar over the mighty empires of Persia and Byzantium within a brief span of ten years is one of the most remarkable stories in military history.

Treaty with the Jews

In Jerusalem, Umar agreed with Christians, giving them the security of life, property and freedom of religion. This is referred to *as Umar's Covenant*; it stipulates the following conditions:

Treaty with the Jews

In the name of Allah, Ever Gracious, Most Merciful.

This is the covenant of peace that Umar, the servant of God and the commander of the faithful, has made with the people of Elia (Jerusalem). This charter, which is vouchsafed to them, guarantees them the protection of life, property, churches, crosses, and those that set up, display and honour these crosses. Their churches shall not be used as dwellings nor destroyed, nor shall they or their compounds, their crosses and their belongings be diminished in any way. They shall not be subjected to persecution in matters about their religion, nor shall they be annoyed. No Jew shall dwell with them in Jerusalem.

It is incumbent on the people of Jerusalem to pay the jizyah as people of other towns do. They must turn out the Greeks and the robbers. Whoever of the Greeks leaves the city, his life and property

---

shall be protected until he reaches a place of safety. Whoever should stay in Jerusalem shall be protected, and he must pay jizyah like the rest of the inhabitants. Whoever should wish to go away with the Greeks and take his property shall leave behind their churches and crucifixes; there is protection for them as well. Their lives, properties, churches and crosses shall be protected till they reach a place of safety. There shall be no payment of tribute till the harvest is gathered in.

Whatever is contained in this deed is under the covenant of God and His Messenger and under the guarantees of his successors and the faithful, as long as the inhabitants pay the jizyah.

Witnessed by:

Khalid bin Walid, Amr ibn al-As, Abdur Rahman ibn Auf, and Muawiyah ibn Sufiyan.

Later, he visited Bethlehem and prayed at the church of Nativity. The following incident is recorded in Le Stranger's book *Palestine under the Muslims*. It is reported that when he was in Bait Lahm, a monk approached him and said: "I would obtain mercy of thee for Bait Lahm". Said Umar; "I know nought of the place but would like to see it." When Umar came, he said to the people, "Ye shall have mercy and safe conduct, but it is incumbent upon us that every place where there are Christians, we should erect a mosque." The monk answered: "There is in Bait Lahm an arched building (Haniyyah) which is built to be turned towards your *qiblah*, take this and make it a mosque for the Muslims and do not destroy the church." Umar spared the church, saying his prayer in that arched building and made it a mosque, laying on the Christians the service of lighting it with lamps and keeping it clean and its repair.

There is another version of the covenant that was reached after a conversation between Umar Abu Ubayda (chief commander in Syria) and Constantine, the eldest son of Heraclius.

These are the terms imposed on the Christians. The rich are to pay forty-eight dirhams, the middle class twenty-four, and the poor twelve. They are not to build churches, not to lift a cross in the presence of Muslims, and to only beat the nakus (bells) inside the churches. They are to share their houses so the Muslims may dwell in them; otherwise, I (UMAR) shall not be straightforward about you.

They are to give part of the churches towards Makkah and have mosques for the Muslims, for they are in the middle of the towns. They are not to drive pigs into the presence of Muslims. They are to entertain them as guests for three days and nights. They are to provide mounts from village to village for those on foot. They are to help them and not betray them. They are not to make agreements with their enemies. He who breaks these conditions may be slain, and his women and children may be enslaved individuals. (AS Tritton, page 11).

As they did with all other cities they conquered, the Muslims had to write a treaty detailing the rights and privileges of the conquered people and the Muslims in Jerusalem. This treaty was signed by Umar and Patriarch Sophronius, along with some of the generals of the Muslim armies.

At the time, this was by far one of the most progressive treaties in history. For comparison, a general massacre was ordered just 23 years earlier when the Persians conquered Jerusalem from the Byzantines. Another massacre ensued when the Crusaders conquered Jerusalem by the Muslims in 1099.

When Umar surveyed Jerusalem from the Jewish temple site after conquering the city in AD638, it was a defining moment in the emergence of the militant faith. Over the decades that followed, the

Muslim victory was consolidated by the construction of the temple mount of the Al-Aqsa mosque and the Dome of the Rock (the supposed site of Mohammed's ascent to heaven after his miraculous 'Night Journey' from Mecca). The Islamic conquerors had every reason to believe history was on their side, while the arrival of the upstart religion shattered the Christian empires of Europe and Byzantium. Within 100 years, the Muslim conquests created an empire that stretched through Spain and into the heart of France. Jerusalem is a city holy to the three largest monotheistic faiths – Islam, Judaism and Christianity. Because of its history that spans thousands of years, it goes by many names: Jerusalem, al-Quds, Yerushaláyim, Aelia, and more, all reflecting its diverse heritage. It is a city that numerous Muslim prophets called home, from Sulayman and Dawood to Isa (Jesus).

The first epoch of 450 years began in 638 when Caliph Umar accepted the surrender of Jerusalem and was surprised when informed that there were no Jews in the city. Over the previous century, the Byzantine emperors, in collusion with the local Christians, had forced the Jews to convert. Those who did not were expelled from Jerusalem and banned from praying at the sacred Temple Wall. Jews often came secretly to the neighbouring hills overlooking the holy site to pray and gaze at the Temple wall. To rectify this injustice, Hazrat Umar encouraged 70 Jewish families to resettle in their ancestral homes and cleared a space around the Temple Wall. He then personally wrote a document clearly defining the rights of the minorities (dhimmis) in conquered lands. This mandate, called Ehed Umaria, is enshrined in the Mosque of Umar in the Christian Quarter of Jerusalem. To commemorate the benevolence of the Caliph, a large area in the Jewish Quarter of Jerusalem is named Umar Ibn Khattab Square.

By 637, Muslim armies began to raid Jerusalem. Jerusalem was under Patriarch Sophronius, a representative of the Byzantine government and a Christian church leader. Although numerous Muslim armies under the command of Khalid ibn al-Walid and Amr ibn al-'As began to surround the city, Sophronius refused to surrender unless Umar came to accept the surrender himself. Having heard of such a condition, Umar left Medinah, travelling alone with one donkey and one servant.

The Muslim generals met the Caliph at Jabia. So, Yazid ibn Abi Sufyan, Khalid ibn Walid and others came and received him at this place. Long residence in Syria had robbed these officers of their Arabian simplicity. When they arrived in Umar's presence, he saw them in silk from the richest looms and their brilliant dresses and flamboyant appearances gave them the look of the Persians. Umar flew into a fit of rage at the sight. He jumped off his horse and picked up a few pebbles scattered about the ground. He pelted them, saying: "So soon have you fallen into Persian habits."

The officers replied that they had cuirasses beneath the silken tunics, implying that they had not lost the art of war and that their warlike spirit was as keen as ever. On hearing this, the Caliph relented and agreed that if such was the case, then there was no actual harm done. Approaching close to the city, Umar got up on a hillock and looked all around. The magnetic fields of Ghota, with their verdure-laden expense, stretched, and Damascus's stately and towering edifices loomed in front of him. He was strangely moved and, in a tone of deep pathos, repeated the following verse from the Qur'an: "They have left many a garden, fountain, park, arbour and riches which they used to enjoy. Thus, it is that We put another community in possession thereof."

Umar sojourned for a long while at Jabia, and the treaty of Jerusalem was drawn there. The Christians of Jerusalem had already been informed of Umar's journey, and some of the nobles of that city proceeded to Damascus to see him. Umar was seated amid the Muslim troops when a cloud of dust suddenly arose in the distance, and several horse riders appeared at full gallop, swords glittering at their sides. The Muslims startled at the appearance, instinctively felt for their weapons. When

Umar enquired about the cause of the alarm, they pointed towards the dashing cavalry.

Quickly, Umar guessed that the approaching horse riders were the Christians of Jerusalem, and he accordingly reassured his men, saying they need not be alarmed as the strangers only came to sue for peace. The peace treaty was drafted, and the Companions' elite subscribed to it. This is Tabari's statement. Balazuri and Azdi, on the other hand, say that the peace treaty was drawn up in Jerusalem.

After the ratification of the treaty, Umar proceeded to Jerusalem. The hoofs of the horse he rode were worn to tenderness, and the animal limped painfully. Umar dismounted on seeing its deplorable condition. His men brought him an acceptable course of Turkish breed. The horse was very aggressive and galloped violently. As Umar mounted it, it began to prance, and he cried out: "Miserable thing I whence this vain and haughty amble?" Thus, saying he alighted and pursued his way on foot. As he entered Jerusalem, Abu Ubaida and other army officers came forth to bid him welcome. The scantiness of Umar's shabby attire and the tattered condition of his scrubby equipage put the Muslims to shame, and their sense of self-respect was shocked when the galling idea crossed their minds as to what the Christians would think of them on beholding their chief. So, they brought a gallant Turkish charger and a handsome dress of valuable materials for him. However, Umar rejected the offer, saying that the honour God had conferred upon him was that of Islam and that that was enough for him. In short, he entered Jerusalem in the same humble guise.

Sophronius, dressed in the gilded attire of his office, came out to meet Umar, expecting to find a royally armoured conqueror. He was surprised to meet a dressed man leading a camel mounted by Umar's manservant. The two had travelled from the north, taking turns riding the camel. The humbly attired Muslim army commander promised Sophronius that the people, property, and holy sites of the city of Jerusalem would be spared. Moved by his pledge, the bishop handed Umar the keys to the city gates and the Holy Sepulcher.

First of all, he bowed before the mosque, and then, while approaching the arch of David, he recited the verse from the Qur'an, which speaks of the Apostle David as bowing down to God and prostrating himself in humble obeisance. He then visited the church of the Christians and walked about the building for some time.

Sophronius ushered Umar to the *Holy Sepulcher*, the holiest church in Christendom and a repository of religious history. Adam, the first man, was buried there. This was the place of Christ's empty tomb, and it was there that Helena, the mother of Constantine the Great, had discovered the true cross and the crown of thorns. For centuries, legends of the beneficial effects of a visit to such sites, just a touch of the sacred stone of the tomb that was said to cure deadly diseases, had been luring pilgrims throughout the world.

When the time for prayer came, Sophronius invited Umar to pray inside the church, but Umar refused. He insisted that if he prayed there, later Muslims would use it as an excuse to convert it into a mosque – thereby depriving Christendom of one of its holiest sites. Instead, Umar prayed outside the church, where a mosque (called Masjid Umar – the Mosque of Umar) was later built. Umar then asked the bishop about the site of the Holy Rock and Solomon's Temple. The bishop didn't know exactly where the temple was, as the plateau it had once stood was now a vast garbage heap. There were piles of bones and human dung, animal skins, and, most shocking of all, Muslim and Jewish pig carcasses.

Out from the nearby crowds, says Muslim legend, a Jew stepped forward. It was he who now offered to help Umar locate the site of the temple and the rock. And the two furrowed their way through the rubbish until they came to the spot. "It is here," the Jew said to Umar. "This is the place you seek." Umar began digging with his own hands.

Once he had cleaned away the debris and wiped the Holy Rock clean with his robe, he performed a prayer.

Umar immediately set about making the city an essential Muslim landmark. Umar and his army (along with some Jews) cleaned it and built a mosque – Masjid al-Aqsa, there.

Jerusalem became a major centre of religious pilgrimage and trade throughout the remainder of Umar's caliphate and into the Umayyad Empire's reign over the city. The Dome of the Rock complemented Masjid al-Aqsa in 691. Several mosques and public institutions were soon established throughout the city.

The Muslim conquest of Jerusalem under the Caliph Umar in 637 was an essential moment in the city's history. For the next 462 years, it would be ruled by Muslims, with religious freedom for minorities protected according to the Treaty of Umar.

As many military officers and provincial Governors had gathered there, Umar prolonged his sojourn in the holy city for many days and issued various necessary orders. One day, Bilal, the Prophet's muezzin, complained to the Commander of the Faithful that the officers treated themselves to such goodies as fowl's meat and white loaves. At the same time, the men could not get even ordinary food - Umar glanced inquisitively at the officers, who replied that edibles of all varieties were cheap in that country. Those white loaves and fowl' meat cost the same there as brown loaves and dates in Hijaz.

Umar could not compel the officers to partake of a more frugal fare, but he issued an order to the effect that in addition to their pay and a fair share of the war spoils, the soldiers should also get free rations.

One day, during prayers, Umar requested Bilal to say the *adhan*. Bilal said that he had made up his mind never to say the *adhan* for anyone after the Prophet but that he would make an exception in his favour and obey him for that only once. So, when his well-known stentorian accents began to summon the faithful to prayers, Bilal's resonant and sonorous cadences painfully reminded the Companions of the blessed times of the Prophet and melted their hearts to tears. Abu Ubayda and Muaz ibn Jabal wept most disconsolately while Umar fell into uncontrollable sobs. It was some time before this scene of deep emotion and pathos turned normal.

During his stay in Jerusalem, Umar once visited the Mosque of Aqsa and sent for Kaab, where the Bishop asked him where to say the prayers. The ancient Prophets have left a stone in this fane as a relic. It is called Sakhrah, and the Jews hold it in the same reverence as the Muslims do the *Hajar Aswad* (the Black Stone). When Umar enquired with Kaab about the direction in which the prayers were to be offered, the latter pointed out Sakhrah as the Qiblah. On this, Umar told him that the Jewish faith still had a holdover in his mind, which had led him, instinctively, as it were, to put off his shoes near Sakhrah. This event shows how Umar regarded such ancient monuments.

To support the above description of the religious tolerance of Umar, let me quote Sir William Muir, a nineteenth-century British historian of early Muslim history:

Mahometan (Muslim) tradition gives no further detail respecting this memorable visit (to Jerusalem). But Christian writers say that Umar accompanied the Patriarch over the city, visited the various places of pilgrimage, and graciously inquired into their history. At the appointed hour, the Patriarch bade the Caliph perform his orisons in the church of the Resurrection, where they chanced to be. But he declined to pray either there or in the church of Constantine, where a carpet had been spread for him, saying kindly that if he did so, his followers would take possession of the church forever, as a place where Muslim prayer had once been offered up. Umar also visited Bethlehem and, having prayed in the church of the Nativity, left a rescript with the Patriarch, who accompanied him on the pious errand, securing the Christians in possession of the building, with the condition that not more than one Mussulman (Muslim) should ever enter at a time.

Islam's advance under Umar

Under Umar's leadership, Islam made its most significant and fastest expansion. During his reign, Muslim forces conquered Syria, Jerusalem, Egypt, Libya, Iraq and Persia. One ingenious means of ensuring the continued expansion of Islam was Umar's decision to forbid Arabs from owning any land. Thus, excluded from acquiring wealth, they were motivated to focus on Because Umar was one of the most adamant opponents of Mohammed's preaching in Mecca, his dramatically sudden conversion to Islam in 615 was a turning point in the career of the Prophet. The fierce loyalty which he gave to Mohammed, both as a warrior in the battles against the Meccans and as an adviser, was reinforced by marriage when his daughter Hafsa married the Prophet.

Nevertheless, in spite of his vigorous support of the Prophet, Umar did not figure prominently in Islamic history until the death of Mohammed in 632, and even then, it is as a supporter of Abu Bakr, the first caliph, whose selection Umar imposed on the divided Muslim community by the sheer force of his personality. Although some modern historians have claimed that Umar was the real power behind the throne during Abu Bakr's short reign (632-634), Umar was careful—if this theory is sound—to stay in the background, perhaps realizing that more vigorous leadership **might be resented** by the Arab Moslems so soon after the death of their beloved Prophet.

Early Conquests

At any rate, upon Abu Bakr's death in 634, Umar assumed the caliphate in his own right, apparently without opposition. The immediate task confronting him was to direct the two-pronged military campaign (which had been launched in 633 by Abu Bakr) against the Byzantines in Palestine and Syria and the Sassanians in Iraq. In both fields of battle, Umar gave new energy to his armies by sending new levies to tribal troops. Thus reinforced, the Syrian army, led by the famous general Khalid ibn al-Walid, captured Damascus in 635 and, in the following year, smashed the Byzantine military in Syria at the battle of Yarmuk. Further successful campaigns in Syria led to the conquest of Jerusalem in 638. Because Jerusalem was the third holiest city in Islam, after Mecca and Medina, Umar himself visited it as a conqueror. Typically, however, he insisted on presenting himself as a spartan desert warrior rather than a mighty potentate.

Simultaneously with the conquest of Syria and Palestine, another of Umar's armies was driving the Persian army from Iraq. Here, the decisive battle was fought in 636 at Qadisiya, where a Muslim victory left the Sassanian capital of Ctesiphon virtually defenceless and open to plunder by the Arabs. Once the conquest of Syria had been achieved, the Syrian army was free to attack upper Mesopotamia from the west, and it came under the control of the caliphate in 640.

Administrative Reforms

The conquest of such a vast area in such a relatively short time soon created formidable administrative problems for Umar. Since the Arabs had no experience as rulers of an empire, they were forced to settle to a great extent in the bureaucracies created by the Byzantine and Sassanian governments. Nevertheless, Umar is credited with introducing several new administrative practices and institutions which, in conjunction with the customary practice of the conquered lands, gave stability to the Arab occupation and allowed the conquests to maintain their momentum.

Tradition would have it that Umar announced his innovations in a speech made to the Arab military leaders during a lull in the fighting between the battle of Yarmuk and the occupation of Jerusalem. Though this tradition may well be a reconstruction of the gradual evolution of early Muslim policy, Umar probably laid down guidelines, at least for the solution of pressing problems. Almost all of these were related to finances: how to pay the troops and support the Muslim community on a long-term basis without disrupting the economy of the conquered lands.

In general, Umar's solution was to leave the conquered peoples in possession of their lands and their religion in exchange for the payment of tribute, which was to be disbursed by the Muslim government to its armies and citizens. To institutionalize this policy, a divan, or register, was drawn up, which regularized the stipends that Muslims were to be paid according to religious and tribal principles. The relations between Moslems and non-Moslems were further stabilized by exempting the latter from military service and guaranteeing them protection in return for the taxes which they paid.

Invasions of Persia and Egypt

Undoubtedly of equal importance to these measures was Umar's decision to establish garrison cities, first in Iraq and later in Egypt, to administer the newly conquered territory and to serve as bases for the invasion of Persia. In this way, Basra and Kufa were founded by Umar in 635, both of which were to become important centres of Islamic civilization. From these cities, Umar launched an invasion of Persia in 640, which was climaxed by the defeat of the Sassanian army at the battle of Nihawand in 642; the resultant collapse of Sassanian power opened Persia to relatively easy conquest.

At the same time that Umar's armies were achieving victory in Persia, another army was still invading Egypt. Between 639 and 642, the Arabs succeeded in driving the Byzantines from Egypt and establishing a Muslim government there. Again, Umar's policy of establishing new garrison cities was followed by the founding of al-Fustât, later becoming Cairo.

With astonishing speed, Umar succeeded in spreading Arab Muslim rule from Persia to Egypt under his political and religious leadership. He was also able to establish a remarkable degree of unity in the empire through the appointment of provincial officials loyal to him and his principles and by setting a stern example of piety and morality at the capital. He is celebrated in Arabic historiography for his unaffected, rough manner, coupled with devotion to his religion—the prototype of the unspoiled Arab ruler. An enslaved individual Persian, outraged by Umar's refusal to reduce a heavy tax, mortally wounded the Caliph in 644 while Umar was leading the prayers. Refusing to name his successor on his deathbed, he established still another precedent by appointing a council to choose the new caliph.

The visit to Jerusalem

The anecdote about Umar's entry into Jerusalem has remained an immortal example of his adherence to Islam's principle of equity. Because he had only one attendant and one camel to ride, they rode the camel by turns. It happened to be the servant's turn to ride on the day when they were to reach Jerusalem. The people who had seen the pomp of great kings were stunned to see the Caliph of Islam walking while his attendant sat on the camel's back!

Fully realizing his responsibility to his charge, Umar personally visited Iraq, Syria and Egypt when, in the year 17 A.H., a great plague swept through those countries, killing thousands of people. Reminded by one Companion about the divine warning against knowingly putting one's life at risk, he answered that he was following another Divine Command.

Another memorable anecdote associated with Umar is his letter. The Coptics were Christians but followed a savage practice of giving a human sacrifice once a year amidst a big festival in the summer. A beautiful maiden dressed as a bride was flowed in the Nile. People felt that the gift was necessary to please the Nile and get an enormous flood of water for their parched fields. If the Nile got displeased, they thought, there would be no flood and no crops.

The Coptics asked the Muslim Governor's permission to sacrifice a maiden as usual. He disallowed the savage act. It so happened that the Nile had very little water that year. Crops failed. Many of the peasants decided to leave the country. Amr bin 'Aas, the Governor, informed Umar, at which point the Caliph sent a letter addressed to the Nile.

It said:

"From the servant of Allah and Commander of the Muslims to the River of the Nile of Egypt. O Nile, if you flow of your own will, then do not flow. But if Allah, the Almighty, controls your flow, we pray to Him to keep you flowing."

This letter was thrown into the river as directed by the Caliph. The river overflowed its banks that year. Such a big flood had not occurred for many years. The country was once again green with crops. The peasants were happy. The savage practice of human sacrifice came to an end forever.

The examples of Umar's practices in letter and spirit as an individual and as the Commander of the Faithful are too many to be enumerated and condensed.

From the Hijra onward, Hazrat Umar was actively involved in every significant development in the formative period of Islam until the revelation of the Qur'an ended and the religion in its great essentials was complete. There was no battle, no negotiation, and no administrative measures put in place without Umar's consultation and his advice influencing the decision.

Umar attained excellence in several fields - in government and administration, in statesmanship and political craft, in the management of armies and conquests, in Qur'anic scholarship and exegesis, in the

Law and the principles of information, and in devotion and servant-hood to God. Achievements.

The new conquests

Umar promised not to send the Muslim armies "into destruction", meaning that he would not send the troops out without evaluating the risks and consideration of the worth of the nation. He promised not to keep the soldiers away from their families for an extended period. He reassured the men that while they were away fighting for the Muslim *ummah,* if they did not return, he, the Caliph, would be the father of their children and the caretaker of their wives. Umar believed the role of the leader was to protect the people. Although he was the leader of a great empire, Umar never felt it necessary to have a bodyguard.

Umar extended Islam's temporal rule over Syria, Egypt, Iraq, and Persia from a purely military standpoint, with astonishing victories. Within four years after the death of the Prophet, the Muslim state had extended its sway over all of Syria and had, at a famous battle fought during a sandstorm near the RiverYarmuk, blunted the power of the Byzantines - whose ruler Heraclius had recently rejected the letter from the unknown Prophet of Arabia.

Vanquishing the Persians

The Romans and Persians, who always looked down upon the Arabs as an uncultured race, viewed the rising power of Islam with alarm and were anxious to subjugate and crush it. The Persians sent reinforcement to the rebels of Bahrain against Islam. They instigated Sajab, who pretended to be a Prophetess in Iraq and marched upon Medinah. Rustam, the famous Persian General, had sworn that he would destroy the entire Arab race. Such designs and machinations of the Persians warned the Muslims of the dangers, but they accepted the challenge as a spirited people. Hence, the war was forced upon the unwilling Muslims, and they could not ignore this threat to their existence.

The first defeat of the Persians came as a great surprise to them as they expected little resistance from the Arabs. They were already alarmed at their unexpected defeats during the time of Abu Bakr. Every disaster on the battlefield only added to the flames of Persian fury. Theirs was a vast empire, and so were their resources. They deployed their forces and materials recklessly to stem the advance of the Arabs and crush their striking power forever. A handful of ill-equipped Arabs were pitted against the formidable forces of Romans and Persians. One can hardly find in recorded history an instance where, despite such disparities between the opposing forces, the weaker one turned out to be triumphant over two powerful opponents. It was reminiscent of the Battle of Badr.

The tempo of war increased when Umar was elected as Caliph. Muslims were fighting on two fronts - in Syria. They fought the powerful forces of the mighty Roman Empire, and in Iraq, they were prosecuted against the formidable forces of Khosroe (Persians). Puran Dikht ascended the Persian throne and appointed Rustam as the army's Commander-in-Chief. All these initiatives could not check the Muslim advance, and the Persians, under the command of Narsi, were routed to Kasker. Rustam appointed Bahman, a sworn enemy of Arabs, as the Commander of Persian forces in Iraq. A highly pitched battle was fought at Beirut in 635A.D.in which the Persians beat a hasty retreat, leaving behind many dead bodies. Muthanna, the Muslim General, declared that he had taken part in several engagements against the Persians in pre-Islamic days. Previously, 100 Persians could have overpowered 1000 Arabs, but the tables.

The battle of Qadisiyah, fought in 635 A.D. under the command of Saad Abi Waqas, was decisive since it sealed the fate of the Persian Empire in Iraq. Rustam, the greatest war hero of Persia, had mustered a strong force against the Muslims. The ill Muslim commander had appointed Khalid Bin Artafa in his place and guided his movements through written instructions. A poet named Abu Mahjan Saqfi, who was in chains for his drunkenness, implored the commander's wife, Salma, to release him for a short while so that he could take part in the battle. He promised to return when the war was over. His request was granted immediately, and Abu Mahjan, with a sword in his hand, literally ran amok and fought bitterly to the end. When the battle was over, he put himself in chains again, but Sa'd released him on knowing of his exploits.

Rustam, who tried to escape, was killed. Umar was very anxious about the result of this battle. He had masterminded military operations in Iraq; for hours, he would wait daily outside Medinah in the hope of good news. Umar made a memorable speech before the Madinites.

Brothers of Islam! I am not your ruler who wants to enslave individual you. I am a servant of God and His people. I have been entrusted with the heavy responsibility of running the caliphate administration. I must make you comfortable in every way, and it will be an evil day for me if I wish you to wait on me now and then. I want to educate you not through my precepts but by my practice.

The Persians made their last stand in Iraq in front of Medinah, the capital. They destroyed the bridge built on the Tigris. Such obstacles could not check the advance of Muslims. Saad, the commander of the faithful, plunged his horse into the river. The rest of the army followed suit and crossed the river without disrupting their formations.

The Persians were terrified at this unusual sight and cried out! "Demons have come". Saying this, they took to flight in utter confusion. A vast treasure fell into the hands of the Muslim conquerors, including the invaluable Persian carpet. This treasure was couriered to Medina and mounted in the courtyard of the Mosque of the Prophet. The great Caliph burst into tears at its sight. The audience asked him the reason for his unusual expression of grief. The Caliph replied promptly, "This wealth was the cause of the downfall of Persians, and now it has come to us to bring our downfall." He ordered that the wealth be distributed among people immediately. On Ali's advice, even the priceless carpets was not spared.They were torn into pieces and distributed among citizens. Umar commended the high character of his soldiers, who did not touch a single souvenir from this colossal booty.

Encountering the Syrians

Syria was another theatre of war, where the Muslims were arraigned against the formidable Roman forces. During his lifetime, Abu Bakr summoned Khalid Bin Walid, the Sword of God, to assist the Muslims in Syria. The Syrian cities, one after another, capitulated to the Muslims. Hems, Hama (Epiphania), Kinnisrin (Chalcis), Aleppo and other vital towns surrendered and opened their gates to the forces of Islam. The city of Damascus, which was held by a large garrison, offered considerable resistance. One night, Khalid bin Walid, stationed on the other side of the city, scaled its walls and opened the gate. The Muslim army entered the city from one side. Immediately, the Romans offered themselves for peace to the commander-in-chief, Abu Ubaidah, who was stationed on the other side of the town. Khalid and Abu Ubaidah, who came from opposite directions, met in the city's centre. Abu Ubaidah asked the Muslims not to plunder anyone as he had accepted the peace terms.

Antioch, the capital of the Roman East, also fell to the Muslims after stubborn resistance. The Roman Governor, named Artabin, had mustered a potent force for the defence of his province. Placing small bodies of troops at Jerusalem, Gaza and Ramleh, he had assembled a large army in Ajnadian. The Muslims, who were deeply concerned about these movements of the Roman forces, withdrew their garrisons from various sectors and advanced to face Artabin. While withdrawing from Hems, Abu Ubaidah, Commander-in-chief of the Muslim troops, asked his Treasury Officer to return the *jizyah* (Protection Tax) to the inhabitants, as they could not undertake the responsibility of protecting their non-Muslim subjects there. The order was immediately carried out, and the whole amount was refunded to the local inhabitants. This unusual generosity of the conquerors touched the Christian population so much that they wept bitterly and cried out, "May God bring you here again." The Jews swore in the Torah to resist the Romans to the last man if they ever ventured to capture the city.

A bloody battle ensued in the plain of Yarmuk in 634 A.D. between Islam and the Romans. The Romans had mustered a strong army of 3 lac soldiers, while the Muslim army comprised 30 thousand unskilled and ill-equipped soldiers only. The Muslims fought like demons and routed the Romans after a fierce conflict. More than a hundred thousand Romans perished on the battlefield, while Muslim casualties hardly exceeded three thousand. When appraised of this crushing defeat, Caesar cried out sorrowfully, "Goodbye Syria", and he retired to Constantinople.

The few Roman soldiers who escaped from Yarmuk found refuge within the walls of the fortified city of Jerusalem. This city was garrisoned by a heavy force and resisted for a considerable time. At last, the Patriarch sued for peace but refused to surrender to anyone except the Caliph. Umar acceded to his request and, travelling with a single attendant without escort, pomp, and pageantry, arrived at Jabia. When he came in the presence of the Patriarch and his men, he was leading the camel while the attendant was riding it. This strange respect deeply moved the Christian priests and their associates for equality exhibited by the Caliph of Islam. The patriarch presented the keys of the sacred city to the Caliph, and they entered the town together.

Umar refused to offer his prayers in the church of Resurrection, saying,

"If I do so, the Muslims in future might infringe on the treaty under the pretext of imitating my example." Just terms were offered to the Christians, while the Samaritan Jews, who had assisted the Muslims, were granted their properties without payment of any tax.

The subjugation of Syria was now complete. Syria bowed under the sceptre of the Caliphs seven hundred years after Pompey had deposed the last of the Macedonian kings. After their previous defeat, the Romans recognised themselves hopelessly beaten, though they continued to raid the Muslim territories. To erect an impassable barrier between themselves and the Muslims, they converted into a veritable desert, a vast tract on the frontiers of their remaining Asiatic possessions. All cities in this doomed track were razed to the ground, fortresses were dismantled, and the population was carried away further north. What was deemed to be the work of Arab Muslim hordes was the outcome of Byzantine barbarism". This short-sighted policy was of no avail and could not stem the tide of Muslim advance. Iyaz, the Muslim commander, passed through Tauras, reduced the province of Cilicia, captured its capital, Tarsus and reached as far as the shores of the Black Sea. His name became a terror to Romans in Asia Minor.

After clearing Syria of the Roman forces, the Muslim army marched on Persia and conquered Azerbaijan in 643A.D., Bostan in 643 A.D., Armenia in 644 A.D., Sistan in 644 A.D. and Mekran in 644 A.D. According to the celebrated historian Billazori, the Islamic forces had reached as far as the plain of Debul in Sind. But Tabari says that the Caliph prevented his army from advancing east of Mekran. The defeated Roman forces had fled Alexandria and threatened Muslim-conquered Syria. Hence, Umar bin Aas implored the Caliph to allow him to advance on Egypt. The request was granted, and Muslim forces under Umar bin Aas captured Alexandria in 641-642 A.D. The Egyptian Christians, called Copts, were treated humanely by the Muslim conquerors and were granted landed properties.

The Arabs also constructed a solid fleet to meet the challenge of Romans as masters of the seas. Thus, the naval supremacy of Arabs was also established, and the Roman fleet fled before them to the Hellespont. The Muslims captured several islands of the Greek Archipelago.

Yazdgard tried to slow the advance of Arab troops by destroying the bridge linking the Tigris River's western shores to Madayen. These tactics, however, proved futile. The Arabs put their horses into the river and waded across to the other shore, and Madayen fell in 637 A.D. The treasures of the Persian capital were now in Muslim hands. Vast amounts of gold, silver, jewels, carpets and artefacts were captured and transported to Medina. A part of the war booty was an elephant that aroused a great deal of curiosity among the ladies in Medinah.

Yazdgard fled Madayen towards Merv in north-eastern Persia. Realizing that the war with the Muslims was not just a skirmish but a full-scale invasion, he called on all Persians and their allies to defend Persia. A vast army of 150,000 was assembled and put under the command of Mardan Shah, who had already seen action against the Arabs at the Battle of the Euphrates. To inspire the Persians, Mardan Shah was vested with the *draft*, the national emblem of Persia. The governor of Kufa, Ammar ibn Yassir, sent this information to the Caliph and asked for additional troops. Umar sent a corps of 30,000 under the command of Numan ibn MuQur'an. Peace talks proved futile, and the two armies met at the Battle of Nahawand. In the initial engagements, Numan ibn MuQur'an was seriously wounded, but the Muslim commanders kept this fact secret. Towards the end of the first day, the enemy lines broke, and the Muslims were victorious. Numan did not survive his wounds and died that evening.

Persian resistance continued from its eastern provinces. Yazdgard set himself up in Merv and took personal command of his forces. Realizing that an injured enemy was a dangerous enemy, Umar resolved to put an end to all Persian resistance. From Nahawand, the Arab armies split up and mounted a multi-pronged drive against Persian strongholds. Abi al Aas captured Persepolis. Aasim ibn Amr took Sistan. Hakam ibn Umair conquered Makran and Baluchistan. Azerbaijan fell to Othba ibn Farqad. Buqair ibn Abdulla subdued Armenia. A contingent under

Ahnaf ibn Qais marched on Khorasan. By the year 650 A.D., the Persian Empire was entirely under the control of Arab armies. Yazdgard fled Persia and died in exile.

Within a decade after the election of Umar ibn al Khattab as the Caliph, the map of West Asia and North Africa was reconfigured. Medinah was now the capital of the largest empire in the world, extending from Tripoli in North Africa to Samarqand in Central Asia. This empire was ruled not by a king or a general but by a revolutionary creed: "There is no deity, but God and Muhammad are His Messenger." The Caliph was no more than a servant of God and the keeper of Divine Laws.

When Caliph Umar came to know of the victories over Persia, he went to the mosque in Medinah and addressed the people: *"O, believers! The Persians have lost their kingdom. They cannot harm us anymore. God has made you inherit their country, properties, and riches so that He may test you. Therefore, you should not change your ways. Otherwise, God will bring forth another nation in place of you. I feel anxiety for our community from our people."*

Freedom of religion in Egypt

Whereas the orthodox church of Byzantine had persecuted the Christians of Syria and Egypt as heretics, Muslims treated the Copt community in Egypt with respect and dignity. It is noteworthy that Coptic Patriarch Benjamin, a fugitive in the desert for the last 12 years, was summoned by Muslim Governor (Amil) Amr ibn al-Asi from his hiding to resume the leadership of the Coptic church. The victorious Muslim commander said to him:

"Resume the government of all your churches and your people and administer their affairs. And if you will pray for me, that I may go to the West and Pentapolis, and take possession of them, as I have of Egypt and return to you in safety and speedily, I will do for you all that you shall ask of me."

Then the holy Benjamin prayed for Amr and pronounced an eloquent discourse, which made Amr and those present with him marvel and contained words of exhortation and much profit for those who heard him. He revealed certain matters to Amr and departed from his presence honoured and revered.

A benign and strategic conqueror

A handful of ill-equipped and unskilled Muslims had overthrown two of the mightiest Empires in the world. The Prophet had infused a revolutionary spirit in the adherents (supporters) of the new faith, who demonstrated enormous courage and tremendous confidence in the new religion.

The wise policy followed by Umar in the selection of his generals and the liberal terms offered to the conquered races were instrumental in the speed of victories registered by Muslims. Umar was a great military strategist; he issued detailed instructions regarding the conduct of operations. A study of the history of Tabari would reveal that Umar-the-great, sitting thousands of miles away, guided his armies on the battlefronts and controlled their movements.

Umar's generosity helped win the conquered people's hearts, which ultimately paved the way for the conquered territories' consolidation and efficient administration. He had strictly forbidden his soldiers not to kill the weak and damage the shrines and places of worship. A treaty, once concluded, would be observed in letter and spirit. Contrary to the repression and ferocity of great conquerors like Alexander, Caesar, Tamerlane, Changiz Khan, and Halaqu, Umar's conquests were both physical and spiritual. When Alexander conquered Sur, a city in Syria, he ordered a general massacre and hanged one thousand respectable citizens on the city walls.

Similarly, when he conquered Astakher, a town in Persia, he beheaded its entire male population. Tyrants like Changiz, Tamerlane and Halaqu were even more ferocious. Hence, their vast Empire crashed. The conquest of the second Caliph of Islam was different. The humane approach to efficient administration added to the consolidation of his Empire in such a way that even today, after 1400 years, the countries he conquered are still in Muslim hands.

10. A MORAL PREACHER

Tarawih prayers

In the month of Ramadan, it was the practice with the Prophet that he would stay in the mosque after the night prayers and offer extra prayers. One night, as the faithful saw the Prophet offering different prayers, they also prayed as the Prophet did. The following night, more Muslims stayed in the mosque after the night prayer to offer extra prayers. On the third night, there was a more extensive gathering of Muslims to perform the different prayers. On the fourth night, when many of the faithful assembled to offer the extra prayers, the Prophet introduced a tradition of extra prayers after the night prayers during Ramzan.

The messages of Unar concerning these prayers were disseminated in Muslim society. Some felt that as the Prophet had not prescribed such prayers, it was unlawful to prescribe such prayers after the death of the Prophet. Umar explained that he was not defining these prayers as a compulsory ritual; they were discretionary prayers, and they were left to the people to decide. Offering such prayers would enhance his righteousness, but if anybody did not do so, that would not bring him any discredit.

Umar and the Holy Qur'an

The Holy Qur'an was revealed to the Prophet in instalments over 23 years. Whenever the Prophet received the revelation, he would dictate it to one of his scribes, who would record it on a piece of leather, date skin, or even bones and stones.

The principal scribe of the Prophet was Zaid bin Thabit. Many Companions committed the entire Qur'an to memory, and these 'Huffaz' could recite the Qur'an as a whole at any time. The Prophet kept all the pieces of leather, date skins, and other materials on which the Qur'an jotted in his custody. During the lifetime of the Prophet, the revelation was a continuous process, and there was no occasion to compile them into a compendium. After the death of the Prophet, the process of revelation came to a close, and it became necessary to organise the entire compendium and preserve it.

In the battle of Yamama, most of the Companions who had learned the Holy Qur'an by heart got martyred. Umar realised a strategy to ensure the preservation of the Qur'an. There was also the danger that a lapse of time might inadvertently allow some interpolations in the text or even deliberately.

Despite the reservation of Abu Bakr, who was then the caliph, Umar persuaded Abu Bakr to formulate a strategy of a team for memorizing the Qur'an and making it a permanent means of ensuring the preservation of the Qur'an. Zaid b. Thabit was commissioned to head the task of collating all the verses of the Holy Qur'an and compiling them in the form of a compendium. Zaid was reluctant but finally decided to agree to the Abu Bakr and Umar project.

A proclamation was declared that whosoever had learned any portion of the Qur'an from the Prophet should produce such a bit. Two witnesses had to attest to the genuineness of the verses. When all the verses were collected, a committee was set up, with Umar as one of the members. This committee supervised the compilation of the Qur'an—sad b. al-As dictated the Qur'an, and Zaid bin Thabit took the dictation. The members of the committee, including Umar, checked this.

When the work was completed, it was further checked by Abu Bakr and finally approved. Abu Bakr kept a copy in his custody. The compilation was given the name of 'Mashaf'.

Umar's reinvigoration of mosques

With the expansion of the Islamic dominion, Umar ordered mosques to be built in all conquered territories. In the newly founded cities of Kufa and Basra, Jami Masjids were built in the centre of the town, and smaller mosques were constructed in each tribal quarter. According to one account, as many as 4,000 mosques were erected during the caliphate of Umar.

Umar had the sacred mosque at Ka'bah extended. In 739 A.D., Umar purchased the surrounding houses at state expense. These were demolished, and the area under them was included in the mosque. Hitherto, there was no wall around the mosque. Umar had a wall constructed for the first time. Umar provided lights for the mosques for the first time. Formerly, the cover of the Ka'bah was made of ordinary cloth. Umar had the cover made of a superior and finer cloth manufactured in Egypt.

The boundaries of the Haram, the sanctuary of the Kaaba, extended to three miles in one direction and seven to nine miles in other directions. The boundaries were not defined, and there was the risk of this area being infringed upon. Umar surveyed the area, and the borders were demarcated. Stone pillars called *Ansab* were fixed to delineate the boundaries.

Umar extended the Prophet's Mosque at Medinah as well. In 739 A.D., the same year as the Ka'bah was extended, Umar purchased the houses that surrounded the Masjid i-Nabvi. After demolishing it to extend the mosque.

Abbas, whose house also surrounded the mosque, refused to sell his house. He sued the state in the Court of the Qadi Ubayy b. Kab. The Court gave its verdict against the state and held that the property could not be acquired compulsorily. Umar accepted the judgment of the Court. Thereupon, Abbas voluntarily gifted his house for the extension of the mosque. Umar took the gift gratefully and provided alternative accommodation to Abbas.

As a result of the extension, the length of the mosque rose from 100 to 140 yards while its width rose from 60 to 80 yards.

Umar was the first to provide lights for Masjid-i-Nabvi. Umar also made arrangements to burn incense in the mosque. The floor of the mosque was paved and covered with mats.

The veiling of women

In Medinah, Muslim women did not observe veiling. Most men in Medinah were pious and careful about their conduct with women. But Umar still doubted some characters and was suspicious of their mischief.

Umar shared his apprehensions with the Prophet and suggested that women should be required to stay at home. Umar was keen that the wives of the Prophet should be provided adequate protection.

On hearing Umar, Zainab, a wife of the Prophet, said: "Umar, you have started interfering in the domestic affairs of the Prophet as well. The revelation comes to our house, and you come up with suggestions of your own."

The Prophet, however, understood Umar and was awaiting revelation, a revelation in this regard.

And then came a detailed revelation on the subject. The revelation was:

"Prophet, say to your wives: if you desire the present life and its beautiful things, come, and I will give you your dowries and send you away handsomely. And if you want Allah and His Prophet and the next world, remember that Allah has in store a great reward for those of you who are righteous. (Q33:28)

Another verse proclaimed:

O wives of the Prophet! Whoever of you commits flagrant indecency will have your punishment twice over. Indeed, it is easy for Allah to double your punishment. As for those who are obedient to Allah and His Apostle and act righteously, we shall give them their reward twice over. We have rare gifts in store for them. (Q 33:30)

And yet another verse said:

O wives of the Prophet, you are like no other women. If you fear Allah, do not be soft-spoken, for it will tempt the man with heart disease. Speak in a dignified tone, stay in your homes, and do not display your beauty as in the days of ignorance. Observe prayer, give alms, and obey Allah and His Apostle. Members of the house of the Prophet! Allah only intends to rid you of your uncleanliness and to purify you completely. Women, keep in mind the revelations of Allah and the words of wisdom that are recited in your houses. Benign is Allah, All-Aware. (Q33:32)"

These verses corroborated what Umar had said. When the Prophet informed Umar of these verses, he felt satisfied that God had ordered what he desired. Turning to Umar, the Prophet said, "Umar, rejoice for once again Allah has spoken through your tongue."

Rumours of the Prophet's estrangement with his wives

Umar felt that while in Makkah, the Qurayshites dominated their women, in Medinah, things had changed, and the women asserted themselves. One day, Umar was unhappy with his wife on some matter, but instead of being quiet, she retorted, "How is it that you feel annoyed at my remonstrance? Go and see that the wives of the Prophet remonstrate with the Prophet. Tonight, one of his wives quarrelled with him all night."

Hearing this, Umar went to his daughter Hafsa and enquired whether she had quarrelled with the Prophet. She said that she had fought because she had a grievance. Thereupon, Umar was perturbed and advised her, "Hafsa, you are incurring a loss. Don't you know by annoying the Prophet, you invite the wrath of God?"

At night, the Ansari neighbour of Umar knocked at his door. As Umar opened the door, his friend told him something grave had happened. Umar thought that perhaps Banu Ghassan, whose attack was expected, had invaded Medinah. Umaya said, "No. Something more serious than that has happened. The Prophet had divorced his wives".

Umar was distraught by the news. He spent the whole night in prayer. Early in the morning the next day, Umar went to Hafsa. He found her weeping. He enquired about whether the Prophet had divorced her. She said that she did not know. Umar rebuked her, saying. "Did I not warn you that you would invite trouble by annoying the Prophet?" Thereupon, Hafsa burst into violent sobs. Umar left her weeping and went to the Prophet's Mosque. The people sat in groups, lamenting that the Prophet had divorced his wives.

The Prophet was in the cell attached to the Mosque. Umar went to the cell and asked the enslaved person at the door to seek the Prophet's permission for entry. The enslaved person replied that the Prophet was unresponsive to the requests.

Umar returned to the main hall of the Mosque and sat dejected. After some time, he rose and went again to the cell of the Prophet. This time, Umar got permission to meet him.

Entering the cell, Umar said:

"O Messenger of God, I have not come to plead for Hafsa. I will wring her neck with my hands if that is your pleasure."

That softened the Prophet, and he smiled at the words of Umar.

Umar said, "I find that in Makkah, our ladies were docile; the environment of Medinah has made them assertive. O Prophet of God, if you have divorced them because of their audacity, God, His angels, and all your followers are with you."

The Prophet smiled and said, "Be assured, I have not divorced my wives. I have only decided to remain separate from them for one month."

"Then may I say so to Hafsa," said Umar.

The Prophet said. "You may if you like."

Umar nervously surveyed the room. The Prophet lay on a bare mat. There was no furniture in the room. There was hardly anything for the Prophet to eat but barley bread. Seeing this plight, Umar began teary-eyed.

The Prophet said, "Ibn-i-Khattab, what makes you weep?"

Umar said, "You are the Prophet of God, and you are living in such straitened circumstances. The people of Persia and Byzantine live in luxury. O Prophet of God, why don't you pray to God to bestow you with wealth?"

The Prophet said. "Do you think He Who made me His Prophet could not make me wealthy? Indeed, He offered me the keys to all the treasures in the world, but I refused them in return for the treasures in the next world. Surely, treasures in the next world will be preferred over petty wealth. And as for the riches of Persia and Byzantine, rest assured all such wealth will lie at the feet of the Muslims. I will not be alive then, but in your lifetime, the Muslims will be overpowered by Persia and Byzantine."

Umar's covenant with citizens

On the occasion of the first Friday prayer, after he assumed office as Caliph, Umar addressed the faithful assembled in the mosque and assured them of fairness and honesty.

Although Umar was the sovereign ruler of the entire Islamic empire, he understood the extent of his power, rights and status very well. Once, while delivering a sermon, he said: "My rights over public funds (the *BaitulMaal*) are similar to those of the guardians of an orphan. If I am well placed in life, I will not claim anything from it. In case of need, I shall draw only as much as is constitutionally allowed to provide food. You have every right to question me about any improper accumulation of the revenue and bounty collections, improper utilization of the treasury money, provision of the daily bread to all, border security arrangements, and harassment caused to any citizen."

On another occasion, he declared: "For Umar, what is permissible from *Baitul Mal* is a length of the cloth sufficient to cover him, a ride for *hajj* pilgrimage and other State tours, and sustenance equal to the requirements of a middle-class family."

Self-introspection

To be accountable to oneself, that is, to be honest about self-criticism is part of a Muslim practice called *al-murabb*a or self-inventory. According to Umar, engaging in *al-murabb*a is "to asses and adjudge yourselves before you are adjudged and assessed on the Day of Judgment, and weigh out your deeds before they are weighed out for you." Umar, a man of his word, used to whip his right foot at night and say to it, "What have you done today?"

Once, he addressed a gathering, saying, "Brothers, if I stray from the right path, what will you do"? A man stood up and said, "We will behead you." Umar shouted to test him. "You dare utter such impertinent words for me?" "Yes, for you," replied the man. Umar was very pleased with his audacity and said, "Thank God, there exist such bold men in our nation that if I go astray, they will set me right."

11. VIGNETTES FROM UMAR'S CALIPHATE

Umar has a multifaceted personality and handles a wide diversity of challenging situations with grace and confidence. A few incidents from his life give us insight and a glimpse of his virtuous attributes.

An Epitome of Justice

Justice is the cardinal value of any civilized society. More than any other element, justice remains the bedrock of all great civilizations. Without it, the entire bulwark of society would collapse. There would be utter chaos, and people would endure constant injustice. The past tells us that all those civilizations which did not nurture the values of justice scripted their doom.

"Man is his star;

and the soul that can.

Render an honest and perfect man,

Commands all light, all influence, all fate."

As Ralph Waldo Emerson rightly proclaimed, all those great rulers whose images gleam through the pages of history were men who lived solely by justice. They harnessed the power of justice to lead people to a life of righteousness. They established an order that would ensure fairness and justice in human affairs. Judicial verdicts may not change hearts, but they can prevent people from becoming heartless.

Justice can take root only if people nourish it for the noble principles of being amenable to the highest standards of honesty, morality and righteousness. Justice is a value that takes birth in our daily actions. It is a social value and an essential virtue for every human interaction. It is not left just to kings, rulers, judges and leaders.

Umar set up an effective system of judicial administration under which justice was administered according to the principles of Islam. Qadis or judges were appointed at all administrative levels for the administration of justice and were chosen for their integrity and learning of Islamic law. High salaries were paid to them, and they were appointed from among the wealthy and those of high social standing so as not to be influenced by the social position of any litigants. The Qadis were not allowed to engage in trade.

The Caliph took particular care in enforcing equality of justice. In the eyes of the law, all equal. He had separated the judiciary from the executive, a remarkable achievement that has not been achieved even in the most modern states of the present day. The court was free from the control of the Governors, and the Qadis imparted justice free from fear or favour.

In the Qur'an, the nature of justice is referred to in several places by directing that Allah commanded, "Lo! Allah commandeth you that ye restore deposits to their owners, and, if ye judge between mankind, that ye judge justly" (Q4:58). It is observed in the same chapter that "O ye who believe? Be ye staunch in justice, witnesses for Allah, even though it be against yourselves or (your) parents or (your) kindred, whether (the case be of) a rich man or a poor man, for Allah is nearer unto both (than ye are). So, follow not passion lest ye lapse (from the truth), and if ye lapse or fall away, then lo! Allah is ever informed of what ye do."

Justice has been epitomized for ages in the inspiring statue of a crusading woman. For centuries, she has been painted blindfolded with a sword in one hand and lifted scales in the other. Why is justice painted blind? Joseph Addison explains: Justice discards party, friendship, and kindred and is therefore always represented as blind. Justice is painted blind to signify that she is impartial and without prejudice. She favours neither one side nor the other and bears no ill will to one or the other. Few people in the scrolls of world history symbolise this lofty vision of justice, and Umar adorns them with grandeur.

Judicial procedure

Umar contributed to developing the judicial system by laying down the broad legal principles and establishing the required judicial procedures for dispensing justice. Umar used to send instructions, called *firman,* from time to time to Abu Musa Ash'ri, the Governor of Kufa, establishing fundamental principles for courts of justice. In one of the *firman* issued to the judges, Umar laid down the following principles to be observed in the Courts:

- Justice is an essential obligation to God. This responsibility is given to you, and you must discharge it with all sincerity and ability to get God's pleasure and earn the people's goodwill.

- All people are equal. Treat them alike so that the weak are not deprived of justice and the well-placed persons are not favoured.

It was further laid down that:

- The onus of proof in a suit lies on the plaintiff. He has to present evidence for his claims. The claims are denied only on oath.

- Compromise is possible if it is lawful and does not turn unlawful into lawful and vice-versa.

- You can change your previous decision if you think that the earlier decision was incorrect after due consideration.

- When you doubt specific issues and do not find any explanation in the Qur'ān and the *sunnah* of the Prophet, think it over again and again, consider the precedents and analogous cases thoroughly, and then decide by analogy.

- A date should be fixed for a person who wants to produce witnesses. If he proves his case, decide in his favour. Otherwise, dismiss the suit.

- All Muslims are eligible to witness except those who are punished or have given false witness or whose integrity is doubtful.

Dispensing justice

Abu Musa Ashari was the Governor of Basra. He held the chief command of the operations in Persia. After the victory of Isfahan, Abu Musa sent a delegation of sixty persons to Medinah. A young man, Zaba bin Mohsin, waited for Abu Musa and a request for his inclusion on the board. Abu Musa regretted his inability as there was a more deserving than Zaba. Zaba felt dissatisfied, and he threatened to complain to the Caliph. Abu Musa informed Umar of the danger of Zaba.

Zaba went to Medina and complained to Abu Musa. Umar recorded the complaint and summoned Abu Musa to Medinah. When Abu Musa came to Medinah, Umar showed him the list of charges against him and asked for his explanation.

The first charge was that sixty prisoners were kept captives in his custody. Abu Musa explained that these captives had applied to be ransomed, and he had kept them with him till they were ransomed. Umar disapproved of this action.

The second charge was that he had paid one thousand dirhams to a poet. Abu Musa said that he had spent the amount out of his money. Abu Musa presented the accounts. Umar felt satisfied and dismissed. this charge

The third charge was that Abu Musa had a maid, Aquila, who got two shares. Abu Musa explained that the maid had some metabolic problems as her food consumption was twice that of an average adult. As such, she needed two shares.

The fourth charge was that Abu Musa had entrusted most of his work to a young man, Ziyad. Abu Musa explained that he had done so in the public interest as Ziyad was most intelligent.

Umar summoned Aquila and Ziyad to Medinah. He verified that Aquila consumed food twice the regular quota for an adult's food. By questioning Ziyad, Umar felt convinced that Ziyad was brilliant and that it was in the public interest to avail of his intelligence. Abu Musa was acquitted of the charges and resumed his office at Basra.

On another occasion, a person came to Umar and complained about Abu Musa. He said that Abu Musa gave him a smaller share at the time of the distribution of the spoils. He protested and urged that he should be given the total share due to him. Thereupon, Abu Musa felt annoyed, struck him with twenty lashes, and had his hair shaded. Umar asked the complainant to return to Basra and level the charge against Abu Musa before a congregation there. If the charge was proven, he could have his revenge on Musa. Umar gave the complainant the necessary authority to do so on this behalf. The complainant returned to Basra and, in the mosque, levelled the charge against Abu Musa. Many in the congregation came forward to support the charge. Turning to the crowd, Abu Musa said, "You can have your revenge. You may beat me or accept me at your option." The complainant said, "Now I feel satisfied, and I forgive you in the name of Allah."

A trusted Governor

Sa'iid ibn Aamir is a name that is not frequently mentioned or even known by many - yet he was a man of enormous faith. Sa'eed left Makkah for Medinah to devote himself to the propagation of Islam. On the death of Prophet Muhammad, 'Amir proved to be a staunch supporter of the Prophet's two successors, Abu Bakr and Umar, whom he actively assisted in administration.

Umaras, the Governor of Homs in Syria, appointed Sa'iid. He refused when he was nominated for that position, saying, "Do not expose me to *fitnah* (trials and tribulations)." But Umar urged him to accept, saying, "By Allah, I will not let you turn me down. Do you lay the burdens of your trusteeship and the caliphate upon my shoulders, then refuse to help me?" Sa'iid ibn Aamir had to accept the position.

Homs was called the second Kufa (Kufa is in Iraq) because its people were notorious for endless mutinies and uprisings. Yet, these people loved and obeyed Sa'iid ibn Aamir.

When some trustworthy people came from Homs in Syria sometime later, 'Umar asked them to list the names of the poor people in Homs. When he noticed that the name of Sa'iid was figured in the list, he was amazed. 'But who is Sa'iid mentioned in the list, he queried. They replied he was their Governor." Umar sobbed at his plight and directed the administration that a thousand dinars be sent to him. When Sa'eed received the money, he became depressed, as if a calamity had befallen him. His wife inquired about the matter. He informed her that temptation had entered his house. Without her knowing, she advised: "Get rid of it." He asked, "Would you help me?" Yes, of course!" was her immediate response. They put the money in small pouches and distributed it to people experiencing poverty. When Umar disclosed that he found it strange that the people of Homs loved and obeyed him, Sa'iid said, "Perhaps they love me because I help and sympathize with them."

But soon, the rebellious nature of these people became evident when they complained to Umar when he visited the city. They said, "We have four complaints against Sa'iid: first, he does not come out of his house until the sun rises high and the day becomes hot; second, he does not see anyone at night (that is, he is not available for us at night); third, there are two days in every month in which he doesn't leave his house at all; fourth, he faints now and then and this annoys us even though we know he cannot help it."

Hearing these complaints, Umar was silent for a while. He prayed to Allah, "O Allah! I know that Sa'iid is one of Your best-enslaved individuals. O Allah, I pray You will not disappoint me about him."

Then he called for Sa'iid ibn Aamir to defend himself. When Sa'iid heard the complaints, he said, "By Allah, I did not wish to make known my reasons, but I have to explain now that these complaints have been brought against me! First, I do not leave my house before noon because my wife does not have a servant, so I knead the dough for her, wait for her to rise, bake my bread, perform ablution and pray and then go out of my house."

Umar's face brightened, and they said, "All praises and thanks to Allah!"

Sa'iid ibn Aamir continued, "As for their complaint that I do not meet them at night. By Allah, I did not wish to make my reasons known, but you forced me to. I have devoted the day to the people and their needs and reserved the night for the worship of Allah."

"As for their third complaint, they do not see me two days a month because I do not have a servant to wash my garment, and I have only one garment. So, I wash it, wait for it to dry, and shortly before sunset, I go out of my house to meet them.

"As for their fourth complaint, that I have fainting fits, it is because I witnessed the martyrdom of Khubaib Al-Ansaari in Makkah. As the people of Quraysh cut his body into small pieces, they said, 'Do you want to save yourself and see Muhammad in your place instead?' And he answered, 'By Allah, I will not accept your offer of setting me free to return to my family safe and sound, even if you lavish me with wealth for letting down the Prophet' This happened as I watched as a disbeliever (he had not embraced Islam then). Now, every time I remember how I stood and watched Khubaib being tortured to death and did nothing to save him, I find myself shaking with fear of Allah's punishment, and I faint!"

There was nothing more to be said except what Umar noted in response to this explanation: "Alhamdulillah! All praises and thanks to Allah!"

Muslim Brotherhood

Once, Umar saw that a man he knew was missing from one of his gatherings. He asked about him since the person regularly attended these gatherings, and the people told him that the man could not let go of his habit of drinking alcohol.

So, Umar sent the man a letter:

"Peace be upon you. I praise Allah, besides whom there is no other God in the Name of Allah, the Most Beneficent, the Most Merciful.

(Qur'an 40:1-3 — *'Haa Meem (These letters are one of the miracles of the Qur'an, and none but Allah alone knows their meaning.) The Revelation of this Book (the Qur'an) is from Allah, the All-Mighty, the All-Knower, the Forgiver of sin, the Acceptor of repentance, the Severe in punishment, the Bestower of favours. La ilaha illa huwa (none has the right to be worshipped but He), to Him is the final return.*"

He sealed the letter and said to his messenger, "Do not give it to him except when he is in a sober mood." He then told those who were with him to pray for that man.

When the letter reached the man, he read it and said, "My Lord has promised to forgive me and has warned me of His punishment," He kept repeating that until he started weeping. He then gave up alcohol and kept away from it.

When news of this reached Umar, he said to his Companions, "This is what you should do. If you see that one of you has slipped (fallen into error), correct him, pray for him, and do not help Satan against him (by insulting him, etc.)."

A great judge of people

Umar was an excellent leader. He used to say, "Do not be deceived by a man's eloquence; whoever fulfils trusts and refrains from hurting people's honour is a real man."

And he used to say, "Do not look at a man's prayer or fasting; rather, look at his reason and honesty."

Once, a man gave testimony in a case, and Umar asked the people if anyone could vouch for the man's character. One person said to him, 'I will vouch for him, *O Ameer ul Mu'minee*n (Leader of the Muslims).'

Umar asked him, "Are you his neighbour?" He said, "No."

He then asked, "Did you spend a day with him and come to know his real character?" The man said, 'No.'

He asked next, "Did you travel with him? Travelling and being away from home reveal a man's true essence." Again, the man said, "No."

Umar said, "Perhaps you saw him in the mosque, standing, sitting, and praying?"

At that, the man said, "Yes."

Umar said, "Go away, for you do not know him."

He used to say to the people, "There are two types of people of whom I have no fear for you: a believer whose faith is obvious and a *kafi*r (disbeliever in Allah and His Messenger) whose *kufr* (disbelief in Allah and His Messenger) is obvious. Rather, I fear for you, the hypocrite who hides behind a show of faith but strives for some other purpose."

Umar's criteria for appointment of Governors

To maintain the administration's integrity, Umar laid down strict criteria for selecting candidates for appointment as Governors. Some accounts have come down to us, which show how scrupulous Umar was in choosing his Governors.

It is related to the time Umar decided to appoint a governor. The Governor designates Umar to get his appointment orders. Umar asked his Secretary to draft the declaration. As the order was being prepared, Umar's younger son came and sat in his lap. Umar caressed the child. Thereupon, the Companion said *Ameer ul Mu'minin*, your children come to you freely, but my children do not dare to come near me". Thereupon, Umar said, "If your children are afraid of you, the people will be still more afraid of you. The oppressed will hesitate to bring forward their complaints to you. As such, you are not fit to be a Governor, and the mandate about your appointment as Governor now stands cancelled."

On one occasion, Umar decided to appoint his companion as Governor. Before the appointment orders were issued, that Companion called on Umar and solicited appointment as a Governor. Umar said:

"I was going to appoint you as a Governor on my account, but now that you have asked for this appointment, I think you are not fit for the office. As you have asked for the office, I fear you will use it as an office of profit, and I cannot allow that. I would appoint only such men who regard such office as a burden to be entrusted to them in the name of Allah."

The appointment of Governor for Kufa became a significant headache for Umar. If he appointed a harsh and stern man, the people complained against him. The people took advantage of his leniency if he set a soft-hearted man. Umar wanted his comrades to advise him regarding selecting a suitable man for the office. One man rose to say he could suggest a man who would be the fittest person for the job. Umar enquired who he was, and the man said, "Abdullah bin Umar." Umar was furious. "May God curse you? You want me to expose myself to the criticism that I have appointed my son to a high office. That can never be".

Around Umar were such prominent persons as Usman Ali, Zubair, Talha, and others. Umar did not offer them any office. Someone asked

Umar why he had not appointed such prominent persons as governors. Umar said, "These notables occupy a high status because of their virtues. I do not appoint them as Governors lest their reputation may get stained on account of any lapse, and they may lose their present prominence."

Once, the post of the Governor of Hems fell vacant, and Umar thought of offering it to Ibn Abbas. Umar called Ibn Abbas and said, "I want to appoint you as the Governor of Hems, but I have one misgiving." "What is that," asked Ibn Abbas. Umar said, "I fear that sometime you would be apt to think that you are related to the Prophet and would come to regard yourself above the law." Ibn Abbas said, "When you have such a misgiving, I will not accept the job." Umar said, "Please advise me what sort of man I should appoint." Ibn Abbas said, "Appoint a good man, and about whom you have no misgiving."

Someone asked Umar, "What is your criterion for selecting a man for appointment as a Governor?" Umar said, "I want a man who, when he is among men, should look like a chief although he is not a chief, and when he is a chief, he should look as if he is one of them."

The stone of justice

During the caliphate of Umar, Amr bin Al-Aas was appointed the Governor of Egypt. One of Amr's first projects was to expand the principal mosque of Cairo, which was surrounded by residents' dwellings. Amr's workers negotiated with the residents to buy their houses so that the land could be available for expansion. All occupants, barring one Coptic Christian, agreed. The Coptic refused on the ground that the place had sentimental value for him. The matter was referred to Amr, who summoned the Copt. Amr offered the Copt double, triple and quadruple the value of his house, but the Copt refused to sell, irrespective of the compensation. The persuasive efforts were of no avail as the Copt appeared determined to have his way. Amr became exasperated and ordered the Copt's house to be destroyed, leaving it to the Copt to accept or refuse the compensation.

The Copt was distraught and believed that this new Muslim Governor of Egypt had wronged him. He was unsure who to seek help from. People advised him to meet the Cali*ph: "Go to Medinah and speak to the Caliph, Umar bin Al Khattab, for no man is wronged in his lands."* So, the Copt decided to travel to Medinah to complain to the Caliph about how he had been unjustly treated by one of his Governors. When he arrived in Medinah and asked to see the Caliph, he was told, "Go to the Sacred Mosque of the Prophet, and there you will find a man sweeping the floor. Speak to him." The Copt went to the Sacred Mosque, hoping that its sweeper would be able to direct him to the Caliph.

When the Copt entered the Sacred Mosque, he found a man sweeping its floor. The Copt asked him if he could help him meet the Caliph. The sweeper asked him, "And what business do you have to speak to the Caliph about?"The Copt replied, "I have been wronged by one of his Governors, so the people asked me to complain to the Caliph as he is a just man and no one is wronged in his lands," and he related to the sweeper the story of what had happened to his house in Cairo.

After attentively listening to the Copt's story, the sweeper picked up a stone, and with another stone, he scratched two lines on it, one crossing the other at right angles. He gave the rock containing the lines to the Copt and told him to give it to the Governor of Egypt with the words, *"This stone is from the sweeper of the Sacred Mosque of Allah's Messenger."* The cop thought the sweeper was mocking him, but the sweeper reassured him to do as he had instructed and assured him that the problem would be solved. The sweeper made no mention of the Caliph. The Copt returned to Egypt with the stone given to him by the sweeper of the Sacred Mosque of Allah's Messenger.

When the Copt returned to Egypt, he went straight to Amr and gave him the stone, saying it was from the sweeper of the Prophet's Mosque in Medinah. No sooner had Amr seen the lines on the rock. His face went pale in fright. Amr apologized profusely to the Copt and immediately ordered that the part of the mosque built over the Copt's house be rebuilt exactly as it was before demolition. Puzzled by this sudden change of heart in the Governor, the Copt asked Amr what the significance of a simple stone with two lines was. Amr related the story behind the stone of justice to him. He told the Copt that the man sweeping the Sacred Mosque of the Prophet was none other than the Caliph himself, Umar bin Al Khattab. Amr understood from the two lines scratched on the stone that if he did not return the house to the Copt, then Umar would cut him into four quarters, not in two halves like the Persian prince. Since Amr knew that whenever Umar said something, he meant it, he took no chances and ordered the Copt's house to be rebuilt, albeit at the expense of destroying a part of the newly built mosque. The Copt was so moved by the whole sequence of events that he forfeited his claim for the reclamation of land used by the rulers for the construction of the mosque.

The justice of King Kisra

During their early adulthood in Makkah before the advent of the Prophet, Umar and Amr bin Al-Aas were business partners, trading in fine Arabian horses. Once, they received an order for a significant number of horses from King Numan, the Arab king of the Al-Mundhir governate, which, under the rule of the Persian Empire, was a buffer region between Arabia and Persia (represented today by parts of modern-day Iraq). King Numan made a down payment to Umar and Amr, who promptly set about finding and training horses to meet the king's requirements. When the horses were ready, the two friends set off to Al-Mundhir to deliver them to their buyer, King Numan.

While travelling through the desert in Al-Mundhir, they came across a royal entourage. It turned out to be that of a Persian prince, a son of Emperor Kisra, who had come on a hunting expedition to Al-Mundhir. The prince saw the fine Arabian horses and asked to see their owners. He offered to buy the horses from the two friends, but they said they had already been sold to a buyer. The prince doubled and trebled his offer, but Umar and Amr refused to go back on their contract with King Numan, so they politely declined the prince's offers. After much haggling, the pompous prince grew impatient and ordered his guards to seize (without payment) the horses from the two men.

Distraught and nervous at this incivility of the prince, Umar and Amr were unsure what to do. Local tribesmen advised them to travel to the capital of the Persian Empire and speak to the emperor Kisra himself. He was known to be just, and no one was wronged in his empire. The two friends journeyed to Persia and eventually reached Kisra's court, weary and dishevelled. They complained to him that their horses had been stolen by a man who claimed to be the emperor's son. Kisra listened intently and then asked the two men to return to him the following day while he looked into the matter. He ordered his palace courtiers to arrange for a stay for the two men as guests of the emperor.

The following day, Umar and Amr went to Kisra, and he came down to them from his throne, asking the two to accompany him. He led them to a courtyard where they saw their stolen horses. Kisra asked them to confirm if these were the horses that the prince had seized from them and, if so, that they should check that they were okay. Umar and Amr carefully checked each horse and informed Kisra that everything was fine. Kisra then profusely apologized to the two for what had happened, and he asked them if he could further assist them. They told him they were satisfied and would like to continue their journey. Kisra ordered his staff to give the men some provisions, and he guaranteed them safe passage until they left the boundaries of his territory. Just before they left, Kisra asked the two to leave the palace grounds from two different gates: the Eastern Gate and the Western Gate.

Umar left via the Eastern Gate and, to his astonishment, he saw hanging half of the body of the Persian Prince, son of Kisra, as if he had been sawn in two. When he rejoined Amr, Amr told him that he had seen the other half of the Prince's corpse hanging from the Western Gate. Kisra was not prepared to let a spoilt son of his damage to his widespread reputation as the beacon of justice. He not only wanted justice to be done, but he wanted that justice must be seen to be seen.

Since the Emperor was just, all his subjects were just, and people felt safe in his lands. Had the Persian Empire not been conquered by a Muslim army whose soldiers established individual justice (through the fear of Allah) and social justice, it may have remained a world superpower until today. The Persians' rejection of the Divine Message eventually led to the decay which destroyed their civilization. When Umar bin Al Khattab came, people forgot the justice of Kisra.

And what was the justice of Umar? Ink will dry, and paper will finish before it is possible to describe all the living examples of justice established by the Prophet and embodied in the legacies of the Rightly-Guided Caliphs who succeeded him. Yet one statement, made by a Roman, reveals a glimpse into the justice of Umar, the second. One afternoon, a Roman emissary arrived in Medinah on crucial diplomatic business with the Caliph. When he enquired about Umar's whereabouts, he was directed to a man sleeping peacefully under a tree with no bodyguards, weapons, fortifications, or security. The Roman messenger marvelled at this sight: the sight of the leader of millions of people sleeping peacefully under a tree without a care in the world. He then remarked on his famous words that remain etched into history today:

O Umar! You ruled.

You were just.

Thus, you were safe.

And thus, you slept.

Such is the security that justice brings to both the ruler and the ruled. Umar was just to his people, so he had nothing to fear from them. He rendered everyone their rights, so they had no grievances against him. His people slept in peace. So, he, too, slept in peace. How the world yearns for this sleep!

O Umar! If only you would return,

To spread justice so the world would learn,

That even a stone of your righteousness,

Would rescue it from this fathomless abyss.

Grooming Umar for Caliphate

During the caliphate of Abu Bakr, Umar was the principal adviser to the Caliph. A story is on record showing the great esteem and regard that Abu Bakr had for Umar and his opinion. It is related that once, Ayanayah bin Hassan and Aqrah bin Habas, two tribal chiefs, waited on Abu Bakr and requested that an estate be awarded to them. They suggested that close to their settlement, there was a wasteland comprising only rock and was therefore totally barren and unproductive. Since it was of no use to the state or the public, they wanted the Caliph to gift it to them because they wanted to put it to productive use and attempt to cultivate it.

Abu Bakr consulted the people around him. They suggested that it was a reasonable proposition for the wasteland to become productive. Abu Bakr accordingly agreed to award them the land in question. A document was drawn up. Umar was not present, and Abu Bakr advised the grantees to have Umar witness it.

The grantees thought that such witnessing by Umar was merely a formality and that there would be no difficulty in obtaining his signature on the document. The grantees went to Umar and requested that he affix his signatures to the document, as Abu Bakr had approved it.

After reading the document, Umar returned it to the grantees, saying that he could not be a party to the deed. In anger, the grantees went to Abu Bakr and reported what Umar had said.

Abu Bakr remained quiet. Turning to the Caliph, the grantees asked, "Are you the Caliph, or is Umar the Caliph?"

Abu Bakr said, "You may take Umar to be the Caliph."

Then Umar came to the Caliph. Abu Bakr enquired what the reason for his refusal to sign the document was.

Umar asked, "Is the land which you have gifted your property, or is it a trust with you on behalf of the Muslim community."

Abu Bakr said, "It is not my personal property; as such, it should be a trust on behalf of the Muslim community."

Umar said, "If that is the position, how can you extinguish the trust by gifting it to A or B? They may take it on lease subject to terms, but it must remain the State property."

Turning to the applicants, Abu Bakr said, "Umar has spoken the truth. I cannot deviate from the law."

Turning to Umar, Abu Bakr said, "I had already requested you to take over the office of the Caliph, but you thrust the burden on my shoulders. I may not be with you for long, and ultimately, you will have to shoulder this responsibility."

A criminal embraces Islam.

By 638 A.D., the entire Syria was under the occupation of the Muslims. Heraclius, the Byzantine emperor, had left Syria and withdrawn his forces. His parting words were:

"Farewell Syria, never again will I come to this beautiful land. What a fine country I am leaving for the enemy."

Some Christian Arabs were grieved at the shame the Christians suffered at the hands of the Muslims. In a passionate spell, they vowed vengeance against the Muslims. Having failed to defeat the Muslims on the battlefield, they decided to use underhand means and murder some high-ranking Muslims. A Ghassanid Arab Wasiq volunteered to slay Caliph Umar.

Wasiq waited on Heraclius at Constantinople, and a deal was fixed to relieve the Byzantine emperor of his enemies. The plan appealed to Heraclius. He paid Wasiq a vast sum and promised to reward him further after he executed the initial project. Motivated by the bounty and promise of his patron, Wasiq decided to proceed to Medinah.

Since he was an Arab, Wasiq faced no problems reaching Medinah incognito. He posed as a Muslim coming from the hinterland of a desert to pay a visit to Medinah. Wasiq carried a poisoned dagger carefully hidden in the folds of his cloak. Having reached Medinah, he was on the hunt for a chance that could put him face to face with the Caliph of Islam and kill him with such speed that he would be caught off guard and with little opportunity for security guards to overpower him. He was surprised to learn in Medinah that there were no bodyguards for the security of the Caliph. Wasiq was excited by this news and felt glad he could execute his plan efficiently.

Wasiq waited for a suitable opportunity. One day at noon, Wasiq found Umar sleeping under a tree, alone and without any guard. No one was close to Umar, not even a plain unarmed guard. Wasiq felt he was blessed with a golden opportunity, and the Caliph appeared to be easy prey for him.

He strolled with measured footsteps so as not to disturb Umar. In a very covert manner, Wasiq removed Umar's sword. He was about to stab the Caliph when his eyes fell on the face of Umar. The sight of the unadorned majesty of the pious Caliph sent a shudder through Wasiq's body. His legs hobbled, and his hands trembled. The sword slipped out of his grip and dropped down. With the noise of the blade dropping, Umar woke up. He was quick to take hold of the fallen sword. He propped up from his bed and confronted the would-be assassin.

Wasiq fell at the feet of the Caliph, implored his forgiveness and embraced Islam.

Sabbath for soldiers

In the wars conducted during the rule of Umar, the soldiers on the front remained absent for considerable periods. Umar introduced the reform that should be granted to every soldier after he had served on the front for four months.

It is related to one night when Umar was on his routine nocturnal round in Medinah. It was late in the night, and there was stillness all around. Umar heard a woman ranting and lamenting from one of the street's dwellings. She was repeatedly grumbling:

"The night is boring and keeps me sleepless;

For I have none to keep me company.

I fear Allah, Who keeps watching over our souls,

And would not take another Companion,

But who could tell Umar,

That he should not be so cruel,

As to keeping my husband away from me,

For such a long period."

The woman's painful and agonizing litany lit up Umar's heart. He knocked at the door, and when the woman came to the door, he said:

"I have heard what you wanted to be conveyed to Umar.

How long has your husband been away?"

The woman said, "About a year."

Umar said, "Rest assured, your husband will return to you shortly."

Umar sought clarification from his daughter Hafsa on the maximum period for a man to remain separate from his wife. She suggested four months. Umar accordingly issued orders that unless a man of the armed forces could take his wife with him, he should be allowed a spell of leave after every four months of active service on the front.

Destruction of the library at Alexandria

Ptolemy II, who became the ruler of Egypt after Alexander the Great in the third century BC, was a great patron of learning. In Alexandria, he established a library which eventually contained some 500,000 books and was a fabled repository of the wisdom and arts of the ancient world. It came to be known as the Great Library at Alexandria and was one of the Seven Wonders of the Ancient World. It has been said that the library was burned on the orders of Caliph Umar ibn Al-Khattab after the Muslims had taken the city. The story goes that the books were used to feed the numerous furnaces which heated the baths of the city. The story also contains the oft-quoted remark, allegedly made by Caliph Umar, "If these writings of the Greeks agree with the book of God, they are useless and need not be preserved; if they disagree, they are pernicious and ought to be destroyed." Thus, the library was burned without even a cursory look at its contents. Or so the story goes. But is it true?

The Encyclopedia Brittanica says that the library had, in fact, been destroyed long before the advent of Islam — in the fourth century AD. Phillip K. Hitti, the great historian of the Arabs, states that the story "is one of those tales that make good fiction but bad history." He continues, "The great Ptolemaic library was burnt in 48 BC by Julius Caesar. A later one, referred to as the daughter library, was destroyed about 389 AD by Emperor Theodosius. At the time of the Arab conquest, therefore, no library of importance existed in Alexandria, and no contemporary writer ever brought up these charges against Umar ibn Al-Khattab."

Professor Bernard Lewis, a modern critic of Islam, has summarized the verdict of contemporary scholarship on the subject: "Modern research has shown the story to be completely unfounded. None of the early chronicles, not even the Christian ones, make any reference to it, and it was not mentioned until the 13th century." Those words were written by Professor Lewis in 1950. In 1990, he said: "Not the creation but the demolition of the myth was an achievement of European scholarship which, from the 18th century to the present day, has rejected the story as false and absurd, and thus exonerated Caliph Umar and the early Muslims from this libel."

Bertrand Russell made the following statement: "Every. Christian has been taught the story of the Caliph destroying the library in Alexandria. As a matter of fact, the library was frequently destroyed and frequently rebuilt. The early Muslims, unlike the Christians, tolerated those whom they called 'People of the Book,' provided they paid tribute. In contrast to the Christians, who persecuted not only pagans but each other, the Muslims were welcomed for their broadmindedness, and it was essentially this that facilitated their conquests."

In the 500 years between the burning of the library and its first being reported, no Christian writer or historian mentions it. However, Eutychius, who was archbishop of Alexandria in 933, described the city's capture by the Arabs in great detail. Colin Wilson, a scientific writer and researcher, expressed his belief that Christian clergy caused the demolition of the library. He wrote, "The Library at Alexandria, which contained, among other things, Aristotle's book collection, was burned down on the orders of the archbishop of Alexandria supported by Emperor Theodosius." No less a historian than Edward Gibbon said that the library had been thoroughly destroyed by Christian fanatics some three centuries before the armies of Islam conquered Egypt.

M.N. Roy, the Indian philosopher, analyzed the issue from a broader perspective. "The Library at Cairo contained over 100,000 volumes, while Cordoba boasted six times as many. This fact gives the lie to the slander, which depicts the rise of Islam as an eruption of savage fanaticism — specifically, the tale of the destruction of the famous library at Alexandria. One must have a pious mind of credulous disposition to believe that those who took delight in founding and supporting such noble seats of learning would have callously set fire to the library at

Alexandria, that those who command the gratitude of humanity for having saved its most precious inheritance, could have possibly begun by contributing to the destruction of that same inheritance. When the dispassionate and scientific study of history dissipates legends and discredits malicious tales, the rise of Islam stands out, not as a scourge, but a blessing for humanity."

Umar's strictness with family

What was especially astonishing about Umar was his integrity. He, almost alone, had been given the inner strength to disregard the importance of his children, his wives, his cousins, his clan and his tribe. This one weakness has pulled down generation after generation of Arab leaders. It is a weakness that, if unchecked, bleeds the most astute statesman into an empty shell. Once, Umar gathered his immediate family and said to them: "I have forbidden the people to do so and so. Now, the people look at you as birds look at flesh, and I swear by God that if I find any one of you doing any wrong, I will double the penalty against him."

Umar set up very high standards of integrity for himself and his family members. He took particular care to see that such standards were followed strictly. Whenever Umar issued any instructions for the people to follow, he brought home to his family members that he expected them to conform to such instructions strictly.

What was especially astonishing about Umar was his integrity. He, almost alone, had been given the inner strength to disregard the importance of his children, his wives, his cousins, his clan and his tribe. This one weakness has pulled down generation after generation of Arab leaders. It is a weakness that, if unchecked, bleeds the most astute statesman into an empty shell. Once, Umar gathered his immediate family and said to them: "I have forbidden the people to do so and so. Now, the people look at you as birds look at flesh, and I swear by God that if I find any one of you doing any wrong, I will double the penalty against him." He issued strict orders that no member of his family should accept any gift from any person. Hence, Umar found a new carpet with his wife, Atika. He wanted to know where the rug had come from. She said that Abu Musa Ashari, the Governor of Basra, had presented it. Umar had the carpet immediately returned to Abu Musa. Abu Musa was reprimanded in solid terms for sending a gift to the wife of the Caliph.

'Abdullah, the son of Umar, purchased some camels. They were lean and were bought at a very cheap price. 'Abdullah sent these camels to the state pasture where they were fattened. These were then sold in the market and fetched a high price. When this was brought to Umar's notice, he ordered that as the camels had been fed at the state pasture, whatever profit had accrued in the sale of the camels should be deposited in the state treasury.

Once, Umar saw a small girl who was lean, thin, and bony. Umar enquired who the girl was. 'Abdullah, the son of Umar, said that she was his daughter and that she had lost weight because, with the allowance that Umar allowed to his family, nourishing food could not be provided. Umar said that he was giving them what he gave to other families, and he could not offer his family anything more than what he did to other families.

Once 'Abdullah and 'Ubaidullah, two sons of Umar went to Basra. There, they obtained a loan from Abu Musa on the condition that the amount be paid to the state treasury in Madinah. With this amount, they purchased some merchandise and sold it at Madinah. They earned considerable profit, which they kept for themselves, and credited the principal amount to the state treasury. When Umar came to know of this transaction, he wanted his sons to credit the entire profit to the state treasury as the money they had traded was state money. 'Abdullah kept quiet, but 'Ubaidullah protested. He said that if there had been a loss, the state would not have shared it. Umar stuck to his decision, but 'Ubaidullah protested again. Some other Companions intervened, and it was decided that the partnership should be treated as a case of partnership. Umar allowed his sons to retain one-half of the profit and to deposit the other half in the state treasury.

Once Umar received a considerable quantity of musk. It had to be weighed and then distributed. Umar was in search of a person who could weigh musk with meticulous care. Atika, Umar's wife, offered to do so as she was an expert on the job. Umar did not accept the offer on the ground that when she weighed and distributed it, some musk would be attached to her hands and clothes, and that would be misappropriation of state property.

Once, Umm Kulthum, Umar's wife, purchased perfume for one dirham and sent it as a gift to the Byzantine empress. The Byzantine empress returned the empty phials of perfume filled with gems. When Umar learned of this, he sold the gems. Out of the sale proceeds, he handed over one dirham to his wife, and the rest was deposited into the state treasury.

Once, some gifts were received in the Baitul Mal. Hafsa waited on Umar and wanted a share. Umar said:

"Dear, you have a share in my personal property, but I cannot give you a special share out of the property that belongs to the Muslims as a whole. You can get only what other Muslims get."

His son-in-law once waited on him and wanted some assistance from the Baitul Mal. Umar paid him some money from his pocket and did not give him anything from the Baitul Mal.

Once after distribution, a lady's scarf was found surplus. The custodian of the Baitul Mal suggested that this might be offered to Umm Kulthum, Umar's wife. Umar said:

"No. Present it to Umm Salit, the lady who carried the water skin on her back on the day of the battle of Uhud to distribute water among the Muslim warriors."

Once, after accounting, one dirham was found surplus in the Baitul Mal. The treasurer gave the dirham to a minor son of Umar. When Umar came to know that, he had the dirham returned immediately.

'Abdullah, a son of Umar, fought in the battle of Jalaula. He got his share of the spoils and sold it on the spot. This fetched a high value. When Umar came to know that, he said that he was allowed the high price because people thought that he was the Caliph's son. He ordered that the profit earned beyond the market value should be credited to the state treasury.

One of Umar's sons drank wine inadvertently in Egypt. He submitted himself voluntarily to the punishment of 80 stripes in Egypt, but Umar was not satisfied. He called the boy to Madinah and flogged him to death. When the boy was on his bed, Umar said to him, "When you meet the Holy Prophet, tell him that Umar is following hi' injunctions strictly."

12. THE INNOVATIONS OF UMA

The Year of the Famine in Madinah and Umar they have resulted in disaster for the people. Muslims have also suffered from these famines. There have been countless examples of famine from the time of the Prophet. One of the most significant of these famines is the famine incident that was effective in Madinah and its surroundings during the khalīfat of Umar bin al-Hattab (d. 23/644). This famine, corresponding to the 6th year of the khalīfat of Umar, had negative consequences. In this period, when the rains were not falling, and the soil almost turned to ash, creatures were harmed, and some deaths occurred. When the opportunities in the city were insufficient to eliminate the shortage, the Khalif asked for help from the surrounding provinces. The coming help eased the situation for the people. In this famine year, which is known as the Remade year, Umar did not collect zakat from the public nor applied a sentence for theft in this period. Umar did everything in his power, but as the effects of the famine did not lessen, he went to the rain prayer for the drought to disappear. When the rain came, life took its ordinary course, and the people who came to Madinah from the rural parts due to the famine were sent back home by the khalīfa. There have been famine incidences in different geographies throughout human history. The Hejaz region in Saudi Arabia was also affected by these natural disasters. Mecca, which has an arid climate, has witnessed countless famines from pre-Islamic times to the present day. Madinah, which became a centre of attraction with the Prophet's migration, struggled with famines in the times of the Prophet as well as in later periods. Among these famines, the famine experienced during the khalīfat of Umar had considerably heavy consequences. The year of the famine in Madinah was recorded as Amurremade, which means the year was given that name because there was no rain at all, and the soil turned into the colour of ash and was swept easily by the wind. The famine, which began in the late 17th year of the Hejira and continued until the beginning of the 18th year, lasted approximately nine months. During this time, the soil dried up, the crops did not grow green, and the animals perished. The public was exposed to starvation and misery and had nothing in their hands. The bazaars and markets got empty. There was nothing left to buy and sell. People dug in the ground to find food and ate the lizards and moles they found. The famine had a more complex impact on the rural areas of Madinah. Those living in the desert had to take refuge in Madinah when they could not find anything to eat.

The severe drought even caused deaths in some tribes. The survivors had to eat whatever they could to stay alive. The animals they butchered had no meat, too. Thus, people removed the skins of dead animals and cooked them and gnawed on them or broke the bones of animals killed and ate the crumbs. When the famine continued for a long time, the living conditions of many people changed. Khalif Umar took some precautions to overcome the people's troubles. First, he gave the food in the central treasury (Beytulmal) in Madinah to the service of those who suffered from famine. When the food in the Beytulmal did not suffice, he called for his governors to send aid to Madinah and its surroundings. The call was answered. Abundant assistance was sent to Madinah from Damascus, Kufah, Basra, Egypt and Yemen.

Thanks to the help sent, people were relieved. The aid sent from the provinces was planned to be distributed equally to both the people of Madinah and the people who came from outside and settled around Madinah. For this, Umar tried to determine the number of people in need by assigning some people. After the number of people was determined, he prepared a list showing the names and needs of those who suffered from famine. Documents bearing Umar's seal were given to the public so that they could buy food. The aid also helped to decrease the prices. Because the prices of almost everything, particularly the bare necessities, had reached very high levels.Khalif Umar, thanks to donations supported by governors, also founded flour silos for those in need. Those who came to Madinah got food such as flour, bread, dates, grapes, etc. In addition, some days, twenty camels were butchered, and those who suffered from the famine were invited to get hot meals. For those who could not come, food was sent. This practice was continued regularly every month until the famine ended. When Umar could not find anything to distribute, he designated one family that had food to host another family that could not find food. After the rains started, the Khalif sent the Arabs, who had come to Madinah in time of the famine, back to their countries. He also funded them from the treasury so that they could reach their homes comfortably. The Arab tribes were delighted and thanked for the excellent treatment Umar showed during the famine. Umar did not collect zakah from the goods during the drought period. However, when famine weakened, he took the zakat of two years together.

In the same way, he did not apply the punishment to those who fed themselves illegally because of necessity. Umar worked hard to resolve the people's hardship and took all precautions during the famine period. However, the famine maintained its hard impact. Therefore, Umar decided to go for rain prayer and asked his governors to go to rain prayer, too. When people learned that Umar would pray for the rain, they all joined him. Caliph Umar, taking Abbas with him, wished for forgiveness from Allah. The prayers were soon answered, with a massive waterfall in and around Medina Madina. There was a waterfall all in and around Mwsina. Took a breath. Umar, the ruler of the Muslims, did not eat anything different from the people during the famine and sometimes was in a worse situation than the others. Many times, he preferred the benefit of others until the famine ended. For this, he was often hungry. This seriously threatened the Caliph Umar's health. These conditions were not limited to the caliph's person but also affected his family. His family members lived in more misery than other families. The conditions continued in this way until the famine lost its effect.

Linking Med To Red

It was 638 CE, the "Year of Ashes" on the Arabian Peninsula. Just six years after the death of the is 638 CE, the "Year of Ashes", there is a beach om wh; I;c;h; is; beset ee; s; I;x; yers Arabian Peninsula, which is plagued by a terrible drought. Just six years after the death of the Prophet Muhammad, phet Muhammad in the holy cities of Makkah and Madinah are besieged by dire peril and refugees from the countryside face starvation. Casting around for assistance, Caliph 'Umar ibn al-Khattab writes from Madinah to 'Amr ibn al-'As, his general in Egypt, urging him to send food to feed the hungry in the Hijaz, the Islamic heartland.

'Amr had not yet wholly subdued Egypt when he received the caliph's orders, but the historical record tells us that he did not stint, sending a vast camel caravan laden with food, most likely wheat and barley, to 'Umar. The caravan made its way from the Nile Valley across the Sinai Peninsula, then south through the Hijaz Mountains to Madinah, a journey of some 1300 kilometres (800 mi) that took a month to complete.

The caravan leader carried a response from 'Amr to the caliph. "I have sent you camels," he wrote. "The first is with you in Madinah; the last is just leaving me in Egypt." In between, says the ninth-century Egyptian historian Ibn 'Abd al-Hakam, an unbroken file of animals carried the bounty of the Nile to the Hijaz. When they reached Madinah, 'Umar allocated one camel, with its load, to each household. The hungry recipients ate both the animals and their cargo. Other

caravans came from lands to the north, and a Phe was thus narrowly averted. The effort had stretched caravan transport to its limits, however, and the lesson of the vulnerability of the Holy Cities, as well as the importance of the bounty of Egypt, was not lost on the caliph. 'Umar wrote again to 'Amr with a plan. "I wish to excavate a canal from Egypt's Nile so that its waters will flow to the sea," Ibn 'Abd al-Hakam quotes 'Umar as saying. "That way, it will be easier to transport food to Makkah and Madinah. Consult among yourselves to settle the matter." David Rumsey map collection

'Umar's idea was not as extraordinary as it first sounds. In fact, it was based on the memory that such a canal had existed when Egypt was under Roman rule and that ships carrying grain from Egypt had indeed sailed to the Hijaz in the past. By the time of the Islamic conquest of Egypt, however, the canal had fallen out of use and was blocked with sand and debris.

The leaders of Egypt's native Copts were particularly displeased, for they doubted the project would be as commercially beneficial for them as it would be for Arabia. Ibn 'Abd al-Hakam reports that they urged 'Amr to impress upon 'Umar that the project "is immoderate. It will not happen. We don't see a way." But 'Umar was not to be deterred. "I shall make it a command that no ship shall sail in the [Red] Sea except with food for the peoples of Makkah and Madinah," he vowed.

When 'Amr realized 'Umar was in earnest, he quickly set about the task of restoring the ancient Nile-Red Sea canal. According to Ibn 'Abd al-Hakam, a Copt showed 'Amr the route of the old Roman canal. In return, he and his family were exempted from the poll tax. For the most part, the Canal of the Commander of the Faithful, as it was named in honour of the caliph, followed the route cut by the Roman canal, with one major exception: It had to find a new connection to the Nile to avoid land already earmarked for the construction of Fustat, Egypt's new Islamic capital, the predecessor of modern Cairo. The new canal mouth was located at the site of today's Sayyida Zaynab Square in the heart of Cairo.

From its mouth on the Nile to its terminus at the Red Sea port of al-Qulzum (modern Suez), the canal coursed a remarkable 170 kilometres (105 mi). The 14th-century Mamluk historian Ibn Duqmaq tells us: "No sooner had ['Amr] brought effort to bear than ships were moving in it as they had before. Ships were arriving in the Hijaz in the seventh month [after the start of excavation]." 'Amr himself travelled on one of those ships to make the pilgrimage to Makkah.

The canal took advantage of some features of the Egyptian landscape. The first section followed the eastern fringe of the low-lying Nile Delta for about 80 kilometres (50 mi) and then struck east for around 65 kilometres (40 miles) along the Wadi Tumaylat. That was a dry east-west valley that had been cut through the northern extension of the Muqattam Hills by an ancient branch of the Nile that had once emptied into the Red Sea instead of the Mediterranean. The final leg south to the sea at al-Qulzum followed the Isthmus of Suez, a tectonic depression along which the modern Suez Canal runs today.

The main advantage of the canal was not so much enhanced speed as its capacity to deliver enormous amounts of strategic food reserves to the granaries of Arabia. The Fatimid-era author Ibn Tuwayr reports that it took five days for a flat-bottomed Nile vessel to travel the length of the canal—two or three days longer than by camel. At al-Qulzum, the cargo had to be transferred onto seagoing vessels, further slowing its journey. Moreover, the canal could only be used for part of the year, during the annual Nile flood from September to February. Nevertheless, a single Nile barge or Red Sea ship could replace a large number of camels and operate at a much lower cost. And the steady northerly winds that blow from al-Qulzum in the northern Red Sea would have enabled ships to arrive at the ports of the Hi jaz in less than two weeks, safe from the predations of desert raiders.

'Umar's canal transformed the fortunes of the Holy Cities, bringing unprecedented food security to the residents of the Hijaz. Egypt had once been the breadbasket of Rome and Byzantium; now, its rich soils could sustain the Islamic heartlands.

The scheme to supply the Hijaz with Egyptian food was not without its teething problems; however, the villains of the piece, financial speculators, are familiar to the modern reader. To ensure fair distribution of Egyptian grain when shipments arrived at al-Jar, the port of Madinah, 'Umar issued ration certificates to the people that entitled them to a share of the supplies. Initially, the situation was desperate, and people were hungry. Soon, a secondary market for certificates emerged, and prices soared. Specific traders, including one dealer named Hakim bin Hizam, were accused of profiteering. 'Umar ruled that trade in certificates for food that had not yet arrived was unethical, and Hakim was ordered to make amends by distributing his profits to people experiencing poverty.

'Umar was the latest in a long line of leaders to have pursued the idea of joining the Red Sea at Suez to the Nile, either to link the Nile Valley to the eastern seas or to serve as a bridge between the Red Sea and the Mediterranean. While the notion of a Suez Canal is usually associated with the great 19th-century engineer Ferdinand de Lesseps today, the Frenchman was actually heir to an ambition that goes back 2500 years and possibly more.

When the Greek historian Herodotus visited Egypt in the mid-fifth century BCE, he saw for himself the first of the Nile-Red Sea canals for which we have clear archaeological evidence: that of the Persian king Darius the Great (522–486 bce). "This [canal] is four days' voyage in length," wrote Herodotus, "and it was dug wide enough for two triremes to move in it rowed abreast"—a width of at least 25 meters (82'), allowing a little for clearance.

Darius himself showed no false modesty about his achievement. He dotted the route of his canal, which started near Bubastis on the easternmost branch of the Nile, with four prominent monuments inscribed in hieroglyphs: Old Persian, Elamite and Babylonian. On them, he boasted: "I am a Persian; from Persia, I seized Egypt; I gave orders to dig this canal from [the] Nile to the sea which goes from Persia. Afterwards, this canal was dug as I had ordered, and ships went from Egypt through this canal to Persia."

Apart from demonstrating Persian imperial power to his Egyptian subjects, Darius's canal was also about booty: exporting the wondrous and often heavy products of the Nile to Persia. Indeed, the famous statue of Darius himself that was discovered by archaeologists in 1972 at Susa—carved in an Egyptian style out of greywacke sandstone quarried in Egypt's Eastern Desert—must have been shipped to Persia via the canal.

There may have been even earlier attempts to cut a canal to the Red Sea. The Greek philosopher Aristotle recounts a story that a pharaoh called Sesostris—probably Senwosret iii (1845–1837 BC)—contemplated digging one but gave up for fear that the sea would flood Egypt. Herodotus himself says that a pharaoh named Neccho, probably the 26th Dynasty ruler Neccho ii, started work on a canal some 12 centuries later but halted when a soothsayer advised him to turn his attention to war in the Levant instead. According to Herodotus, 120,000 people died in the excavation attempt.

We do not know for sure that the Persian canal ever truly fell out of use, but Ptolemy ii Philadelphus, who reigned from 283 to 246 BC, claims credit for having excavated a new one. In fact, several ancient Greek authors, their anti-Persian prejudices showing, falsely claim that Ptolemy II was the first to succeed in cutting a canal to the sea and that Darius before him had failed.

If Darius's canal was about transporting imperial loot out of Egypt, then the Ptolemaic canal reversed that direction. Under the dynasty established by the successor of Alexander the Great, Egypt was no longer the vassal of a foreign power but the seat of an empire in its own right. Ptolemy faced competition abroad from the Seleucids, who had inherited the eastern territories of Alexander's empire. They had access to war elephants from India, and to match them in the imperial arms race, the Ptolemies needed elephants of their own. The solution lay in an expedition south along the African coast of the Red Sea to what today are Sudan and Eritrea. A hieroglyphic stone uncovered by Swiss archaeologist Douard Naville at Tell al-Maskhuta in Wadi Tumaylat in the late 19th century boasts of Ptolemy's excavation of the canal. It tells how the pharaoh sent one of his generals on an expedition via his newly excavated canal to establish a colony: "He made their fields and cultivated them with ploughs and cattle. He caught elephants in great numbers for the king, and he brought them as marvels for the king on his vessels on the sea. He brought them also on the Eastern Canal; no such thing had ever been done by any of the kings of the whole earth."

But it was the first-century Roman emperor Trajan whose canal-digging efforts left the most significant legacy for 'Umar to exploit in his seventh-century relief of the Holy Cities. Earlier canals had departed from the Nile along its easternmost branch. By Trajan's time, however, that branch was beginning to dwindle, so his engineers came up with the idea of extending the new canal south, upstream, beyond the head of the Delta, to the fort of Babylon in today's Old Cairo. Probably more than any other act, this decision determined the location of Egypt's capital today.

The emperor Diocletian (reigned 284–305 CE) added new fortifications to the fort and the canal mouth in the late third and early fourth centuries CE, and it was there, 350 years later, that Egypt's Byzantine rulers made their last stand against 'Amr's army. It was outside the walls of the fort that the besieging 'Amr pitched his tent, and it was around his tent that the new Islamic capital of Fustat was founded. Three centuries later, it was nearby, along the Trajanic canal's east bank, that the Fatimids would lay out their fabulous new city of Cairo in 969 CE.

Trajan's canal looked east to naval dominance of the Red Sea, to links with the newly conquered province of Arabia Petrea, to the mines and quarries of Egypt's Eastern Desert, to the critical incense-producing lands of Arabia Felix and the growing trade in luxury goods with India and East Africa. However, the canal also served more regional trade. The large number of late-Roman Egyptian amphorae that archaeologists have found at Aqaba, at modern Jordan's southern tip, suggest that Egyptian wine might have been one of the canal's exports. From the writings of Ibn 'Abd al-Hakam, it appears that Egyptian grain was also being traded in the Hijaz, implicitly via a canal, in the period before Islam.

Building the canal, in any era, was no mean feat. Herodotus's claim that Neccho's attempt cost 120,000 lives smacks of hyperbole, but it may be based on a kernel of truth. In the early 19th century, when the Egyptian ruler Muhammad Ali built a new 80-kilometre (50-mi) canal from Cairo to Alexandria using conscript labour and hand tools, reports said that 20,000 people died in the process. The much longer Red Sea canal probably required the removal of more than 24 million cubic meters of earth (31.5 million cubic yards), almost ten times the volume of the Great Pyramid of Cheops at Giza. From scratch, that would probably have taken 18,000 people working every day for a year to achieve. With silt carried by the river and sand blown in from the desert, maintaining the canal as a working waterway would have been a never-ending process. In that respect, 'Amr's re-excavation of the Roman canal would have been relatively more straightforward since it was essentially a case of clearing out the course of the defunct Roman canal. 'Amr's route diverged from the Roman one only in making a new connection to the river that avoided Fustat.

The fact that the Nile–Red Sea canal operated seasonally also made maintenance of the waterway easier. From about January to August, the water level of the Nile was too low to fill the canal, rendering it idle. During this time, workers could have laboured to keep it clear.

When the Nile began to rise in June, the entrance of the canal, like those of others throughout Egypt, would have been blocked by a temporary earth dam. Medieval historians tell us that it was only when the Nile reached 16 cubits (about 8.3 meters, or nearly 28') on the scale of the great Nilometer on Roda Island in Cairo that the signal to break the dam was given. Grand festivities surrounded that event since the 16-cubit mark meant not only that the canal would flow again but also that the annual flood was considered "complete": Egypt would be irrigated, famine averted, and authorities would be able to levy the total land tax at harvest time.

What became of Caliph 'Umar's canal? It operated for about 114 years, carrying agricultural produce to Arabia, until, in 754 and 755 CE, there was an uprising in Madinah against the new Abbasid caliphate in Baghdad. The caliph, al-Mansur, ordered the canal blocked to cut the supply of food to the Holy Cities and choke off the rebellion—an exact reversal of 'Umar's motivation for reopening it in the first place. The Canal of the Commander of the Faithful continued to flow through Cairo and as far as the central Wadi Tumaylat—about half its original length—throughout the medieval period, becoming known as the Cairo Canal.

On seeing the relics of the canal in 1776, the Franco-Hungarian officer Baron de Tott reckoned that it could be restored with only a little excavation work. Maps from the early 19th century still showed its course running all the way to Suez. Early in the 20th century, the French archaeologist Claude Bourdon found extensive remains of the ancient canal mouth and its associated harbour in the sea lagoon at Suez, and more recent work by Peter Sheehan, who directed archaeological work in Old Cairo by the American Research Center in Egypt, has pinpointed the entrance of the Roman canal under the modern buildings and streets there.

Although it had remained visible for millennia, the last 150 years have not been so kind to what is left of the ancient Suez Canal: Its traces have been almost entirely obliterated by agricultural and urban development. At Suez, where 90 years ago Bourdon had been able to map the concrete wharves and jetties of the ancient Roman and Islamic harbour, urban expansion, land reclamation, unregulated dumping, and excavation for fish farms have heavily encroached upon the archaeological remains.

The last surviving stretch of the canal with water in it, the portion running through Cairo, was filled in and paved in 1898 to combat cholera. If you go to Cairo today, you will be hard-pressed to find any explicit evidence that the canal ever existed. Yet its route through the city is marked by the broad Port Said Street, which cuts the metropolis in two. The belvederes and ornate balconies of the few remaining Ottoman mosques and houses on the street, which today give views of the city's unending traffic snarl, would once have looked out over scenes of summer pleasure boats plying the canal's waters.

For another relic of the canal, head for the unprepossessing Fumm al-Khalig Square on the modern Nile Corniche beside Roda Island. Its name, which means "Canal Mouth Square," marks the final mouth of the Islamic-era canal. It is this unremarkable corner of Cairo that bears the last witness to the waterway that once linked Egypt to Arabia and that assisted the Holy Cities in the earliest years of the Islamic state.

The *Hijri* calendar-The Turn of a Century

For Muslims, the Latin term Gregorian, or Western calendar, means "the year of the Hijra." It refers to the Prophet Muhammad's migration from Mecca to Medina, which is taken as the starting point of the Islamic calendar.

The Hijra occurred in the year 622 A.D. - as the Western world measures it - a year of great importance, for it marked the beginning of the first organized Muslim community, the predecessor of today's worldwide community.

To most laypeople today, the organization of calendars is a total mystery. And even experts are hard-pressed to give lucid explanations of why 1979, in China, is the year 4676, why "leap years" are vital, why February, in the Gregorian calendar, usually has only 28 days, and why, to quote the schoolday mnemonic rhyme, "thirty days hath September, April, June and November."

Calendars were always confusing. The confusion, in fact, was one of the elements that persuaded 'Umar, the second caliph, to establish a purely Islamic calendar.

Until the time of 'Umar, exact calendars in the Arab World were of minimal importance to the Muslims. However, as the Islamic empire grew, so did the problems of administration. 'Umar, for example, found himself faced with extensive correspondence with his generals and regional governors, as well as with the daily tasks of regulating the financial affairs of the community. And one man, Abu Musa al-Ashari, later the governor of Kufa, finally wrote to 'Umar, tactfully pointing out a problem. "You are sending us undated letters," he said.

Pondering this, 'Umar saw how undated correspondence might lead to confusion and consulted with his advisors. What he found was that the various systems of dating then used in the empire were bewildering in their variety.

The Christian and Jewish communities, for example, used calendars calculated from the date of the creation of the world, a date about which there was, understandably, a good deal of doubt. The Coptic community in Egypt used a calendar based on the date of the accession to the throne of Emperor Diocletian; other communities used the "Era of Alexander", and there were two calendars in use in Iran: one based on the date of the accession to the throne of Yazdegird III, the other based on the date of his death. Because of this confusion - and the fact that the various calendars in use were intimately linked to different religions or rival states - 'Umar decided to establish an Islamic dating system.

The Islamic New Year, or the Hijri New Year, marks the start of the Muslim lunar calendar. This year, it is set to fall during the second week of August 2021.

The calendar has been observed for more than 1,440 years and is used to date important Muslim events, including the beginning of Ramadan (month of fasting), Eid al-Fitr and the start of the Hajj pilgrimage. Running for 354 or 355 days it is approximately 11 days shorter than the solar Gregorian calendar. The year is 12 months, beginning with Muharram and ending with Dhul al-Hijjah. Each month starts with the sighting of the new moon.

The date when the new Hijri year begins is determined by various techniques – including the use of scientific and astronomical calculations or conducting an official moon-sighting exercise. The method adopted differs from country to country.

The Islamic new year starts with the migration, also known as the Hijrah, of Prophet Muhammad and his companions from Mecca to Medina in 622 AD, after they were repeatedly persecuted and threatened.

The Hijrah, considered one of the most important events in Islamic history, was chosen as the starting point for the calendar in 639 AD by Umar ibn al-Khattab, the second caliph.

The first ten days of Muharram hold considerable significance for Muslims – especially Shia Muslims – who mourn the death of Husayn Ibn Ali al-Hussein, the grandson of Prophet Muhammad, who died at the Battle of Karbala in 680 AD.

Ashura, the annual commemoration of the death of al-Hussein on the 10th day of Muharram, is marked by Shia Muslims in several ways, including with public expressions of mourning and by visiting the shrine of al-Hussein in Karbala, Iraq.

Shia pilgrims gather between the Imam Hussein and Imam Abbas's shrines during Ashura in Karbala, Iraq, October 1, 2017 [File: Abdullah Dhiaa Al-Deen/Reuters]

Because the Qur'an (Sura 10:5) establishes the use of lunar months for Muslims - that is, a calendar based on the phases of the moon - the Islamic year does not correspond with the Gregorian calendar, which is based on a solar year, as an astronomical lunar month contains 29 days, 12 hours, 44 minutes and 3 seconds, a year composed of 12 such lunar months comprises 354 days, 8 hours, 48 minutes and 36 seconds - which is approximately 11 days shorter than the solar year.

The months of the Muslim year, by convention, have 29 and 30 days alternately. This means that the Hijra - or, more exactly, the Hizri-year contains exactly 354 days. The 8 hours, 48 minutes and 36 seconds difference (11/30 of a day) between this figure and the astronomical lunar year adds up to 11 days in every cycle of 30 years. These 11 days are inserted into the calendar by establishing leap years. Every period of 30 years, therefore, has 11 leap years of 355 days instead of 354. These are normally the 2nd, 5th, 7th, 10th, 13th, 16th, 18th, 21st, 24th, 26th, and 29th years of the 30-year cycle. The "leap day", which is added to these years, is always assigned to the end of the month of Dhu al-Hijja, the month of the Hajj - the Muslim pilgrimage to Mecca - and the last month of the year. In just the same way, the Gregorian calendar adds an extra day to February every four years.

Since the Hijri year is 11 days shorter than the Gregorian year, the beginning of each Hijri year falls 11 days earlier in the Gregorian calendar each year. Thus, the Hijri year moves backwards in relation to the Western calendar. This retrograde motion has a necessary consequence: Muslim festivals fall at different times each year, according to the Western calendar, although always, of course, in the same month of the Hijri year. Every 33 years, the months of the Muslim calendar make a complete backwards circuit of the seasons. This explains why the Hajj, for example, sometimes falls in midwinter and sometimes in summer. The months of the Hijri year, unlike the Gregorian year, bear no relation to the seasons.

The conversion of Gregorian to Hijri dates and vice-versa is no easy matter, particularly if one is trying to find the exact day. The matter is further complicated by the fact that the Gregorian calendar used now did not come into use until 1582 in Europe and not until the early 18th century in England. Dates before then, therefore, must be calculated according to still another system: the Julian calendar. Given this final complication, the easiest way to find the correspondence between a Gregorian and a Hijri date is to refer to a table.

Converting years is much easier. A simple rule of thumb is that each Gregorian century equals approximately 103 Hijri years and that, conversely, every 100 years of the Hijri calendar equals 97 years of the Gregorian. A useful benchmark is that the year 1300 A.D. corresponded with 700 A. H.

A more exact calculation can be made by using the following formulae, where G = Gregorian year and H = Hijri year:

$G = H + 622 - (H/33)$

- $H = G - 622 + \{(G-622)/32 \}$

Justice all

A son of `Amr ben Al `Aas, the Governor of Egypt, once struck a lower-class man. The man swore that he would complain to Umar. `Amr ben Al Aas's son told the man to do so, boasting that the Caliph would never punish him since he was the son of the noble ruler of Egypt. Later, during the pilgrimage season, when the Caliph Umar, his entourage, `Amr ben `Al `Aas, and his son were assembled, the man whom `Amr's son had struck went to the Caliph and pointed to the son of `Amr ben Al `Aas and said: "This man struck me unjustly and when I threatened to complain to you, he told me that he was the son of a nobleman and that you would never punish him."

The Umar looked at `Amr ben Al `Aas and uttered his famous words, "What right have you to enslaved individual people whose mothers gave birth to them as free people?" He then gave the man who had lodged his complaint a whip and told him to strike the son of the nobleman - the son of `Amr ben Al `Aas - as he had struck him.

The humility of a mighty ruler

During his caliphate, Umar Ibn Al-Khattab marched upon Damascus with his army. Abu Ubaydah was with him, and when they came upon a little lake, Umar descended from his camel, took off his shoes, tied them together, and hung them on his shoulder. He then took the halter off his camel, and they entered the water together. Seeing this in front of the army, Abu Ubaydah said: "O Commander of the Believers! How can you be so humble in front of all your men?" Umar answered, "Woe to you, Abu Ubaydah! If only someone else other than you thought this way! Thoughts like this will cause the downfall of the Muslims. Don't you see we were indeed a very lowly people? God raised us to a position of honour and greatness through Islam. If we forget who we are and wish other than the Islam which elevated us, the one who raised us surely will debase us.

Exemplary honesty and integrity

Honesty and integrity were the highest virtues in Umar's character. Once, during his illness, his physician prescribed honey for him. Tonnes of honey were kept in the *Baitul Mal*, but he did not take a drop of it unless the people's committee permitted him. His wife, Umme Kulthum, once presented a few bottles of perfumes to the Empress of Rome. The Empress returned the bottles filled with precious stones. When Umar learned of it, he deposited the jewels in the *Baitul Mal*. The Caliph had great respect for social justice. This virtuousness profoundly struck the Patriarch of Jerusalem for social equality, as shown by the esteemed Caliph when he observed the enslaved person riding the camel and the Caliph leading him by the rope.

Once, Ali was sitting in Umar's company. A Jew entered and complained about the former. Addressing Ali as "Aba Hassan," the Caliph asked Ali to defend himself. Ali submitted his explanation, and as the Jew failed to establish his case, the Caliph dismissed the case on merit. As soon as the complainant left the room, the Caliph asked Ali why he had frowned when he asked him to tender an explanation. Ali replied that he was not at all displeased; on the contrary, he frowned because the Caliph had addressed him with a term of endearment, "Aba Hasan." Being one of the parties to the suit, with the Caliph as the judge, the mode of address was not consonant with the spirit of justice.

Amru bin Qais Abu Musa Ashari was a one-time administrator of the state treasury during Umar's Caliphate. Once, during the cleaning of the treasury building, Abu Musa found a dirham on the floor. He gave it to Umar's son, who was standing nearby. On inquiry, Umar was told that Abu Musa gave the child this dirham. Umar called for Abu Musa and said, "Could you not find a better enemy than Umar's son? Do you want people to question me about this lousy dirham on the Day of Judgment"? The dirham was duly deposited in the treasury.

When the spoils of Median and Jalula (Iraq) arrived in Medinah, the Caliph was found weeping. Asked why he was crying, he replied that in these spoils, he saw the ruin of his people. He was right in his judgment because the events that unfolded after the arrival of fabulous wealth stained the character of Muslims, who slowly became corrupted and began to get trapped in various vices.

On one occasion, Umar asked Salman Farsi, one of the illustrious Companions of the Prophet, whether he was a Caliph or a King. Salman replied," If you extort money from the people, if you misappropriate money from *Bait al-Mal*, then you are a king, else a Caliph." By God, said Umar, I know not whether I am a Caliph or a King. And if I am a King, it is a fearful thing."

Perhaps of all Muhammad's successors, the second Caliph, Umar, is the chief exemplar of integrity in Islam. Although he lacked Muhammad's humour and charm, Umar matched him in scrupulous honesty and uprightness in financial matters, in his passion for impartial justice and adherence to the straightforward, open and approachable Bedouin leadership style.

Umar's simplicity, honesty, and humility echoes in the sanctions of the Qur'an:

And do not walk upon the earth exultantly. Indeed, you will never tear the earth [apart], and you will never reach the mountains in height. (Q 17:37)

And do not turn your cheek [in contempt] toward people and do not walk through the earth exultantly. Indeed, Allah does not like everyone who is self-deluded and boastful. (Q31:18)

No compromise on justice

During the reign of Umar Ibn Al-Khattab, Jabalah ibn Al-Ayham, the king of the Ghassani Arabs in Syria, he once visited the Ka'bah in Makkah. This occurred after he joined the Muslims and split ranks with the Romans, with whom he had joined ranks during the early years of Islam. When Islam became victorious, he embraced Islam. While he was circling the Ka'bah while performing Haj, a man stepped on his garment, and it fell to the ground. Jabalah smacked the man's face and broke his nose. The man complained to Caliph Umar, who summoned Jabalah. Umar informed him that the man had the right to avenge his broken nose by striking him on the nose. Or, the man may forfeit his freedom if he elects to do so.

He also said to Jabalah, "Here is your foe! Try to strike a deal with him; otherwise, he has the right to avenge what you did to him!" Jabalah said, "How can this be? I am a king, and he is nobody!" Umar then explained to him that Islam has made them equals. Then, he asked for a grace period to think about this matter. Before the morning, Jabalah escaped to his people, converted from Islam, and rejoined the Romans. Later, he regretted his decision, sobbing at times, although the Romans were very generous with him.

Rehabilitation of enslaved individual people

When Islam appeared on the world stage, the world economy was based on enslaved individualry. Islam was the first religion to raise its voice against enslaved individualry. Among the early converts to Islam, many were enslaved individuals. Indeed, one of the reasons for the hostility of the Quraysh against Islam was that they saw in Islam a threat to enslaved individuals on which the economy of Mecca was based.

When Umar became the Caliph of Islam, he took particular measures to eliminate the evils of enslaved individuals as far as possible. He took a bold step when he declared that no Arab could be enslaved individuals. Arabia was thus the first country in the world, under the impact of Islam, to abolish enslaved individualry. During the apostasy wars, many Arabs were taken captive and enslaved individuals. Umar emancipated all such enslaved individuals people.

Umar also decreed that enslaved individual women who had borne a child to their master stood emancipated.

The Holy Qur'an laid down:

"If you see good in them (enslaved individuals), agree with them."

Umar implemented this injunction and laid down that an enslaved person could agree with the master that he would pay so much within the specified period to secure his freedom. Anas, an enslaved individual, was named Sirin. The enslaved person wanted to agree with his master, but Anas refused. When the matter was reported to Umar, he made Anas decide with his enslaved individual.

In the matter of stipends allowed by the state, Umar made no distinction between the enslaved individual and the enslaved person.

The enslaved individual people were given grants on the same scale as their masters.

Umar issued orders that enslaved individual people could not be separated from their kindred. Under these orders, the child was not to be separated from their mother. If there were two brothers, both needed to be purchased by one master.

Umar was so considerate that he instructed that when some very highly placed person was taken captive, he should be ransomed and not kept as an enslaved person. When the daughter of the emperor Heraclius in Syria was taken captive, she was returned to her father. When Armanusa, the daughter of Maqauqas, was taken captive in the battle of Babylon, she was returned to her father.

To raise the status of enslaved individual people, Umar enjoined that the master should generally take meals with their enslaved individuals. Occasionally, Umar invited enslaved individual people to dine with him. Umar said:

"The curse of God be upon those who feel ashamed to sit to meals with enslaved individuals."

Umar laid down that if an enslaved individual Muslim gave protection to a non-Muslim, such protection was to be honoured like the protection provided by any other Muslim.

Umar took pains to provide facilities for enslaved individual people to rise to the position of importance in the state. During the caliphate of Umar, Ikramah, who came to be regarded as an Imam of *hadith*, was an enslaved individual. Nafi, who was the teacher of Imam Malik, was an enslaved individual. Many other enslaved individual people rose to eminence during the caliphate of Umar.

Allowances and stipends for Muslims

After the battles of Yarmuk and Qadisiyya, the Muslims won heavy spoils. The coffers at Medinah became full to the brim, and the problem before Umar was what should be done with this money. Someone suggested that money should be kept in the treasury for public expenditure only. This view was not acceptable to the general body of Muslims. A consensus was reached that whatever was received during a year should be distributed.

The next question for consideration was what system should be adopted for distribution. One suggestion was that it should be distributed on an ad hoc basis, and whatever was received should be equally distributed. Against this view, it was felt that as the spoils were considerable, that would make the people very rich. It was that instead of ad hoc division, the allowance amount to the stipend should be determined beforehand, and this allowance should be paid to the person concerned regardless of the spoils. This was agreed.

About the fixation of the allowance, there were two opinions. Some held that the allowance amount for all Muslims should be the same. Umar disagreed with this view. He held that the allowance should be graded according to one's merit concerning Islam.

Then, the question arose as to what basis should be used for placing some above others. Everyone suggested that a start should be made with the Caliph, and he should get the highest allowance. Umar rejected the proposal and decided to start with the clan of the Prophet.

Umar set up a committee to compile a list of persons near the Holy Prophet. The Committee produced the list clan-wise. Bani Hashim appeared as the first clan. Then, the clan of Abu Bakr was placed third, followed by the clan of Umar. Umar accepted the first two placements but delegated his family to lower the scale concerning nearness in relationship to the Holy Prophet.

The members of the clan of Umar objected to Umar's order, but he rebuked them, saying, "You desire that you should stand on my neck and deprive me of my good deeds. I cannot permit that." "I have decided the scale according to merit by entry into Islam and not by position."

In the final scale of allowance that Umar approved, the main provisions were:

The widows of the Prophet received 12,000 dirhams each;

Abbas, the uncle of the Prophet, received an annual allowance of 7,000 dirhams;

The grandsons of the Prophet Hasan and Hussain got 5,000 dirhams each;

The veterans of Badr got an allocation of 6,000 dirhams each;

Those who had become Muslims by the time of the Hudaibiya pact got 4,000 dirhams each;

Those who became Muslims at the time of the conquest of Mecca got 3,000 dirhams each;

The veterans of the apostasy wars got 3,000 dirhams each.

The veterans of Yermuk and Qadisiyya got 2,000 dirhams each.

In announcing this scale, Umar said:

In this award, Umar's son Abdullah got an allowance of 3,000 dirhams. On the other hand, Usama got 4,000. Abdullah objected to this distinction, and Umar said: "I have given Usama more than you because he was dearer to the Holy Prophet than you, and his father was dearer to the Holy Prophet than your father."

Equality before law

Umar personally visited several courts to gain practical experience. Once, he had to attend the court of Qadi Aaid bin Thabit as a defendant. The Qadi showed some preferential respect to him, which the Caliph resented and warned him, "Unless you consider an ordinary man and Umar as equals, you are not fit for the post of Qadi."

Jablah bin Al Aiham Gassani was the ruler of a small state in Syria. He was converted to Islam, and one day, while he was engaged in hajj, a part of his gown was unintentionally trampled upon by a poor Arab. Jablah slapped him. He, too, paid him in the same coin. The infuriated Jablah hastened to the Caliph and urged him to deal severely with the Arab. Thereupon, the Caliph said that he had already had justice. Jablah retorted, saying, "Had he done such an insult to me in my land, he would have been hanged." The Caliph replied calmly: 'Ubai was a common citizen. He charged Umar, the Caliph, in the Qadi Zaid bin Thabit court. The Caliph presented himself before the court in a simple dress. The Qadi offered his respect to the Caliph. He was reprimanded, 'This is your first act of injustice." And he seated himself by the side of 'Ubai.

'Ubai had no proof for his claim. Caliph Umar disowned the claims. 'Ubai wanted the Caliph to take an oath as was the practice. The Qadi suggested that 'Ubai should exempt the Caliph from this formality. Umar himself disapproved of this. He said, "Unless 'Ubai and Umar are not equal in your court, you do not deserve to hold the high office of the Qadi." "All veneration comes to us through following the religion of Allah. Islam is the only mark of exaltation."

13. FOUNDATION OF THE CALIPHATE

Umar's political capacity first manifested as the architect of the caliphate after Prophet Muhammad died on 8 June 632. While the funeral rituals were organised, a group of Prophet'sMuhammad's followers who were natives of Medina, the *Ansar* (helpers), organised a meeting on the outskirts of the city, effectively locking out those companions known as *Muhajirs* (The Emigrants), including Umar. [1] Umar found out about this meeting at Saqifah Bani Saadah and, taking with him two other Muhajirs, Abu Bakr and Abu Ubaidah ibn al-Jarrah, proceeded to the meeting, presumably to head off the Ansars' plans for political separation. Arriving at the conference, Umar was faced with a unified community of tribes from the Ansar who refused to accept the leadership of the Muhajirs However, Umar was undeterred in his belief the caliphate should be under the control of the Muhajirs, Though the Khazraj were in disagreement, Umar, after strained negotiations lasting one or two days, brilliantly divided the Ansar into their old warring factions of Aws and Khazraj tribes. Umar resolved the divisions by placing his hand on that of Abu Bakr as a unity candidate for those gathered in the Saqifah. Others at the Saqifah followed suit, with the exception of the Khazraj tribe and their leader, Said ibn 'Ubada, who was isolated. The Khazraj tribe is said to have posed no significant threat as there were sufficient men of war from the Medinan tribes, such as the Banu Aws, to organize them into a military bodyguard for Abu Bakr immediately.[37]

Umar judged the outcome of the Saqifa assembly to be a falta [translated by Madelung as 'a precipitate and ill-considered deal' because of the absence of most of the prominent Muhajirun, including the Prophet's own family and clan, whose participation he considered vital for any legitimate consultation (shura, mascara). It was, he warned the community, to be no precedent for the future. Yet he also defended the outcome, claiming that the Muslims were longing for Abu Bakr as for no one else. He apologized, moreover, that the Muhajirun present were forced to press for an immediate oath of allegiance since the Ansar could not have been trusted to wait for a legitimate consultation and might have proceeded to elect one of their own after the departure of the Mekkans.

According to various Twelver Shia sources and Madelung, Umar and Abu Bakr had, in effect, mounted a political coup against the Saqifah. [1] According to one version of narrations in primary sources, Umar and Abu Bakr are said to have used force to try to secure the allegiance of Ali and his party. It has been reported in mainly Persian historical sources written 300 years later, such as in the History of al-Tabari, that after Ali refused to pay homage, Abu Bakr sent Umar with an armed contingent to Fatimah's house where Ali and his supporters are said to have gathered. Umar warned those in the House that unless Ali succumbed to Abu Bakr, he would set the House on fire [and under these circumstances, Ali was forced to capitulate. This version is generally rejected by Sunni scholars who, in view of other reports in their literature, believe that Ali gave an oath of alliance to Abu Bakr without any grievance. But then other Sunni and Shia sources say that Ali did not swear allegiance to Abu Bakr after his election but six months later, after the death of his wife Fatimah, putting into question al-Tabari's account. Either way, the Sunni and the Shia account both accept that Ali felt that Abu Bakr should have informed him before going into the meeting with the Ansar and that Ali swore allegiance to Abu Bakr.

Appointment as a caliph

Abu Bakr appointed Umar as his successor before dying in 634 CE. Due to his strict and autocratic nature, Umar was not a very popular figure among the notables of Medina and members of Majlis al-Shura; accordingly, high-ranking companions of Abu Bakr attempted to discourage him from naming Umar. Nevertheless, Abu Bakr decided to make Umar his successor. Umar was well known for his extraordinary willpower, intelligence, political astuteness, impartiality, justice, and care for people experiencing poverty. Abu Bakr said to the high-ranking advisers:

His (Umar's) strictness was there because of my softness. When the weight of the Caliphate is over his shoulders, he will no longer be strict. If I will be asked by God to whom I have appointed my successor, I will tell him that I have appointed the best man among your men.

Abu Bakr was aware of Umar's power and ability to succeed him. His was perhaps one of the smoothest transitions of power from one authority to another in the Muslim lands. Before his death, Abu Bakr called Uthman to write his will, and he declared Umar his successor. In his will, he instructed Umar to continue the conquests on the Iraqi and Syrian fronts.[citation needed]

Caliphate

Umar was a pioneer in some affairs:

Umar was the first to introduce the public ministry system, where the records of officials and soldiers were kept. He also kept a record system for messages he sent to Governors and heads of state.

He was the first to appoint police forces to keep civil order.

He was the first to discipline the people when they became disordered.

Another critical aspect of Umar's rule was that he forbade any of his governors and agents from engaging in any business dealings whilst in a position of power. An agent of Umar by the name of Al Harith ibn K'ab ibn Wahb was once found to have extra money beyond his salary, and Umar enquired about his wealth. Al Harith replied that he had some money, and he engaged in trade with it. Umar said: *By Allah, we did not send you to engage in trade!* And he took from him the profits he had made.[

Canals

Since Medina, with a rapidly growing population, was at risk of recurring famines when crops were lacking, Umar sought to facilitate the import of grain. He ordered the building of a canal connecting the Nile to the Red Sea and an improvement of port infrastructure on the Arabian coast. When Basra was established during Umar's rule, he started building a nine-mile canal from the Tigris to the new city for irrigation and drinking water. Al-Tabari reports that Utba ibn Ghazwan built the first canal from the Tigris River to the site of Basra when the city was in the planning stage.[citation needed] After the town was built, Umar appointed Abu Musa Ashaari (17-29/638 – 650) as its first governor.[citation needed] He began building two crucial canals, the al-Ubulla and the Ma'qil, linking Basra with the Tigris River. These two canals were the basis for the agricultural development of the whole Basra region and were used for drinking water. Umar also adopted a policy of assigning barren lands to those who undertook their cultivation. This policy continued during the Umayyad period and resulted in the cultivation of large areas of barren lands through the construction of irrigation canals by the state and by individuals.[66]

Reforms

Under Umar's leadership, the empire expanded; accordingly, he began to build a political structure that would hold together the vast territory. He undertook many administrative reforms and closely oversaw public policy, establishing an advanced administration for the newly conquered lands, including several new ministries and bureaucracies, and ordered a census of all the Muslim territories. During his rule, the garrison cities (*Ramsar*) of Basra and Kufa were founded or expanded. In 638, he extended and renovated the Masjid al-Haram (Grand Mosque) in Mecca and al-Masjid al-Nabawi (Mosque of the Prophet) in Medina.[citation needed]

Umar also ordered the expulsion to Syria and Iraq of the Christian and Jewish communities of Najran and Khaybar. He also permitted Jewish families to resettle in Jerusalem, which had previously been barred from all Jews. He issued orders that these Christians and Jews should be treated well and allotted them the equivalent amount of land in their new settlements. Umar also forbade non-Muslims from residing in the Hejaz for longer than three days, which was needed. He was the first to establish the army as a state department.

Umar was founder of Fiqh, or Islamic jurisprudence. Sunni Muslims regard him as one of the greatest Faqih, and, as such, he started the process of codifying Islamic Law.[citation needed]

In 641, he established Bayt al-mal, a financial institution and started annual allowances for the Muslims. As a leader, Umar was known for his simple, austere lifestyle. Rather than adopt the pomp and display affected by the rulers of the time, he continued to live much as he had when Muslims were poor and persecuted.[citation needed] In 638, his fourth year as caliph and the seventeenth year since the Hijra, he decreed that the Islamic calendar should be counted from the year of the Hijra of Muhammad from Mecca to Medina.

Visit to Jerusalem in 637 CE

Umar's visit to Jerusalem is documented in several sources. A recently discovered Judeo-Arabic text has disclosed the following anecdote:

"Umar ordered Gentiles and a group of Jews to sweep the area of the Temple Mount. Umar oversaw the work. The Jews who had come sent letters to the rest of the Jews in Palestine and informed them that Umar had permitted the resettlement of Jerusalem by Jews. Umar, after some consultation, permitted seventy Jewish households to return. They returned to live in the southern part of the city, i.e., the Market of the Jews. (They aimed to be near the water of *Silwan* and the Temple Mount and its gates). Then, Commander Umar granted them this request. The seventy families moved to Jerusalem from Tiberias and the area around it with their wives and children."

It is also reported in the name of the Alexandrian Bishop Eutychius (932–940 CE) that the rock known as the Temple Mount had been a place of ruins as far back as the time of Empress Helena, mother of Constantine the Great, who built churches in Jerusalem. "The Byzantines," he said, "had deliberately left the ancient site of the Temple as it was and had even thrown rubbish on it so that a great heap of rubble formed." It was during Umar's Umar marched into Jerusalem with an army that he asked Kaab, who was Jewish before he converted to Islam, "Where do you advise me to build a place of worship?" Kaab indicated the Temple Rock, now a gigantic heap of ruins from the temple of Jupiter. [71] The Jews, Kaab explained, had briefly won back their old capital a quarter of a century before (when Persians overran Syria and Palestine). Still, they had not had time to clear the site of the Temple, for the *Rums* (Byzantines) had recaptured the city. It was then that Umar ordered the rubbish on the *Ṣakhra* (rock) to be removed by the Nabataeans, and after three showers of heavy rain had cleansed the Rock, he instituted prayers there. To this day, the place is known as *ḳubbat es ṣakhra*, the Dome of the Rock.

Military expansion

The military conquests were partially terminated between 638 and 639 during the years of great famine in Arabia and plague in the Levant. During his reign, the Levant, Egypt, Cyrenaica, Tripolitania, Fezzan, Eastern Anatolia, and almost the whole of the Sassanid Persian Empire, including Bactria, Persia, Azerbaijan, Armenia, Caucasus and Makran were annexed to the Rashidun Caliphate. According to one estimate, more than 4,050 cities were captured during these military conquests. [73] Before he died in 644, Umar had ceased all military expeditions apparently to consolidate his rule in recently conquered Roman Egypt and the newly conquered Sassanid Empire (642–644). At his death in

November 644, his rule extended from present-day Libya in the west to the Indus River in the east and the Oxus River in the north.

Great famine

In 638 CE, Arabia fell into severe drought followed by a famine. Soon after, the food reserves at Medina began to run out. Umar ordered caravans of supplies from Syria and Iraq and personally supervised their distribution. His actions saved countless lives throughout Arabia. [74] The first governor to respond was Abu Ubaidah ibn al-Jarrah, the governor of Syria and supreme commander of the Rashidun army.

Later, Abu Ubaidah paid a personal visit to Medina and acted as an officer of disaster management, which was headed personally by Umar. For internally displaced people, Umar hosted a dinner every night at Medina, which, according to one estimate, had an attendance of more than a hundred thousand people.

Great plague

While famine was ending in Arabia, many districts in Syria and Palestine were devastated by the plague. While Umar was on his way to visit Syria, at Elat, he was received by Abu Ubaidah ibn al-Jarrah, governor of Syria, who informed him about the plague and its intensity and suggested that Umar go back to Medina. Umar tried to persuade Abu Ubaidah to come with him to Medina, but he declined to leave his troops in that critical situation. Abu Ubaidah died in 639 of the plague, which also cost the lives of 25,000 Muslims in Syria. After the plague had weakened, in late 639, Umar visited Syria for political and administrative re-organization, as most of the veteran commanders and governors had died of the plague.

Welfare state

To be close to people with low incomes, Umar lived in a simple mud hut without doors and walked the streets every evening. After consulting with people with low incomes, Umar established the first welfare state, Bayt al-mal. The Bayt al-mal aided the Muslim and non-Muslim poor, needy, elderly, orphans, widows, and the disabled. The Bayt al-mal ran for hundreds of years, from the Rashidun Caliphate in the 7th century through the Umayyad period (661–750) and well into the Abbasid era. Umar also introduced child benefits and pensions for children and older people.

Free trade

Local populations of Jews and Christians, persecuted as religious minorities and taxed heavily to finance the Byzantine–Sassanid Wars, often aided Muslims in taking over their lands from the Byzantines and Persians, resulting in exceptionally speedy conquests. As new areas were attached to the Caliphate, they also benefited from free trade while trading with other regions of the Caliphate (to encourage commerce, in Islam, trade is not taxed, but wealth is subject to the zakat).[Since the Constitution of Medina, drafted by Muhammad, the Jews and the Christians continued to use their laws in the Caliphate and had their judges.[

Death & Legacy

In 634 CE, whilst offering prayer in congregation, Umar was stabbed repeatedly in the back by an enslaved individual Persian named Lu'lu. Some say that the enslaved person had some personal grudge against the Caliph. At the same time, other prominent historians (such as Saunders) claim that it was an act of retribution for the Persian defeat in the Battle of Nihavand – the man was stricken with shame at the loss of his **civilization** and decided to avenge his brethren who had fallen in the field.

Umar was a practical person and realized that his wounds were fatal when he was taken to his home. Upon his inquiry about his assailant, he expressed relief in knowing that a fellow Muslim had not killed him. He then appointed a six-member committee comprised of men who were able to elect a new caliph. Umar declared his honesty in the matter and stated that he had not selected his son or any one of his relatives; after Umar's death, Uthman was chosen as Umar's successor. The old Caliph died, leaving behind a lasting legacy that will be carried on for centuries after his death. In his book *A History of Medieval Islam*, historian John Joseph Saunders entitled him as the "real founder of the Arab empire". He was buried near the Prophet's gravesite (part of the al-Masjid an-Nabwi in Medina).

Successful reign

In his successful reign of ten years, not only did Umar rule effectively, but he also managed to take all of the Sassanian dominions and a significant chunk of the former land of the Caesars. These military gains, which were a prelude of things to come, would continue to bring heaps of revenue to the empire – which would, in time, be used to finance grand projects, such as the Al-Aqsa mosque, whose foundations were laid down by Umar in Jerusalem (subsequent rulers would further aggrandize it).

Umar's administrative system would form the basic framework on which Islamic Caliphates would continue to be managed by his successors after his death. The Islamic calendar – one of the most important heritage of Muslims, was formulated by him; based on the Arabian lunar calendar, it holds the year of the *hegira* as year zero, i.e. 0 AH / Zero "After Hegira" (Prophet Muhammad's migration from Mecca to Medina in 622 CE).

Controversy among schools of thought

Umar's personality and his legitimacy have been subject to controversy. While the Sunnis (who hold the claim of all four Rashidun Caliphs as equally legitimate) view him as a man of uncompromising standards of morality and justice, Shias, on the other hand, regard him as a cruel person. Moreover, while mainstream Sunnis see his claim of Caliphate as being legitimate, the vast majority of the Shias consider him a usurper (alongside Abu Bakr and Uthman). Though such debates continue to rage on among the Muslims even centuries after his death, and there seems to be no end to them in sight, no rational person can undermine his achievements.

Rule of law

Despite much rhetoric on the part of governments of various hues, good governance, rule of law and real democracy is a dream that, unfortunately, does not seem to come true in the Islamic world. Fsincere government, however, has a lot to learn from the way Hazrat Umar, the rightly-guided second caliph, ruled more than a hundred years ago. The total area of his caliphate was around 23 lakh square miles, continuously expanding its frontiers. To rule over such a big caliphate stretched from Libya to Makran and from Yemen to Armenia, Hazrat Umar had to establish an entirely new administrative system. For the Arab .sthis the first central government was established. Hazrat Umar believed in shura and what we call the devolution of power today. He would not have decided without consulting the assembly of the great Companions. Ordinary people were also consulted on matters of particular significance. He used to say: "There is no concept of a caliphate without consultation". The roots of modern democracy can be clearly seen in the administration of Hazrat Umar at a time when despotic kings and emperors ruled the whole world. Hazrat Umar divided the entire country into provinces and smaller units.

Stringent discipline

He followed a stringent standard for the appointment of governors and took particular care in appointing men of approved integrity to high offices under the state. He kept a watch over them like a hawk, and as soon as any lapse on their part came to his notice, immediate action was taken. Before assuming his responsibility, a governor was required to declare his assets and a complete inventory of his possessions was prepared and kept in record. If an unusual increase was reported in the holdings of a governor, he was immediately called to account, and the state confiscated the unlawful property. At the time of appointment, a governor was required to pledge: (1) that he would not ride a Turkish horse; (2) that he would not wear fine clothes; (3) that he would not eat sifted flour; (4) that he would not keep a porter at his door; and (5) that he would always keep his door open to the public. This is how it was ensured that governors and principal officers would behave like ordinary people and not like extraordinary or heavenly creatures.

Hierarchy of governors

The governors were required to come to Makkah on the occasion of the Haj. In public assembly, Hazrat Umar would invite all those who had any grievance against any office to present the complaint. In the event of complaints, inquiries were made immediately, and grievances were redressed on the spot. The rightly-guided caliph also established a particular office for the investigation of complaints against the governors. The department was under the charge of Muhammad bin Maslamah Ansari, a man of undisputed integrity. In essential cases, the caliph deputed Muhammad bin Maslamah to proceed to the spot, investigate the charge, and take action. An inquiry commission was constituted to investigate the charge. On occasions, the officers against whom complaints were received were summoned to Medinah and put on trial by the caliph himself. Umar was a man of inflexible integrity. He believed in simplicity and had contempt for pomp and luxury. A strong sense of justice, accountability before law, and equality for all were some of his cherished ideals. He took particular pains to provide practical, speedy and impartial justice to the people.

He was the first ruler in history to separate the judiciary from the executive. Qazis/judges were appointed in sufficient numbers at all administrative levels for the administration of justice. They were chosen for their integrity and learning in Islamic law. High salaries were fixed for them, and they were not allowed to engage in trade. In one of his ordinances issued to judicial officers, Hazrat Umar laid down the following principles: "Verily justice is an important obligation to God and man. You have been charged with this responsibility. Discharge the responsibility so that you may win the approbation of God and the goodwill of the people. Treat the people equally in your presence, in your company, and your decisions so that the weak despair not of justice and the high-placed have no hope of your favour..."

An Islamic social system

Umar took particular steps to build a social order according to the teachings of Islam. He brought about far-reaching reforms in the social, economic and political spheres of collective life. It is but he who could say: "If a dog dies at the bank of Euphrates, Umar will be responsible for that".

As a consequence of large-scale conquests in Iraq, Persia and elsewhere, a question arose as to the administration of land in the conquered territories. The army, following the old maxim "spoils belong to the victors", insisted that all agricultural lands should be distributed among the conquering army, and the inhabitants should be made serfs and enslaved individual people. However, Hazrat Umar, after prolonged counselling and contemplation, rejected the army's demand and decreed that the conquered land would be the property of the state and not of the conquering forces. The former occupants of the lands would not be dispossessed. This was a revolutionary decision. His general decree was that land belonged to the person who could cultivate it and that a person was entitled to possess only that much land that he could grow. The caliph upheld the principle that there was no coercion in religion, and the non-Muslim population was guaranteed life, liberty, and property. The non-Muslims were treated as full citizens of the state.

There was to be no discrimination between Muslims and non-Muslims in the eyes of the law. Even on his death-bed, the caliph thought of the state's responsibility to the non-Muslim citizens. In his legacy to his successor, he said: "My legacy to my successor is that covenants with ahl-ud-dhimma, i.e. the People of the Covenant or Obligation, should be observed faithfully. They should be defended against all invasions. No injustice should be done to them. They should be treated as full-fledged citizens and should enjoy equality before the law. Their taxes should be fair, and no burden should be imposed on them which they cannot bear."

The high standards of integrity that Hazrat Umar set for himself and his family members should be emulated by the rulers of today, particularly those of the Muslim world. The allowance that he drew was just enough for a person of average means. When the people around him insisted that his allowance should be raised, he refused to accept any increase. He ate the most ordinary food and wore the coarsest clothes. Once, he was late for the Friday prayer, and the explanation that he offered was that his clothes had been washed, and that took some time to dry, which delayed his departure for the mosque. When the envoy of the Byzantine emperor came to Medinah, he expected that the caliph would be living in a heavily guarded palace. The envoy found no palace and no guard. He saw the caliph sitting in the mosque in the company of ordinary people. When he went to Palestine to receive the surrender of the city of Jerusalem, the world witnessed the strange spectacle of his enslaved individual riding the camel, and he walked on foot, holding the reins of the camel.

Once, Hazrat Umar's wife, Umm Kulsum, purchased perfume for one dirham and sent it as a gift to the Byzantine empress. The Byzantine empress returned the empty phials of perfume filled with gems. When Hazrat Umar came to know of this, he sold the gems. Out of the sale proceeds, he handed over one dirham to his wife, and the rest was deposited into the state treasury. Hazrat Umar's son Abdullah was a very talented man, but he refused to give him any office. Hazrat Umar was a great social and political reformer and a man of extraordinary vision. He was the first Muslim ruler to establish public treasury courts of justice, appoint judges, set up an army department and assign regular salaries to the men in the armed forces.

Revenue system

He created a land revenue department and was the first ruler under whom survey and assessment work of land was undertaken. He was the first Muslim ruler to take a census, strike coins, organize a police department, and set up jails. He established guest houses in all cities and rested houses on the roadside from Medinah to Makkah for the comfort of travellers. Hazrat Umar took extraordinary measures to minimize enslaved individualry. He ordered that any female captive who gave birth to a child could not be sold as an enslaved person. He established schools throughout the country and gave generous salaries to school teachers. He fixed stipends for people with low incomes and people in need and provided for the care and upbringing of orphans. His caliphate was, in fact, a great welfare and egalitarian state.

Hazrat Umar (581-644 A.D.) was a great companion and a loyal friend of the Holy Prophet. May the peace and blessings of Allah be upon him. Before his death, Hazrat Abu Bakr, with the consultation of the Companions, had appointed him as the caliph. During the ten years of his rule, from 634 to 644 A.D., Hazrat Umar changed the course of history.

Under his wise and courageous leadership, the Islamic caliphate grew at an unprecedented rate, taking Iraq and parts of Iran from the Sassanids, thereby ending that empire, and taking Egypt, Palestine, Syria, North Africa and Armenia from the Byzantines. He was assassinated by a Persian free enslaved individual, Abu Lulu Fairoz, and embraced shahadat on the first of Muharram, 24 Hijri.

14. THE FORGOTTEN ECONOMIC GENIUS OF UMAR IBN AL-KHATTAB

Whenever we think of the great Kings of the world, one name often comes to mind — Alexander the Great. For obvious reasons, he deserves this reputation, but many are unaware that there was another important figure in history who was more significant than many influential kings in every respect. This man has been written about, analysed, reviled, praised, overlooked, and misunderstood even by his people. The personality in question is none other than 'Umar al-Faruq ibn al-Khattab[ra], the second Caliph of Islam. Holding this position between 634 and 644 C.E., 'Umar ibn al-Khattab's[ra's] contributions to Islam are distinguished by his wisdom, practical intelligence, and outstanding leadership.

Indeed, with the same pioneering spirit as the Prophet Muhammad[sa], his thoughts and policies concerning various economic issues are so impressive that one is left dumbfounded. In order to acknowledge his immense achievements in the field of economic development or wealth redistribution, one must understand the context of his time. During this period of history, titanic changes took place, with the rapid and geographic spread of Islam and the collapse of old empires.

However, it would be unjust if we solely spotlight his achievements as an individual. Before recounting his successes, we must not forget that it was not his personality which helped him to establish such significant economic reforms. Had Islam not existed, 'Umar would not have become *Faruq the Great*. It was Islam that moulded his personality and understanding, and it was Islam that put forth a magnificent ideal (the Prophet Muhammad[sa]) for him to emulate, ultimately enabling him to trigger the second economic revolution of Islam.

The Caliphate's Rapid Geographical Expansion

The year 632 C.E. witnessed the most dramatic change in the lives of early Muslims: the death of the Prophet Muhammad[sa]. His death was inevitable and expected, with the Qur'an reminding Muslims that he is. Still, a mortal messenger like those before him, warning them against any setback that might erupt after his demise (*Holy Qur'an, 3: 145*). The shock was severe, but there was eternal hope. Before the Prophet's burial, two groups of Muslims debated the right to the caliphate (succession): the Medinite supporters (the *Ansar*) and the Meccan Emigrants. The dispute was resolved by the oath of allegiance to Abu Bakr al-Siddiq[ra], the Prophet's close companion, as the first Caliph of Islam.

Of the many 'Caliphates' that have come after the death of the Holy Prophet[sa], the "Rightly-Guided Caliphate" (*al-Khilafa al-Rashida*) is the most highly esteemed in Muslim minds and the most associated with righteousness and high spiritual values. From a religious perspective, the many political 'Caliphates' which came after the Rightly-Guided Caliphs were Caliphates in name only, not sanctioned by Islam as legitimate spiritual authorities. The Rightly-Guided Caliphate covered the years 632 to 661 C.E. and comprised four Caliphs: Abu Bakr al-Siddiq[ra] (632-634), 'Umar ibn al-Khattab[ra] (634-644), 'Uthman ibn Affan[ra] (644-656) and 'Ali ibn Abi Talib[ra] (656-661).

Before he died in 634, Caliph Abu Bakr[ra] designated 'Umar ibn al-Khattab[ra] as his successor. The designation was in the form of a recommendation, subject to the approval of the community. Indeed, there was nothing at all binding about it, and the community could have rejected it if they had wanted to (Shaban, 1971). The Qur'an emphasized the importance of mutual consultation (*Shura*) as the fundamental principle which should guide Muslims in the transactions of their national affairs (*Holy Qur'an, 42:39*). Muslims, however, approved his choice and 'Umar[ra] became the second Caliph.

Having begun under Abu Bakr[ra], Islamic external conquests reached a high peak at the time of 'Umar. Indeed, the second Caliph started his Caliphate by completing the task which his predecessor had started: winning the war for Syria and Iraq. During the 7th century, two powerful Empires surrounded Arabia: the Byzantine in the west and the Sassanid in the east. Having seen the rapid rise of the Muslims in Arabia, they quickly mobilised to destroy the nascent empire. Thus, the early Islamic empire was directly in conflict with the two superpowers of its day. These Empires had no tinge of justice in their governance. Power was in the hands of the kings and lords, and the general public was the victim of all kinds of atrocities.

On the Byzantine front, Damascus fell in 636 after a series of battles. When Khalid ibn al-Walid[ra], the general in charge, reached the Euphrates, he was welcomed by the Christian Arabs who lived in Syria. He made a treaty with the people whereby no Jews or Christians would be persecuted, freedom of religion would be ensured, and protection of people would be guaranteed. The Syrians also gladly accepted Muslims because they had ethnic and linguistic ties — both were Arab and spoke Semitic languages. Also, the Syrians were fed up with Byzantine oppression and outrageous taxes.

Later, in 638, 'Umar's forces conquered Jerusalem; Caesarea fell in 641, and Ascalon too in 644. Meanwhile, led by 'Amr ibn al-'As, Muslim troops also marched into Egypt and the same pattern was repeated. The Monophysitic Egyptians felt alienated from the Byzantines, who spoke a different language, believed in a different form of Christianity and thought they were superior. The Byzantine governor, Cyrus, made every attempt to convert the 'Copts' and applied the usual exorbitant taxes. Muslims thus entered the country to the relief of the Egyptians and defeated the Byzantines near Heliopolis in 640, resulting in the fall of Babylon. This victory allowed them entrance into Alexandria in 642. Cyrus was actually in favour of surrendering; however, the emperor of Byzantines, Heraclius, refused to allow him to sign a peace treaty with 'Amr ibn al-'As. Only after the emperor's death in 641 was peace finally established in Egypt. The new Muslim inhabitants kept the same Byzantine administration and did not oust the Coptic officials from their posts. They imposed a softer tax on Christians and Jews was imposed, and no forcible conversion took place (Al-Baladhuri; Hitti, 1936; Holt, 1970; Hart, 1978).

On the Persian front, Muslims had similar successes. 'Umar's[ra] forces met those of Emperor Yazdagird in Qadisiyya, known as the "gateway of Persia". Rustam, the Sassanid commanding general, led an army six times that of the Muslims. Despite this enormous disadvantage and an early defeat in 634, Muslims achieved a decisive victory in 636, and they claimed all of Iraq west of the Tigris River. Ctesiphon, the capital of the Sassanid Empire, fell in 637. A final victory in Nahavand in 642 sealed the fate of the Sassanid Empire. That put an end to the Persian resistance in Iraq and forced Yazdagird to retreat to Istakhar, the old Persepolis. Oddly enough, he was killed by a local Persian in 651. After that, 'Umar[ra] did not want to pursue the Persians any further, and Muslims concluded somewhat similar treaties with Persian cities as was previously done in the Byzantine territories (Al-Baladhuri; Al-Tabari; Hitti, 1936; Holt, 1976).

Keeping the Muslim community united, 'Umar[ra] kept the native administrations of the countries that the Muslims entered and just appointed governors; this limited tension and discord. In general, there was overwhelming support for his leadership, and this kept the community unified (Hold, 1970). This unity strengthened his administration and avoided internal bickering.

Ownership of Land

The expansion of the Islamic Empire brought with it changes in Islamic society that necessitated a fresh outlook in dealing with economic issues.

The most notable example of the novelty in Umar's economic thinking was demonstrated in his attitude towards the ownership of land as a factor of production. Indeed, the Caliph was of the view that if land, as a building block of economic activity, were utilised correctly, it would generate wealth and commerce (El-Ashker & Wilson, 2006).

After the conquests, Muslim warriors advocated that in accordance with the rules of the Qur'an, the conquered lands of Iraq and Syria should be distributed among them. Caliph 'Umar[ra] disagreed. He was of the opinion that the land should be kept in the hands of the State, i.e. that it should be nationalised. He advised that a tax be imposed on the original owners, from which Muslims would be paid stipends. To understand the character of this problem and Caliph 'Umar's[ra's] approach to solving it, it is worth looking into the system of dividing the spoils of war among the warriors as stated in the Qur'an.

The allocation of spoils (*Ghanima*) was ordained in the Qur'an as follows:

"And know that whatever you take as spoils in war, a fifth thereof is for Allah and the Messenger and the kindred and the orphans and the needy and the wayfarer."

The Holy Qur'an, 8: 42

In this distribution, the warrior would keep four-fifths of what he gained in the battle and pay the Prophet, or the head of the State, one-fifth (*Khums*), which would be distributed among the Muslims. During the time of the Holy Prophet[sa], the remaining four-fifths were divided among the soldiers because they were paid no salaries and, in general, had to incur the expenses of wars themselves. This was an exigency measure adopted to meet the conditions then found, as there was then no regular army and no State treasury.

Thus, Muslim warriors claimed the right to four-fifths of the spoils, including land, with one-fifth to be paid to the State — the *Ghanima* distribution. Caliph 'Umar[ra] disagreed by making a difference between mobile and immobile assets (El-Ashker & Wilson, 2006). For mobile assets, the Qur'anic rules were to be applied (one-fifth to the State and the rest to the soldiers). However, immobile assets, particularly those of land, were to become the property of all citizens through the State. With the right of ownership resting with the State, the land would remain in the hands of the original owners, who would utilise them and be liable for the payment of a land tax (*Kharaj*).

The reasons that led 'Umar[ra] to make such a decision were both religious and economic (Abu Yusuf). According to him, the land that Muslim soldiers conquered had the potential to turn Islamic society into a feudalistic society, where the warriors became the aristocracy who held all the new land and, thus, all the new wealth. He knew that the distribution of land to Muslim soldiers was bound to create a powerful class of landlords who could become a parasite for the flourishing economy. Indeed, at a time when a feudal system was in vogue around Arabia, people were accustomed to permanent proprietary rights over land.

But Caliph Umar[ra] opposed this strongly and took a revolutionary step: he abolished absentee landlordism and, through nationalisation, changed the entire system of land ownership in the Islamic Empire. To justify this, he referred to the Qur'anic verses on the distribution of new wealth. He concluded that whatever method of distribution was adopted must prevent the circulation of wealth only amongst the rich:

Whatever Allah has given to His Messenger as spoils from the people of the towns is for Allah and the Messenger and for the near of kin and the orphans and the needy and the wayfarer, that it may not circulate only among those of you who are rich.

The Holy Qur'an, 59: 8.

Lastly, the welfare of future generations, according to Caliph 'Umar[ra], should not be sacrificed for the well-being of the present one. He is reported to have said, "*If I distributed land, nothing would be left for those who will come after you and who will find that the land had already been distributed and inherited*" (Abu Yusuf). In other words, the distribution of the new land among soldiers would have limited tax revenues and thus the ability of the State to establish the system of social security 'Umar[ra] envisaged. Although his council was divided, the debate ended with the approval of the proposal of the Caliph.

'Umar[ra] reformed laws pertaining to land distribution and taxation

National Development

Suppose the policies of the second Caliphra regarding the conquered land are analysed in a broad economic context. In that case, they depict his awareness of two main economic issues in the early Islamic state: national economic development and wealth distribution. The efficiency of using natural resources in general, and the productivity of land in particular, seemed to have been a primary target in 'Umar's[ra] economic development. His attitude regarding the conquered lands was akin to an economist's attitude towards land as a means of production (El-Ashker & Wilson, 2006). He left the land in the hands of the original owners, who were more capable than the Arabs of cultivating it. Furthermore, in imposing land tax (*Kharaj*), the base was the cultivable land regardless of whether the land was actually being cultivated It meant increasing the utility of the land as a means of production.

A closer look reveals similarities between *Kharaj* and the modern economic idea of a Land Value Tax (LVT). The latter seeks to raise public revenue by means of an annual charge on the value of land. Indeed, taxing land is seen as practical and non-distortionary because land is an immobile asset. It is also seen as efficient because it encourages landowners to use the land as productively as possible. In economic theory, an LVT is a straightforward attempt to collect tax on what economists traditionally called the 'unearned betterment' part of the value of a property — the rise in value that has nothing to do with the owner's efforts and everything to do with the community's.

The emphasis of the second Caliph[ra] on the efficiency of using land as a means of production was demonstrated further in the cases of reclaiming barren land and owning more land than one could afford to look after. In the case of reclaiming barren land, Caliph 'Umar[ra], in line with the Islamic teachings, instructed, *"Whoever revives dead land becomes its owner"* (Abu Yusuf). When no one had ownership over barren land, no argument was likely to arise, but a dispute might erupt if the land had an original owner. For the second case, the Caliph emphasised, *"there is no right to the holder after three years of no utilisation"* and *"if someone else, or a group of people, came along and utilised the abandoned part he, or they, may claim the ownership of that part"* (Abu Ubaid; Al-Mawardi).

The second Caliph's awareness of the need for the full use of economic resources did not stop at the level of land as a means of production; it went further to reach human resources and capital. His policies on labour were characterized by encouraging people to have an occupation, to learn and train, to give up laziness under the pretence of religious devotion, and to strive through work for the sake of God. Furthermore, the second Caliph[ra] seemed to have realised the relationship between unemployment and civil unrest as early as the mid-seventh century. In his directions, he is, *"God has created hands to work. If they cannot find work in obedience, they will find plenty in disobedience, so keep them busy in compliance before they get you busy with defiance"* (Al-Ghazali).

Besides land and labour, capital as a means of production also occupied the attention of the second Caliph[ra]. He stressed the importance of spending only what is needed for the sake of increasing savings and maximising the ability to invest. In his stand on the rationalisation of consumption for the sake of saving, 'Umar[ra] advised that people should limit their consumption and not be excessive in their purchases, as is taught in the Holy Qur'an *(25: 68)*. Furthermore, to help people with starting capital, the Caliph[ra] took the initiative of distributing barren land to those who were capable of utilising it, granted them its ownership, and offered financial help to those who were in need for assistance in cultivating it (Abu Yusuf).

If, during the Caliphate of Abu Bakr[ra], the State could be considered economically weak, then during the Caliphate of 'Umar[r], with the first wave of victories, wealth began pouring in. As a result, 'Umar[ra] considered it necessary to thoroughly reform this vast territory, whose area was enlarged after the conquests of Syria, Iraq and Egypt. Having reorganised the territorial organization of the Muslim provinces, Caliph 'Umar[ra] gave the Public Treasury (the *Baitul Mal*) the shape of an economic institution. Indeed, after the conquests, the income that reached the centre (Medina) was so huge that he had to think about how to utilise it wisely for long-term prosperity. At the same time, the burden of the organisation of armies and the administration of conquered lands also increased. Money was also needed for public welfare plans. Hence, this wealth is not required to be spent haphazardly but be kept safe in some place. This led to the creation of the institution of the *Baitul Mal*.

Caliph 'Umar[ra] was very careful about the management and safety of the treasury. He was aware that if mismanagement were once allowed, it would one day go beyond control. With this view in mind, he took every possible care in the selection of treasurers, for which he selected only those whose ability and honesty were beyond doubt. Another critical step that he took to ensure the proper management of the treasury was that it was not mixed with the executive. In provinces, officers in charge of the treasuries were independent of the governors, and they had full authority to use their powers. Each province had a collector of taxes (*Sahib al-Kharaj*) and a Treasury Officer (*Sahib Bait al-Mal*).

Wealth Distribution

Regarding wealth distribution, the other factor in economic welfare, we find that this was taken care of in two principal ways. The first was the institution of Zakat, which was already established in the Qur'an, while the second was a system of stipends that were introduced by Caliph 'Umar. Revenues of Zakat were to be spent in a particular manner specified in the Qur'an in which the beneficiaries are *"the poor and the needy, those employed in connection in addition to that, those whose hearts are to be reconciled, and for the freeing of slaves, those in debt, for the cause of Allah, and the wayfarer."* (The Holy Qur'an, 9: 60). A further reinforcement to Zakat revenues came, as mentioned earlier, from that of *Khums,* which is one-fifth of the spoils of war.

The second tool of wealth distribution in the community was a stipend system, which was introduced by Caliph 'Umar. The allowances were of two types: monetary allowances and allowances in kind. He institutionalized the new social structure based on an Islamic hierarchy by creating what came to be known as *Diwan Umar* – loosely meaning the Ministry of Umar, or the *Umar Plan.* This hierarchy, with its material underpinnings in the form of stipends, had its foundation in Islam (*al-sabiqa fi al-Islam*). The earlier one accepted Islam, the higher one's position and stipend was; those who joined Islam before the Battle of Badr received higher stipends (5,000 dirhams each annually) than those who joined after the conquest of Mecca (3,000 dirhams each annually). The Prophet Muhammad's[sa] family members received special honour and were placed in a higher category than the rest. The Prophet Muhammad's[sa] wives and uncles, for example, received an annual stipend of 12,000 dirhams; Hasan[ra] and Husain[ra], the Prophet's[sa] grandsons, each received 5,000 dirhams (Al-Tabari; Al-Baladhuri). The reason for the disparity was apparent — those who joined earlier made much more tremendous sacrifices, suffering for years under persecution.

A similar system for the distribution of stipends was established in the provinces. This system was also based on the date of first participation in the Islamic expansion; those who fought in the early battles received higher stipends than those who joined later when most of the battles had been won. There were three categories: those who participated in the earliest battles of the expansion (*ahl al-Ayyam*), those who participated in the decisive Battle of Qadisiyya (*ahl al-Qadisiyya*), and the latecomers (*rawadif*). The first category received an annual stipend that ranged over time from 5,000 to 3,000 dirhams, with extra for additional valour; the second received between 3,000 and 2,000 dirhams. The third category received stipends ranging between 200 and 1,500 dirhams, based on the date they moved to the provincial capitals to be registered.

Women and infants from the day they were born also received a share, 200 and 100 dirhams, respectively (Al-Baladhuri; Hinds, 1971). Every infant, in addition to their allowance, received a portion of corn monthly. On attaining the age of one year, the allowance was doubled (i.e., 200 dirhams annually), and on reaching the age of maturity, every child received 300 dirhams annually. Orphans were kept in line with other children. They received an allowance of 100 dirhams, which is an increase compared to ordinary cases. Guardians of such children were given separate pay and allowance. Clothing, shelter, and education for such children were a state duty (Ra'ana, 1975). Thus, we say that the Caliph Umar pioneered a social welfare system that even today's most progressive politicians could not match.

The Caliph's Personal Empathy

Caliph 'Umar's sense of justice (*'adl*) does not seem to have been merely theoretical. Indeed, there are many accounts of his being a true *man of the people*, patrolling the streets in person to see the state of the population under his responsibility.

One account says that one day, Caliph 'Umar[ra] saw, in the presence of a man named Aslam, a campfire outside the city of Medina. As they approached the fire, they saw a woman with some young children screaming. The Caliph[ra] greeted the woman and asked if he was allowed to approach her. The woman returned the greeting and replied: "*Bring us some good or leave us alone.*" The Caliph[ra] then asked her what had happened to the children. She told him that nightfall and cold had overtaken them and that hunger was making her children cry. She had a pot set up over the fire, and the Caliph[ra] asked what was in it. She told him there was water for her children. Not recognizing the Caliph, she added: "*I ask God to judge between us and 'Umar!*" The Caliph[ra] replied: "*God have mercy upon you, how can 'Umar know anything about you?*" To this, she replied: "*He is in authority over us, and yet he neglects us.*"

The Caliph was famed for his sense of personal responsibility for each individual under his care.

Visibly shaken, the Caliph[ra] left with Aslam and went to the flour store, where he took out a measure and put a ball of fat into it. When the Caliph[ra] started carrying all this, Aslam proposed to have it on his behalf. But 'Umar[ra] insisted and said: "*Will you carry my burden for me on the Day of Resurrection, you wretch?!*" He thus took all the food, and they rushed to get back to the woman. The Caliph[ra] gave her the food and began to cook the bread with her. Once it was made, he told her to feed her children until they were satisfied. Gratefully, she said: "*God give you a good reward. You have done better in this matter than the Commander of the Faithful!*". Keeping his identity hidden, 'Umar[ra] replied: "*Speak well of him, for when you come to the Commander of the Faithful, you will find me there, God willing*". After slightly stepping away from her, Aslam said to him that they should leave now as he had other things to do. But the Caliph[ra] remained silent until he saw that the children had fallen asleep. After praising God, he turned to Aslam and said: "*Hunger kept them awake and made them cry. I did not want to leave until I could see them doing what I see now!*" (Al-Tabari).

Custom duties ('Ushur)

Besides *Kharaj*, another tax introduced by Caliph 'Umar[r] was the *'Ushr* or custom duties. At the recommendation of one of the Caliph's governors, Abu Musa al-Ash'ari, the tax was initiated as a reciprocal tax to that which Muslim merchants paid to foreign states on crossing their borders. The rate of the tax was one-tenth, or *'Ushr* (the plural of which is *'Ushur*), which was determined to be retained while imposed by foreign countries on Muslim merchants. In the words of Abu Musa in his letter to 'Umar, *"Muslim traders from our dominion go to the country of the enemies, and they levy 'Ushr (one tenth) on them"*, to which 'Umar replied, *"Take 'Ushr from them just as they charge from the Muslim traders"*. Other characteristics of the 'Ushur tax were that the tax had a threshold of 200 dirhams below which it would not be taxed, it was levied once a year on the same goods transferred regardless of the number of times they crossed the borders, and it was imposed on external trade with no levy on the transfer of goods among the state provinces (Abu Yusuf).

Public works and infrastructure investment

Caliph 'Umar^ra took a keen interest in public works and built many canals, buildings, and cities—the canals that were needed for the expansion of agriculture. Among them was the "Abi Musa Canal". It was 9 miles long and was brought from the river Tigris to supply water to the people of Basra, who had complained to Caliph 'Umar^ra about the scarcity of water in their city. Another worth mentioning is the "Amir al-Mu'minin Canal". This canal joined the Nile and the Red Sea and was the most helpful canal at that time. Around 640-641, when Arabia was affected by a severe drought and famine, the Caliph ordered the provincial governors to send food grains to the capital. This order was complied with, but the land route from Egypt and Syria being very long, it took a long time for the food grains to reach Medina. Caliph 'Umar decided to connect the Nile and the Red Sea by a canal to reduce the distance and enable the provisions to reach Medina efficiently. He sounded the governor of Egypt on the matter, who completed a 69-mile-long canal in six months. It also helped increase sea traffic ; in the first year, twenty ships carrying a large amount of food grains reached Jar, the port of Medina (Ra'ana, 1975).

Urbanization

One of the practices which took root in the Islamic world through Caliph 'Umar[ra] was the art of managing the fiscal and accounting affairs of the public treasury. Other practices included urban planning and deliberate architecture, with the result that, upon the order of the Caliph, two cities (Kufa and Basra)were built in Iraq and one in Egypt (Fustat). When Kufa and Basra were constructed, much attention was paid to the groundwork infrastructure development.s, such as the width of the streets and the centrality of the mosque in both cities. These cities and the investments made in them also facilitated the process of development. All these measures allowed the accumulation of wealth and capital in the economy of the early Islamic period. For this reason, aggregate supply increased in tandem with aggregate demand; consequently, the value of money and price levels remained stable, except during the few years of drought (Sadr, 2016).

Conclusion

It is clear from the above that the second Caliph[ra] attached great importance to natural resources as a means of production and endeavoured to maximise the benefits generated from these resources. 'Umar's[ra] policies, with regard to ownership of means of production, were neither capitalistic nor communistic, to use modern economic terms, but a reflection of Islamic economic teachings. Private ownership is highly regarded in Islam, provided it is not abused. If it is abused, the State has the right to step in and rectify the situation. After all, the ownership is ownership by trusteeship between a man who is delegated to own and God who owns everything. Nationalisation was not, therefore, one of the State's general policies. It was only a necessary step taken to rectify the situation and prevent the misuse of economic resources.

In addition, Caliph 'Umar's policy on wealth distribution was based on a compromise that benefited the many. This was demonstrated by the fact that everyone, including infants, received a share of the wealth following the conquests. It is for this reason that his Caliphate is considered the first primary Welfare State in the world and served as a model for subsequent nations.

One thing is for sure: his shadow and his example will continue to prevail and dominate us for a long time. a'Umar[ra] was a great ruler, and he had a lasting impact not only on his reigning region but also on the entire world. It is high time that we grant him back, according to the expression of historian Lucien Febvre, his "right to history".

15. UMAR'S ADVICE TO THE INSTITUTIONS & CALIPH WHO COME AFTER HIM

Umar Bin Khattab offered critical advice to the caliph, who was to come after him and lead the ummah. He said: "I advise you to fear Allah alone, with no partner or associate. I advise you to treat the first *Muhajireen* well and acknowledge their seniority. I advise you to treat the Ansar well, show approval of those who do well, and forgive those who make mistakes. I advise you to treat the people of the outlying regions well, for they are a shield against the enemy and conduits of fay' (booty); do not take anything from them except that which is surplus to their needs. I advise you to treat the people of the desert well, for they are the original Arabs and the protectors of Islam. Take from the surplus of their wealth and give it to their poor. I advise you to treat *Ahl Al-Dhimmah* (Jews and Christians living in Muslim lands under government protection) well, to defend them against their enemies and not burden them with more than they can bear if they fulfil their duties towards the believers or pay the jizyah with willing submission, and feel themselves subdued.

I advise you to fear Allah and fear His wrath, lest you do anything wrong. I advise you to fear Allah with regard to the people, but do not fear the people in relation to Allah. I recommend you treat people justly and devote yourself to looking after them and protecting them against their enemies. Do not show any favour to the rich over the poor. That will be better for your spiritual well-being and will help to reduce your burden of sin, and it will be better for your Hereafter until you meet the One Who knows what is in your heart. I instruct you to be strict with regard to the commands of Allah, His sacred limits, and disobedience with all people, both relatives and others. Do not show any mercy to anyone until you have settled the score with him according to his offence.

Treat all people as equals, and do not worry about who is at fault or fear the blame of the blamers. Beware of showing favouritism among the believers with regard to the fay' that Allah has put you in charge of, lest that lead to injustice. Keep away from that. You are in a position between this world and the Hereafter. If you conduct your affairs justly in this world and refrain from indulgence, that will earn you faith and divine pleasure. But if you let whims and desires overwhelm you, you will incur the displeasure of Allah.

I advise you not to let yourself or anyone else do wrong to *Ahl Al-Dhimmah*. I am offering you sincere advice; seek thereby the Countenance of Allah and the Hereafter. I have chosen advice for you that I would provide to myself or my son. If you do as I have advised you and follow my instructions, you will have gained a great deal. Suppose you do not accept it or pay attention to it and do not handle your affairs in the way that pleases Allah. In that case, that will be a shortcoming on your part, and you will have failed to be sincere because whims and desires are the same, and the cause of sin is blessed, who calls man to everything that will lead to his doom. He misguided the generations who came before you and led them to Hell. What a terrible abode. What a lousy deal it is for a man to take the enemy of All& as his friend, who calls him to disobey Allah. Please adhere to the truth, strive hard to reach it, and admonish yourself.

I urge you by Allah to show mercy to the Muslims, honour their elderly, show compassion to their young ones and respect the knowledgeable ones among them. Do not harm them or humiliate them, and do not keep the fay' for yourself lest you anger them. Do not deprive them of their stipends when they become due, thus making them poor.

Please do not keep them away from campaigns for so long that they end up having no children. Do not allow wealth to circulate only among the rich. Do not close your door to the people lest that let the strong oppress the weak. This is my advice to you, as All& is my witness, and I greet you with peace."

This advice is indicative of 'Umar's farsightedness with regard to matters of ruling and administration, which clearly reflects an integrated methodology and system of ruling and administration.[2] This advice covers a number of critical issues. It deserves to be viewed as a precious document because it includes basic principles of the ruling, which incorporate the religious, political, military, economic, and social aspects of the rule, which include the following:

Advice to fear Allah

A. Strong advice to fear Allah in secret and public, in word and deed, because the one who fears Allah will be protected by Him. "I advise you to fear Allah alone, with no partner or associate." "I advise you to fear Allah and fear His wrath."

B. Imposing suitable punishments on relatives and strangers alike. "Do not worry about who is at fault or fear the blame of the blamers" because hudood punishments are set out by sharī'ah and are part of the religion and sharī'ah that leaves people with no excuse, so their words and deeds are gauged according to accordingly, and neglect it will corrupt religion and society.

C. Firm adherence to Islam

"So stand (ask Allah to make) you (Muhammad) firm and straight (on the religion of Islamic Monotheism) as you are commanded" [Hood 11:112].

This is essential in both religious and worldly terms and is something that is required of the ruler in both word and deed, as well as of the people. "Admonish yourself." "Seek thereby the Countenance of Allah and the Hereafter."

Advice regarding political matters

A. Adhering to justice, which is the basis of rule, and establishing justice among the people gives the ruler authority and respect and brings political and social stability. It enhances the position of the ruler in the eyes of the people. "I advise you to treat the people justly." "Treat all people as equal."

B. Taking care of the first Muslims from among the Muhajireen and Ansar because of their seniority in Islam and because the Islamic religion and the political system that is based on it were established as the result of their striving, and they are its bearers and guardians. "I advise you to treat the first Muhijireen well and acknowledge their seniority. I advise you to treat the Ansar well, and show approval of those among them who do well, and forgive those among them who make mistakes."

Advice regarding military matters

A. Pay attention to the army and prepare it properly because of the great responsibility that is placed on its shoulders in order to guarantee the safety and security of the state—paying attention to the needs of the fighters.

B. Not keeping the fighters away from their families on the borders for too long so as to avoid the boredom, anxiety and loss of morale that may lead. It is essential to give them leave at specified times and let them go back to their families, where they can renew their energy so that they will not cease to produce offspring. "Do not keep them away on campaigns for so long that they end up having no children." "I advise you to treat the people of the outlying regions well, for they are a shield against the enemy."

C. Giving each soldier the fay' and stipend to which he is entitled in order to guarantee a fixed income for him and his family, which will motivate him to fight in jihad and prevent him from worrying about his financial affairs. "Do not keep the fay' for yourself lest you anger them." "Do not deprive them of their stipends when they become due, thus making them poor."

Advice regarding economic and financial matters

A. Taking care to distribute wealth among the people in a just and fair manner, avoiding anything that could lead to the accumulation of wealth among one class to the exclusion of others. "Do not allow wealth to circulate only among the rich."

B. Not burdening Ahl Al-Dhimmah with more than they can bear if they fulfil their financial obligations to the state. "[Do] not burden them with more than they can bear if they fulfil their duties towards the believers."

C. Protecting the people's financial rights and not neglecting them; avoiding the imposition of more than they can bear. "Do not take anything from them except that which is surplus to their needs." "Take from the surplus of their wealth and give it to their poor."

Advice regarding social matters

A. Taking care of the people, checking on them, meeting their needs and giving them their rights. "Do not deprive them of their stipends when they become due."

B. Avoid selfishness, favouritism, and following whims and desires because these things pose the danger of the leader being led astray, leading to corruption in society and the disruption of human relations. "Beware of showing favouritism among the believers with regard to the fay' that Allah has put you in charge of." "Do not show any favour to the rich over the poor."[3]

C. Respecting the people and being humble towards them, young and old, because this will lift human relations to a higher level and lead them to unite behind the leader and love him more. "I urge you by Allah to show mercy to the Muslims, honour their elderly, show compassion to their young ones and respect the knowledgeable ones among them."

D. Being accessible to the people by listening to their complaints, judging among them and settling scores. Otherwise, relations will be adversely affected, and society will be unstable. "Do not close your door to the people lest that allow the strong to oppress the weak."

E. Following the truth and striving to establish it in society in all situations and circumstances because this is a social necessity that must be achieved. "Adhere to the truth, strive hard to reach it." "Treat all people as equal, and do not worry about who is at fault."

F. Avoiding wrongdoing in all shapes and forms, especially with Ahl Al-Dhimmah, because justice is to be established among all those who come under the state's rule, Muslims and otherwise, so that all may benefit from the justice of Islam. "I advise you not to let yourself or anyone else do wrong to Ahl Al-Dhirnmah."

G. Taking care of the people of the desert and looking after them. "I advise you to treat the people of the desert well, for they are the original Arabs and the protectors of slam."[4]

H. Further advice offered by 'Umar to the one who came after him was: Do not leave anyone who was appointed during my reign for more than one year, but leave al-Ash'ari for four years.

References

[1] at-Tabaqat by bn Saad, 3/339; al-Bayan wa'l-Tabyeen by al-Jahiz, 2/46, Jumhurat Khutab al-'Arab, 1/263-265; al-Kamil fi-Tareekh, 2/210; al-Khaleefa al-Farooq 'Umar ibn al-Khattab by al-'Aani, p. 171, 172

[2] al-ldarah al-lslamiyyah fi 'Asr 'Umar ibn al-Khattab, p. 381

[3] Al-Khaleefah al-Farooq 'Umar ibn-Khattab by al-'Aani, p. 174, 175.

[4] al-Khaleefah al-Farooq 'Umar ibn al-Khatab by al'Aani, p. 173-175

[5] 'Asr al-Khilafah al-Rashidah, p. 102

Umar's philosophy of tolerance

During 'Umar's caliphate, the dhimmis (religious minorities in the Islamic State) enjoyed complete religious freedom and civil liberties. They had the full right to practise their religious rituals and rights. They played their bugle, punctually held their socio-religious fairs, and carried the cross in procession. As for the issue of enforcing conversion to Islam, Caliph 'Umar and his administrators never adopted such policies, and they always maintained the Qur'anic principle that there is no compulsion in religion.

Not only did non-Muslims have the right to complete religious freedom, but they also enjoyed the right to equal citizenship During the reign of 'Umar, a Jew was disposed of a plot of land and a mosque was constructed on the site. Learning of this incident, 'Umar ordered the demolition of the mosque and restored the land to its original owner. A Lebanese Christian scholar, Professor Cardahi, wrote in 1933 that "this house (with the above piece of land) of the Jew, known as Bait al Yahudi, still exists and is well known".

One extraordinary episode of tolerance and coexistence occurred during the reign of 'Umar when the city of Jerusalem was freed from the Roman forces. The Patriarch of Jerusalem refused to give the city's keys to anyone except the Caliph. Therefore, 'Umar travelled to Jerusalem and met the Patriarch at the gate, and they went together to visit the historical Church of Resurrection. When the time of prayer came, the Patriarch courteously requested that the Caliph offer his prayer in the church. 'Umar kindly declined his invitation and said, "If I do so, the

Muslims may sometime in future infringe upon your rights by pretending to follow my example." Instead of praying inside the cathedral, he offered his prayers at its steps outside.

The atmosphere of coexistence was disseminated during the whole reign of 'Umar's caliphate, during which adherents to all religions enjoyed full and sedulous rights and protection. Non-Muslims continued to have their properties and land possessions, and a ban was imposed on Muslim citizens of the State with regard to the purchase of lands belonging to the dhimmis. Such policies were put into effect during the pact of Ileliyah in which Caliph 'Umar pledged the following,

"This is a peace granted by God's servant, Amir al-Muminin, 'Umar, to the people of Ileliyah extending to their life, property, churches, healthy, diseased and their co-religionists. Their churches will not be made into residential places, nor shall they be destroyed. Neither shall their territories be damaged, causing the loss. The number of their crosses and their assets will not be reduced, and they will not be asked to become Muslims…"

The interests of the non-Muslims were highly regarded in areas where Islam spread, such as in Syria, Mah Dinar, Jurjan, Azerbaijan, and Moqan. All non-Muslim subjects were given a pledge for the safety and security of their lives, properties, religion and customs. When Syria was conquered, 'Umar ordered Abu 'Ubaidah "to prevent Muslims from oppressing the dhimmis, from causing any loss to them, from dispossessing them without reason, and finally stick tenaciously to the fulfilment of the promises given to them."

In Homs, Muslims took the jizyah from the Christian and Jewish population in exchange for their protection from the Roman forces. To the surprise of Abu 'Ubaidah, the supreme commander, the Roman forces intensified their military forces, and the Muslim army had to retreat, as he was not going to be able to protect the city of Homs. Abu 'Ubaidah returned the tax money that the people of Homs paid due to their failure to keep their pact of security and safety intact. Such a generous act moved the people of Homs, and they pledged that they would protect their city and would not let the Romans conquer them in the hope that Muslims would return.

Another example is that of the Patriarch of Alexandria, who suffered severe persecution from the Romans in 20 A.H. The Muslim forces divested the Romans from their authority over Egypt and restored the fugitive Patriarch to his former post. It was during these days that one of the distinguished ecclesiastical heads remarked, "Today I witness in this city of Alexandria salvation and contentment reigning after a long period of persecution by the Roman rulers."

'Umar followed the leading example of the Prophet Muhammad and the Caliph Abu Bakr in dealing with religious minorities who resided within the boundaries of the Muslim state. During 'Umar's reign, extreme leniency and liberality were shown to minorities even when they committed dangerous acts against the Islamic state. For example, the inhabitants of Arbasus, a town near the frontiers of Syria, agreed with the victorious Muslim army, which guaranteed peace and protection to them in exchange for their loyalty. While this pact was still intact, the Christian residents of Arbasus worked for the Romans, who were political opponents of the Muslims. The commander 'Umair bin Sa, consulted the Caliph on this issue of treason and 'Umar responded with the following, "The commander should ask the offenders to resettle elsewhere, offering them double cost for their flocks and property or that he should wait for one year to see if they change their conduct for the better." The final decision was to banish the dangerous elements of Arbasus from the Islamic State for dishonouring their agreement with the Muslims and for committing treason, an act which barred them from becoming citizens of the Islamic State.

In another incident, the governor of Yemen sent multiple complaints to the Caliph about the conspiracies of some minority groups and sought his direction. The governor suggested their banishment from the Islamic territory. Caliph 'Umar refused the governor's proposal of banishing the defaulters for fear that this action might adversely affect innocent families. Hence, he suggested instead that these groups should be resettled into some other part of the Islamic state. However, they were to be provided with better housing arrangements and compensation for their properties in cash. This group preferred to settle in Syria, and the government accepted their choice and gave them both lands and houses.

Caliph 'Umar integrated non-Muslims into his administration. In the famous history book titled "Al-Ansab", it was reported that 'Umar wrote to his Syrian governor asking him to send a Greek who could adequately assess the accounts of the revenue department. Therefore, a Christian was appointed as the head of the accounts portfolio in the Prophet's city. The non-Muslim communities used to be consulted in economic, administrative, and military matters of the state, especially when they were directly pertinent to them. Non-Muslims also served in the Muslim armies, but they were not obligated to do so, and those who chose to do so were recruited on a voluntary basis.

'Umar introduced an equitable inaugurated economic system based on equal opportunity. The religious minorities were free to enter transactions, make agreements in business, spend and keep money and have a total share in commercial prosperity. No specific taxation was introduced to harass them. As for the jizyah, it was introduced as a taxation for maintaining protection and security in exchange for not being recruited into the Muslim army. The jizyah tax was not levied upon the needy, the oppressed, women, children, religious heads and the sick people of the non-Muslim communities. When it came to collecting tax revenues on land, revenues were collected leniently, and the terms of the agreement with the landlords were lenient.

It is a known fact that during the reign of Caliph 'Umar, poor Jews and Christians were maintained at the expense of the State and on the alms and donations collected from the Muslims. 'Umar encountered an old Jewish man begging, so he gave him some money from the government treasury and directed the cashier to give him monthly financial support.

The spirit of love, compassion, and sympathy were significant elements of Islamic society among all different religious votaries. Abdullah ibn 'Umar, the son of the second Caliph, would not eat the meat of a goat slaughtered for him until he had sent some of it to his neighbours. The tradition of feeding one's neighbours was a common Prophetic tradition that was widespread among the companions.

When it came to war booty, Muslim soldiers were not despoilers and were not aiming at looting booties. 'Umar had always been very cautious when it came to war spoils and always warned the soldiers not to indulge in worldly gains. The famous speech of 'Umar that he delivered to a dispatched army shows the true essence of jihad,

"Do not show cowardice in an encounter. Do not mutilate when you have the power to do so. Do not commit excess when you triumph. Do not kill an older man, a woman or a minor, but try to avoid them at the time of the encounter of the two armies, at the time of the heat of victory and at the time of expected attacks. Do not cheat over booty. Purify jihad from worldly gains. Rejoice in the bargain of the contract that you have made with God, and that is the great success."

Muslim armies marched to war with a high sense of morality and ethical conduct, as they were commanded not to destroy lives and destroy properties. Landowners whose crops or produce were damaged due to the movement of the troops received ample compensation for what they had lost. At one time, the Caliph satisfied a tiller by giving him 10,000 dirhams from the State Treasury because the army had spoiled his harvest. Before the advent of Islamic conquests, non-Muslim populations suffered the brunt of Roman and Persian colonization of their lands.

Sir William Muir, the Scottish Orientalist, said, "The people of Syria, too, apart from the religious persecution to which they had been subjected, suffered from increased taxation, and in consequence remained passive spectators of the invasion of their country, hoping more, indeed, from an occupation by the Arabs, who abstained from pillage, and whose rule was mild and tolerant, than from the continuance of the status quo" (The Caliphate, p. 65).

To sum up the treatment of non-Muslims during the reign of 'Umar, we can honestly say that Islam, with its moral principles, introduced to the world a much-needed sense of justice, moderation and coexistence among world religions and predominantly minority religious groups within Muslim nations. Encouraging religious pluralism was a new phenomenon in ages whose annals were stained with episodes of religious persecution and where religious discord and strife were only suppressed with much bloodshed.

Islam brought a new dawn of civil liberties and religious freedom to all religious communities when it gained political prominence, which revolutionized conditions in the conquered countries.

16. THE PACT OF UMAR

The Pact of Umar

We heard from 'Abd al-Rahman ibn Ghanam [died 78/697] as follows: When 'Umar ibn al-Khattab, may God be pleased with him, accorded peace to the Christians of Syria, we wrote to him as follows:

In the name of God, the Merciful and Compassionate. This is a letter to the servant of God 'Umar [ibn al-Khattab], Commander of the Faithful, from the Christians of such-and-such a city. When you came against us, we asked you for safe conduct [4] for ourselves, our descendants, our property, and the people of our community, and we undertook the following obligations toward you:

We shall not build, in our cities or their neighbourhood, new monasteries, churches, convents, or monks' cells, nor shall we repair, by day or by night, such of them as fall in ruins or are situated in the quarters of the Muslims.

We shall keep our gates wide open for passersby and travellers. We shall give board and lodging to all Muslims who pass our way for three days.

We shall not give shelter in our churches or our dwellings to any spy nor hide him from the Muslims.

We shall not teach the *Qur'an* to our children.

We shall not manifest our religion publicly nor convert anyone to it. We shall not prevent any of our kin from entering Islam if they wish it.

We shall show respect toward the Muslims, and we shall rise from our seats when they wish to sit.

We shall not seek to resemble the Muslims by imitating any of their garments, the *qalansuwa*,[5] the turban, footwear, or the parting of the hair. We shall not speak as they do, nor shall we adopt their *kunyas*.[6]

We shall not mount on saddles, nor shall we gird swords, bear any arms, or carry them on our persons.

We shall not engrave Arabic inscriptions on our seals.

We shall not sell fermented drinks.

We shall clip the fronts of our heads.

We shall always dress in the same way wherever we may be, and we shall bind the *zunnar*[7] ªround our waists.

We shall not display our crosses or our books on the roads or markets of the Muslims. We shall use only clappers in our churches very softly. We shall not raise our voices when following our dead. We shall not show lights on any of the roads of the Muslims or in their markets. We shall not bury our dead near the Muslims.

We shall not enslave individual people who have been allotted to Muslims.

We shall not build houses overtopping the houses of the Muslims.

(When I brought the letter to 'Umar, may God be pleased with him, he added, "We shall not strike a Muslim.")

We accept these conditions for ourselves and the people of our community, and in return, we receive safe conduct.

If we in any way violate these undertakings for which we stand surety, we forfeit our covenant,[8] and we become liable to the penalties for contumacy and sedition.

'Umar ibn al-Khattab replied: Sign what they ask, but add two clauses and impose them in addition to those which they have undertaken. They are: "They shall not buy anyone made prisoner by

> the Muslims," and "Whoever strikes a Muslim with deliberate intent
> shall forfeit the protection of this pact."

In the name of God, the Merciful, the Compassionate!

This is writing to Umar from the Christians of such a city. When You
[Muslims] marched against us [Christians], we asked of You protection
for ourselves, our posterity, our possessions, and our co-religionists, and
we made this stipulation with You that we will not erect in our city
or the suburbs any new monastery, church, cell or hermitage; that we
will not repair any of such buildings that may fall into ruins, or renew
those that may be situated in the Muslim quarters of the town; that we
will not refuse the Muslims entry into our churches either by night or
by day; that we will open the gates wide to passengers and travellers;
that we will receive any Muslim traveller into our houses and give him
food and lodging for three nights; that we will not harbour any spy in
our churches or homes, or conceal any enemy of the Muslims. [At least
six of these laws were taken over from earlier Christian laws against
infidels.]

That we will not teach our children the Qu'ran [some nationalist
Arabs feared the infidels would ridicule the Qu'ran; others did not want
infidels even to learn the language]; that we will not make a show of
the Christian religion nor invite anyone to embrace it; that we will not
prevent any of our relatives from embracing Islam if they so desire. That
we will honour the Muslims and rise in our assemblies when they wish
to take their seats; that we will not imitate them in our dress, either in
the cap, turban, sandals, or parting of the hair; that we will not make use
of their expressions of speech, nor adopt their surnames [infidels must
not use greetings and memorable phrases employed only by Muslims];
that we will not ride on saddles, or gird on swords, or take ourselves
arms or wear them, or engrave Arabic inscriptions on our rings; that we
will not sell wine [forbidden to Muslims]; that we will shave the front of

our heads; that we will keep to our style of dress, wherever we may be; that we will wear girdles round our waists [infidels wore leather or cord girdles; Muslims, cloth and silk].

That we will not display the cross upon our churches or display our crosses or our sacred books in the streets of the Muslims, or their market-places; that we will strike the clappers in our churches lightly [wooden rattles or bells summoned the people to church or synagogue]; that we will not recite our services in a loud voice when a Muslim is present; that we will not carry Palm branches [on Palm Sunday] or our images in procession in the streets; that at the burial of our dead, we will not chant loudly or carry lighted candles in the streets of the Muslims or their market places; that we will not take any enslaved individual people that have already been in possession of Muslims, nor spy into their houses; and that we will not strike any Muslim.

We promise to observe all this on behalf of ourselves and our co-religionists and receive protection from you in exchange. If we violate any of the conditions of this agreement, then we forfeit your protection, and you are at liberty to treat us as enemies and rebels.

Source

Jacob Marcus, *The Jew in the Medieval World: A Sourcebook, 315-1791*, (New York: JPS, 1938), 13-15

Later printings of this text (e.g. by Atheneum, 1969, 1972, 1978) do not indicate that the copyright was renewed)

The Pact of Umar was a 'treaty' forged during the conquest of Jerusalem more than 1400 years ago, at the beginning of Islamic history. It contributes to laying down the foundations of coexistence between Muslims and non-Muslims. In it are answers to most contemporary issues, such as: How do we deal with our enemies who fight us, how do we treat women and children during times of war, is every means permissible to kill enemies, who use women and boys as a human shield, etc. These questions have been addressed in an enlightened manner by modern laws and customs with the aim of preserving human values and dignity.

On comparing modern rules of engagement and laws of war that establish the safety of civilians during times of conflict with Islamic thought and jurisprudence, we find many convergences. The reflection of the Islamic approach can be drawn from the instructions of the first Caliph, Abu Bakr al-Siddiq. May Allah be pleased with him, who gave me the army of Osama bin Zaid before the latter's campaign: "Stop, Oh people, that I may give you ten rules for your guidance on the battlefield. Do not commit treachery or deviate from the right path. Do not mutilate dead bodies. Neither kills a child, nor a woman, nor an aged man. Bring no harm to trees, nor burn them with fire, especially those which are fruitful. Slay not any of the enemy's flock, save for your food. You are likely to pass by people who have devoted their lives to monastic services; leave them alone." (cf. History of Al Tabari, Part 3, p 226).

This text is replete with humanitarian profundity and dates back 1,400 years. Even in modern times (especially the 20th century), these values were acknowledged, for example, in the Introduction to International Humanitarian Law, Geneva: International Committee of the Red Cross under the section titled Islamic Arab history.

We have witnessed the emergence of religious and ideological divisiveness in all its horror, which presents a bleak picture of the Arab world.

In a conscious look at the long-standing Arab-Islamic heritage, we can see how keen it is to assert egalitarian traditions by adding to its humane character and urging adherence to them in terms of mutual respect. This is consistent with the provisions and spirit of international humanitarian law, which protects the rights of combatants and victims of armed conflict.

This tradition was evident in the era of the Holy Prophet), the first Caliph Abu Bakr) and was passed on to the second Caliph Umar ibn al-Khattab, who laid the foundations of coexistence between Muslims and non-Muslims.

This is exemplified in the incident when the Caliph Umar ibn al-Khattab travelled from Jabiyah in Damascus to Jerusalem. In accordance with a pact between him and the Christians, he entered Jerusalem and set up a separate room, which he cleaned with his companions and prayed in.

Being the leader of the victorious army, he could have prayed in the Church of the Holy Sepulchre, but he did not. When asked why he did not pray inside the church, he answered: "If I had prayed inside the church, I was afraid Muslims would say, 'This is where Umar prayed', and then may try to establish a mosque in its place." This shows The Pious Caliph's great wisdom and commitment to the values of tolerance.

Review Islam with new knowledge

In light of these glorious Islamic traditions, why don't we tackle the issue of tolerance and coexistence in our times, where religious and sectarian wars have again raised their ugly head and have destroyed countries like Syria?

We have witnessed the emergence of religious and ideological divisiveness in all its horror, which presents a bleak picture of the Arab world.

While speaking about Islam, we are aware that it is capable of rational interpretation. In spite of several interpretations of religious texts at present, we believe there is room for re-interpretation in the light of new knowledge in disciplines of sociology, politics and history through which we could review traditional understanding of sacred texts in order to promote the spirit of tolerance and respect for pluralism and human rights.

17. PRACTICING COMPASSION WITH THE IMPOVERISHED

Here are a few episodes from Umar's life that give us glimpses of the compassion of this great exemplar of justice.

Umar cooks and feeds a starving family

During one of his nocturnal rounds with his aide, Caliph Umar heard a plaintive wail waft out of a minor, humble dwelling. The alarmed Umar immediately headed towards it. He gently tapped the door. Pushing aside the curtain, he peeped in and found a lean woman cooking meals. She was surrounded by her brood of wailing children who appeared to be extremely hungry. The woman was desperately trying to calm down her unrelenting children. A pan was boiling on the fire. When Umar enquired about the reason for the children's distress, the woman said they had been starving for the whole day. "And what are you cooking," asked Umar. The woman said that there was only water and stones in the kettle. She was trying to console them with the impression that she was cooking food.

Umar was torn with guilt. He believed that in his reign, the people were being governed well. He was appalled and astonished at the plight of his citizens, and he appeared dismayed with his administration. Umar went straight to the state treasury. He called for a sack of rice, loaded it on his back, and, weighed down with this heavy load, trudged through the streets.

On his way, he chanced to meet a Muslim man who, recognizing him, said: 'Caliph, let me carry your burden.' The Caliph replied: 'No, for who will carry the burden of my sins when I meet my Lord?'

Umar arrived at the woman's house and, knocking at the door, went in. The children had not yet gone to sleep. They were still crying. Umar made bread with his own hands and cooked some food. He offered bread and food to the children. The children were so hungry that they scraped the plate clean to the last crumbs before they went to sleep.

Umar asked the woman why she had not complained to the Caliph. The woman said that despite her poverty, she had some self-respect and believed she should not go and beg the Caliph for any favour.

Umar was visibly moved. "You are right. I offer my apologies. For the future, it will be my responsibility to see that every individual of my kingdom can lead a decent life." After making sure that all was well in the house, Umar left.

When the woman realized that the man who had come to her relief was the Caliph himself, she was overwhelmed and smacked her forehead, amazed at the humility of such a powerful ruler. "No Caliph can be so humble and noble," she exclaimed in gratitude as she inconsolably invoked the Lord's blessings for him.

Humility at its zenith

During his travels, Umar would take no tent but throw his gown over a low bush and lie down in the shade. He performed the pilgrimage nine times during his caliphate. Piety, abstinence, and downright simplicity were the hallmarks of his character. "His walking stick," wrote one Muslim historian," struck more terror in those who were present than another man's sword." He would spend several nights visiting townships and going about the streets of Medinah to find out if anyone needed help or assistance. The general social and moral tone of Muslim society at that time is well illustrated by the words of an Egyptian who was sent to spy on the Muslims during their Egyptian campaign. He reported: "I have seen people, every one of whom loves death more than he loves life. They cultivate humility rather than pride. None is given for material ambitions. Their mode of living is simple. Their commander is their equal. They make no distinction between superior and inferior, between an enslaved individual and an enslaved person. When the time of prayer approaches, none remains behind...."

Al-Awza'i once narrated: "Umar came out in the depths of the night and was sighted by Talha, a renowned Companion of the Prophet. 'Umar went and entered a house and then entered another one. The following morning, Talha went to this house, where he saw a blind, disabled old lady. He said to her, 'Why does this man come to you?' She said, 'he has taken care of me since such and such. He comes, helps me with what is good for me, and takes away the harm.' Talha said, 'O Talha, may your mother be bereft. Are you following the slips of 'Umar?'" (*The Virtues of 'Umar ibn Al-Khattab*, by Ibn al-Jawzi, p. 68)

Justice on display

Once, Umar purchased a horse from a Bedouin. However, after travelling some distance, Umar noticed an infirmity in the horse. He rode back to the seller, who requested that he take it back since it was defective. The man grinned and was annoyed. He refused to take it back because the horse was alright at the time of the transaction. "How come this issue has cropped up after I have already sold the animal and the transaction is complete." The seller's stand took aback Umar. He had not anticipated this response. He decided to refer the matter to an arbitrator. He suggested that the man identify a judge to whom they could direct their dispute. The man chose Shurayh bin Al-Haarith Al-Kindi, and Umar accepted his choice.

After the judge had heard the Bedouin's testimony, he turned to Umar, asking: "Was the horse normal when you bought it?" 'Umar replied: "Yes, it was."Shurayh pronounced: "Then keep what you bought or return it as you took." Umar looked at Shurayh, was overwhelmed and exclaimed: "Thus justice should be - statement, distinguishing words and fair justice… I give you the position of Chief Justice of Kufah in Iraq."

Umar did not insist on his choice of a judge or threaten or even influence the judge. Umar accepted the judgment with humility. There was no trace of bitterness or hatred in him.

The power of righteousness

Umar once presided over a packed courthouse when he noticed two men dragging a boy inside. Seeing the commotion, he enquired what about the matter. The men said the boy had killed their father. Umar questioned the boy about the charge. The boy admitted that he had killed their father, but he said it was accidental and not deliberate. "My camel used to graze on their property. One day, their father hit a rock at the camel, which struck its eye. Seeing the pain and suffering of the camel, I got infuriated and threw a stone at their father, who hit his head and killed him."

Umar then asked the two men if they would forgive the boy. They said they wanted retribution, meaning the boy had to be executed for expiation. Umar then asked the boy if he had any last request or desire before he was punished. The boy said his father had passed away, and he had a young brother. His father had left some money for him, and he would require three days to retrieve the hidden cash and hand it over to his brother. Umar then asked if he could produce a guarantor to assure that he would return. The boy looked at the packed courthouse for sympathy but received no response. The people looked the other way, to his utter surprise, when he cast a hopeful glance at them. Then suddenly, a hand in the last row went up. Abū Dhar al-Ghifari al-Kinani, the Prophet's illustrious companion (sahabah), was the fourth or fifth individual to embrace Islam. "I am consenting to come forward to stand guarantee for the poor hapless boy."It meant that in case the boy did not turn up in three days, Abu Dhar would have to get his head chopped off. The boy was allowed to leave and report back within three days.

The first day passed, but the boy could not be, and the second day passed, too, with the boy still not back. On the third day, the two men went to Abu Dhar and asked him to accompany them to the courthouse. Abu Dhar insisted that there was still time till the day to end. The prayer call for sunset prayers was still minutes away. Meanwhile, tension had built up in Medinah, and the town was abuzz with news that Abu Dhar would have to suffer the punishment for the boy.

The boy appeared with just a few minutes to go for the prayer call. He was gasping but relieved that he could make it by the deadline. Umar asked the boy what prompted him to return when he had not sent any spy or an escort to follow him. He said he didn't want people to say that a Muslim had made a vow and failed to fulfil it. Umar then turned to Abu Dhar and asked him what had made him stand up for the boy, mainly when the risk involved was high, as the boy was a total stranger. Abu Dhar replied that he didn't want anybody to say that a Muslim wanted a guarantee, and no Muslim came forward. The two men who lost their father turned emotional. "When there are such honest and pious people in this world, we don't want people to say that a Muslim asked for pardon but couldn't produce one. We would like to forgive the boy." The boy was forgiven. Such was the level of righteousness during the caliphate of Umar.

The righteousness of a poor boy

The great thinker Al Ghazzali records an incident in the life of Caliph Umar. Abdullah Ibn Dinar relates that the Caliph was travelling from Medinah to Makkah. On his way one morning, he noticed a flock of sheep at the base of a hillock. A Negro boy, who was an enslaved individual of a shepherd, was leading the flock. During his travels, Umar would always talk to village inhabitants to ascertain their standard of righteousness and character, as it would help him understand the spiritual health of the kingdom. He asked the boy if he could sell him one sheep. The boy answered an emphatic no without batting his eyelids or pausing for even a moment. "But why?" asked the Caliph. Because the flock belonged to the owner, and he was just a labourer doing his job to earn his bread. "It is my master's, and I am his enslaved individual!" "What's wrong with selling it?" asked the Caliph with his eyes fixed on the boy's innocent face. "Take this money and give that sheep to me, and go and tell your master that a wolf snatched away his sheep." The words chilled the boy. He was appalled and shocked at the treacherous suggestion. He was susceptible to the divine retribution that would befall him for the evil act. He stared hard at the Caliph and eyed him with deep suspicion. The poor fellow did not know whom he was staring at. He gazed at the crest of the hill, and it conjured in his mind the sight of his master. His tone changed and became more arduous. "I can cheat my master over there on the other side of the hill. But can I deceive that Great Master who is seeing both of us and listening to our entire conversation?" the boy exploded. Umar could not hold back his tears when he heard this answer from the boy and remembered the Qur'anic verse: "We verily created man, and We know what his soul whispereth to him, and We are nearer to him than his jugular vein." (Q50:16) Tenderly he asked the boy to lead him to his world master, the owner of the flock. On meeting him, the Caliph enquired how much he had paid for this enslaved person." So much," replied the owner! "Here is that much. Take it and set the boy free," said Umar. What an immense satisfaction Umar must have derived from this profound experience. He paid the amount and freed the boy. He said to him, "This word freed you in this life, and I hope it will free you in the Hereafter." *(Al-Ghazali, Ihya' vol. 4, p. 396)*

The boy was illiterate and had never read the Qur'an. But he was aware of its teachings and the grave implications of dishonesty. A believer must always consider this question, "Where is God?" God is not far away; God is not at a distance. God is not unaware of what we do. God knows everything, and He sees everything. The more we have this faith in our hearts and minds, the more we will do the right deeds, and the more we will be at peace with ourselves and others. The Qur'an says, "We verily created a man, and We know what his soul whispereth to him, and We are nearer to him than his jugular vein."

No substitute for good people

In one of the homes of Medinah, Umar was sitting with a group of his Companions. He asked them, "Make a wish. What is your greatest wish in this world?"

One of them replied, "I wish to have as much gold as would fill this whole house so that I could spend it all for the sake of Allah."

Umar did not pay much attention to this response and then again asked another companion to make a wish. What is your dearest wish in this world?"

The Companion said, "I wish this house were full of jewels and pearls so that I could spend it all for the sake of Allah."

Yet again, Umar did not give much attention to this reply and asked for the third time, "Make a wish! What is your greatest wish?"

Frustrated, his Companions said, "We don't know what to say (what do you mean), O leader of the believers."

Thereupon Umar replied:

"I wish this house was full of men, like Abu 'Ubaydah Ibn Al-Jarraah, Mu'aadh ibn Jabal and Saalim who worked for Abu Hudhayfah (names of some of the Companions who died in the service of Islam) to use them to spread the word of Allah."

Umar understood the value of people who had a sense of mission and purpose. Men and women who will carry the banner of Islam, be bearers of the message and be unwavering in their dedication and commitment to moving Islam forward. Because no amount of gold or silver can replace people, no amount of money can replace "among the believers (those who) are true to what they have promised (to) Allah [...]" (Q 33:23).

He also made the same point when he sent Abdullah ibn Mas'ud to teach the people of Kufa. He said to them, "I have given preference to you over myself in sending Abdullah to you."

Religious tolerance

The greatness of Caliph Umar is apparent from his sympathetic treatment of his non-Muslim subjects. Before the advent of Islam, the rights of other races in the Roman and Persian Empires were worse than those of enslaved individual people. Even the Syrian Christians had no right over their lands, so much so that they were transferred with the transfer of their land. When Umar conquered these countries, he returned the lands to their tillers, who were primarily non-Muslims. According to Imam Shafi, once, when a Muslim murdered a Christian, he was brought to the notice, which allowed the heirs of the Christian to avenge the murder, and the Muslim was beheaded. He consulted non-Muslims in State matters. Their voice carried much weight in the handling of affairs concerning them. The Caliph had been too indulgent to non-Muslims and even pardoned their treasons, which no present-day civilized government could tolerate. These unusual sympathies of the conquerors so much moved the non-Muslims that they sided with them in preference to their co-religionists. The Christians and Jews of Hems prayed for the return of Muslims.

The Caliph, no doubt, imposed *jizyah,* a protection tax on the non-Muslims, but such tax was not realised by those non-Muslims who joined the Muslim army. Abu Ubayda, the Commander-in-Chief of Muslim forces in Syria, returned the *jizyah* realised from the inhabitants of Hems when he had to withdraw his garrison from Hems due to an emergency. Therefore, he could not take responsibility for their protection. The people of Jarjema refused to pay the *jizyah* because they had enlisted in the Muslim army.

He demonstrated justice in defining the rights and privileges of non-Muslims, an example of which is the next contract with the Christians of Jerusalem:

"This is the protection the servant of God, 'Umar, the Ruler of the Believers, has granted to the people of Eiliya [Jerusalem]. The protection is for their lives and properties, churches and crosses, sick and healthy, and co-religionists. Their churches shall not be used for habitation, nor shall they be demolished, nor shall any injury be done to them or their compounds, or their crosses, nor shall their properties be injured. There shall be no compulsion for these people in religion, nor shall any of them suffer any injury on account of religion. Whatever is written herein is under the covenant of God and the responsibility of His Messenger, of the Caliphs and the believers, and shall hold good as long as they pay *jizyah* [the tax for their defence] imposed on them."

Those non-Muslims who took part in defence with the Muslims were exempted from paying *jizyah,* and when the Muslims had to retreat from a city whose non-Muslim citizens had paid this tax for their defence, the tax was returned to the non-Muslims. The public treasury and the zakat funds provided for the old, poor, and disabled Muslims and non-Muslims.

Non-Muslims did not perform a military duty; instead, they paid tribute. They were given jurisdiction over their canon law, a sort of partial autonomy. Those who took part in the defence of the Islamic State were exempted from paying *jizyah*. If the Muslim army had to retreat from a city whose non-Muslim citizens had paid their tax for their defence, the tax was duly returned to them. The tale of the Christian tribe of Banu Taghlib (Christian Arabs) is remarkable in this respect. The Muslim commander Waleed pressed them to recant their faith. Umar was displeased with his actions and instructed: *"Leave them in the profession of the gospel."* The tribe sent a delegation to Umar to request that they be allowed to pay double the zakat (*sadaqa*h) instead of the poll tax as they were too proud to pay the taxes of the 'uncircumcised.' The Caliph allowed them to pay double the amount of zakat and that they not christen their children.

Umar's strictness with family

What was especially astonishing about Umar was his integrity. It is a weakness that bleeds the most astute statesman into an empty shell if unchecked. He issued strict orders that no family member should accept any gift. Hence, Umar found a new carpet with his wife, Atika. He wanted to know where the rug had come from. She said that Abu Musa Ashari, the Governor of Basra, had presented it. Umar had the carpet immediately returned to Abu Musa. Abu Musa was reprimanded in solid terms for sending a gift to the wife of the Caliph.

'Abdullah, the son of Umar, purchased some camels. They were lean and were bought at a very cheap price. 'Abdullah sent these camels to the state pasture where they were fattened. These were then sold in the market and fetched a high price. When this was brought to Umar's notice, he ordered that as the camels had been fed at the state pasture, whatever profit had accrued in the sale of the camels should be deposited in the state treasury.

Once, Umar saw a small girl who was lean, thin, and bony. Umar enquired who the girl was. 'Abdullah, the son of Umar, said that she was his daughter and that she had lost weight because, with the allowance that Umar allowed to his family, nourishing food could not be provided. Umar said he was giving them what he gave to other families, but he could not offer his family anything more than what he did to other families.

Once 'Abdullah and 'Ubaidullah, two sons of Umar, went to Basra. There, they obtained a loan from Abu Musa on the condition that the amount be paid to the state treasury at Medinah. With this amount, they purchased some merchandise and sold it at Medinah.

They earned a considerable profit, which they kept for themselves and credited the principal amount in the state treasury. When Umar knew of this transaction, he wanted his sons to credit the entire profit to the state treasury as the money with which they had traded state money. 'Abdullah kept quiet, but 'Ubaidullah protested. He said that the state would not have shared a loss if there had been a loss. Umar stuck to his decision, but 'Ubaidullah protested again. Some other Companions intervened and decided it should be treated as a partnership case. Umar allowed his sons to retain half of the profit and deposit the other half in the state treasury.

Once Umar received a considerable quantity of musk. It had to be weighed and then distributed. Umar was searching for a person who could weigh musk with meticulous care. Atika, Umar's wife, offered to do so as she was an expert on the job. Umar did not accept the offer on the ground that when she weighed and distributed it, some musk would be attached to her hands and clothes, which would be a misappropriation of in-state property.

Once, Umm Kulthum, a wife of Umar, purchased perfume for one dirham and sent it as a gift to the Byzantine empress. The Byzantine empress returned the empty vials of perfume filled with gems. When Umar came to know of this, he sold the jewels. Out of the sale proceeds, he handed over one dirham to his wife, and the rest was deposited into the state treasury.

Once, some gifts were received in the Baitul Mal. Hafsa waited on Umar and wanted a share. Umar said:

"Dear, you have a share in my personal property, but I cannot give you a special share out of the property belonging to the Muslims. You can get only what other Muslims get."

His son-in-law once waited on him and wanted assistance from the Baitul Mal. Umar paid him some money from his pocket and did not give him anything from the Baitul Mal.

Once after distribution, a lady's scarf was found in surplus. The custodian of the Baitul Mal suggested that this might be offered to Umm Kulthum, Umar's wife. Umar said: "No. Present it to Umm Salit, the lady who carried the water skin on her back on the day of the battle of Uhud to distribute water among the Muslim warriors."

Once, after accounting, one dirham was found surplus in the Baitul Mal. The treasurer gave the dirham to a minor son of Umar. When Umar came to know of that, he had the dirham returned immediately.

'Abdullah, a son of Umar, fought in the battle of Jalaula. He got his share of the spoils and sold it on the spot. This fetched a high value. When Umar knew of that, he said he was allowed the high price because people thought he was the Caliph's son. He ordered that the profit earned beyond the market value be credited to the state treasury.

One of Umar's sons drank wine inadvertently in Egypt. He submitted himself voluntarily to the punishment of 80 stripes in Egypt. Umar was not satisfied. He called the boy to Medinah and flogged him to death. When the boy was on his deathbed, Umar said to him, "When you meet the Holy Prophet, tell him that Umar is following his injunctions strictly."

It is not a private matter for individuals but is both private and public. It permeates the whole fabric of society and covers not only rituals, beliefs, and ethics but also a detailed code of conduct covering every aspect of life, art, politics, hygiene, dress, and diet.

The archangel Gabriel asked Muhammad about three increasingly higher and deeper levels of religiosity. The Prophet answered sequentially, saying Islam (whole-hearted submission to God), faith, and loveliness (*Ihsan*). This third quality the Prophet identified as worshipping God as if we could see the Divine, and if we cannot, to always remember that God nevertheless sees us.

The sequence is fascinating, as it reveals that what we think of as Islam (the attestation to Divine Unity, the performance of the prayers, the pilgrimage to Makkah, the paying of the alms tax, the fast of Ramadan, mark only the very first layer - though the foundational layer - of religiosity. Above that is faith, and above is the spiritual and mystical layer of spiritual beauty, for Ihsan is the realm of actualizing and realizing beauty and loveliness (husn), bringing beauty into this world and connecting it to God, who is the All-Beautiful.

Throughout Islamic history, this realm of *Ihsan* was pursued vehemently by the mystics of Islam, the Sufis. Historically, this mystical realm of Islam formed a powerful companion to the legal dimension of Islam *(shari'*a). Indeed, many of the mystics of Islam were also masters of legal and theological realms. The cultivation of inward beauty and outward righteous action was linked with many critical Islamic institutions. In comparing Islam with Judaism, the mystical dimension of Islam was much more prominently widespread than Kabbalah. And unlike the Christian tradition, the mysticism of Islam was not cloistered in monasteries. Sufis were - and remain - social and political agents who sought the Divine in the very midst of humanity.

Here are a few episodes from Umar's life that give us glimpses of the nobility of this great exemplar of justice.

Umar picks a milkmaid as a daughter-in-law.

Caliph Umar used to sneak out of his palace at night to mingle, in disguise, with ordinary people and learn what they were thinking. One night, Umar moved through his capital with his aide Ibn Abbas. They walked from one settlement to another till they came to a locality inhabited by impoverished families. While passing by a small hutment, Umar overheard a quarrel in a house, and he could guess that trouble was brewing inside. He stopped and overheard the conversation.

The mother was insisting that her daughter adulterate the milk by adding water. She said the money they earned by selling their milk was not enough to sustain them. She recounted that when she was young, she would add water to milk to boost her profits. She insisted that it was the only way they could increase their income.

The girl was taken aback at her mother's arrogance. She baulked at this preposterous suggestion and retorted: "That was when you were not a Muslim. Now that we are Muslims, we cannot do it. Dishonesty is a heinous offence."

The mother stood unmoved and was in no mood to relent. She stuck to her stand, saying Islam did not prevent her from doing business the way she wanted.

The daughter was equally determined and stood her ground. She tried her best to dissuade her mother from this evil plan. "Have you forgotten the Caliph's order? He has prohibited selling milk mixed with water."

The mother was stubborn. "But the Caliph does not know us; we are so poor, how else can we earn our bread?"

The daughter was annoyed. "I cannot practice deception. This income will be unlawful. It will violate the Caliph's mandate. I can't think of such dishonesty."

The mother tried to counsel her, "But how will the Caliph or any of his officers know about it? You are foolish; you do not know how to do business. From tomorrow, I will manage it myself. I do not need you anymore."

The girl remained stubborn. "But remember, I will not allow you to do it. I will respect my conscience and will resist your bad intentions. I can't be dishonest to my Caliph. He may not come to know of this dishonesty, but have you ever thought about Allah, who has His eyes on every speck of the earth?"

Sensing the rebellious mood of her daughter, the enraged mother put off the discussion. She turned off the lamp, and both went to sleep.

Umar spent a restless night mulling over the daughter's conversation with her mother and was heady about his people's high level of righteousness.

In the morning, Umar sent his attendant to purchase milk from the girl. To Umar's utter disbelief, the milk was pure. The girl had kept up her resolve. Umar was overwhelmed by the girl's virtuousness. Tears rolled down his eyes at this rare display of honesty.

Umar turned to his colleague and sighed with a heavy heart. "The girl has defied her mother for the sake of Allah. I recommend a reward for her?"

"We can reward her with cash", replied Ibn Abbas.

Umar found it too inappropriate for such a great virtue. "Such a girl would become a great mother. Her honesty cannot be weighed on a few coins. I shall offer her a reward truly befitting her."

The Caliph invited the daaughter and the mother to his court. The mother trembled as she stood before the mighty ruler, wondering why they had been summoned. But the girl faced the Caliph confidently and with great equanimity. There was an impressive dignity about her.

Umar narrated the entire episode to the audience. He recounted how he had overheard the conversation between the mother and the daughter and how the daughter remained truthful to the commandments of Allah.

Someone suggested that the mother be tasked with misguiding the daughter. The Caliph remarked that ordinarily, he would have upbraided the mother, but he had forgiven her for the sake of her daughter. Turning to the girl, the Caliph said: "Islam needs daughters like you, and as a Caliph of Islam, I feel the best reward I can give you is to own you as a daughter".

The Caliph called his sons and addressed them. He said: "Here is a gem of a girl who would make a great mother. My cherished desire is that one of you should take this girl in wedlock. I cannot think of a better wife than this girl with such sterling character. In matters of wedlock, it should be the character and not worldly status that should count."

Abdullah and Abdur Rahman, the elder sons of the Caliph, were already married. Asim, the third son, was still unmarried. He immediately accepted Umar's offer. With the consent of the milkmaid mother, the marriage was solemnized, and the girl became the daughter-in-law of the legendary Caliph. From this union was born a daughter, Umm Asim, who later became the mother of Umar bin Abdul Aziz. Umar bin Abdul Aziz became a Caliph. Historians consider him one of the greatest caliphs in Islamic rule.

While other caliphs of the Umayyad dynasty revelled in luxury, Umar bin Abdul Aziz followed in Umar's footsteps. If ever there was a noble caliph after the 'rightly guided Caliphs', it was Umar bin Abdul Aziz. By his wise choice of the milkmaid as his daughter-in-law, the Caliph had unknowingly laid the foundation of a great and noble dynasty. We need great mothers if we are to build great nations.

Umar's wife acts as a midwife.

One night, Umar saw a Bedouin sitting outside a tent. As Umar approached him, he heard a groaning sound coming from the tent. Upon inquiry, the man remarked that he was a desert-dweller and his wife was in labour. He had come to Medinah to seek help from the Commander of the Faithful - a title for the Caliph. Umar asked him to relax and leave all his worries to him. The Bedouin was in a daze about the man's identity but was nevertheless at peace with himself." Don't worry, God has answered our prayers," he comforted his wife, who was groaning in pain.

Meanwhile, Umar promptly went home and shared the problem with his wife, Umm Kulthum, who readily offered to accompany him to the tent. She packed food, and they soon reached the tent. Umm Kulthum assisted the woman in labour while Umar made a fire and began cooking a meal for them. After some time, Umm Kulthum cheerfully announced, "O Commander of the Faithful! Congratulate your guest on the birth of a son." The Bedouin was flabbergasted. And in the lady's words, he got a confirmation of the identity of the Caliph. He was transfixed in disbelief. He blessed him in an obsequious tone, turning to Umar, "I am overwhelmed with your benevolence." He broke down. Umar held him and extolled God's mercy, "I thank God that I was able to serve you. Come to me in the morning, and I will find ways to help you further." "God is praised," the Bedouin remarked, "I came to seek Umar, and God sent Umar to seek me." The man's amazement would have been redoubled had he known that the lady who handled the entire midwifery, Umm Kulthum, was the daughter of Fatimah and granddaughter of the Prophet.

A responsible ruler

On one occasion, Umar was walking through the capital when he heard loud and boisterous noises of revelry. Rude songs were echoing in the house. An angry Umar jumped into the house through the chimney. A man and a woman, who Umar knew were not married, and they were drinking and amusing themselves. Umar was furious and wild with rage. He yelled at them: "Do you not fear God that you can commit such great sins?"

The man showed no shame as he remorselessly rattled off a volley of accusations at Umar. "Calm yourself, please, O 'Umar! We confess we have sinned, but what about you; you have committed three. God prohibited spying on people's sins, but you spied. God commanded that people enter houses through their doors, but you jumped in through the chimney. God commanded that people must greet the house dwellers when they enter, but you didn't greet us. The rules that apply to us are meant for you as well. Do you intend to tell us that a Caliph can do no wrong?" There was a note of scorn in the man's voice.

The answer jolted and enraged Umar, who could not comprehend this mood of defiance. Umar went pink on his face. But his sense of restraint prevailed. His senses didn't desert him in his anger. He regained his calm. Umar masked his anger and preferred silence because, as a wise and mature ruler, he knew that silence has its grace, just as speech could be, at times, graceless and ugly. Umar immediately left the house without uttering a word. The couple had transgressed decency limits and deserved a heavy punishment for their obscene acts. But Umar was conscious of his folly. Justice had to be fair and beyond reproach. Umar decided to close the matter and not pursue it any further.

Several months after that incident, Umar happened to cross that man. Umar remembered the whole incident, but he greeted the man usually and quipped:

"Believe me! I have not told anyone what I witnessed months ago".

The man, too, responded politely: "Believe me! I have never committed that sin again".

As a caliph, Umar could have surely avenged his insult. But he bore it patiently. But the man who offended him was overwhelmed by the caliph's response to the incident. He recoiled and immediately reformed himself. This incident demonstrated the fairness of Umar's actions with his citizens.

During one of his patrols, he passes by a house. (Those days' houses didn't have a front yard or back yard or a vast garden or soundproof walls. These were very modest mud-brick buildings. The house is basically composed of a few rooms, and that's it. Hassan Al Basri said the ceiling of the house of Prophet Muhammad (PBUH) could be touched by hand.) So you could hear what was happening inside these houses. Umar bin Khattab is walking very late at night, and he hears women. This woman was reciting the lines of poetry.

Basically, this woman was the wife of a Mujahid. Her husband was away for a very long time, and she felt very lonely. She had no children, and she was staying at home alone. So, she was reciting the lines of poetry.

This night is very, very long, and I have no companion to be with me

If it weren't for Allah, I would have been with another man

So basically, she is saying that if it weren't for Allah, I would have committed Haraam. But then she said but because I fear Allah and because there is an eye that is watching me all the time. If that weren't the case, I would have been with another companion.

Umar Bin Khattab said: May Allah have mercy on you. He wasn't speaking to her, but he was making dua for her.

He then goes to his daughter Hafsa. He knocks on the door. Seeing him, Hafsa said, "Oh, my father, why did you come in this late hour? It must be something very urgent. So he comes and says, "For how long can a woman wait for her husband? How long can she stay alone? How long will her patience last? Hafsa said, "One month, two months, three months and then after four months, her patience runs out."

Umar bin Khattab immediately issued an order that no Muslim soldier should stay away from her wife for more than four months. So, the rotation is for four months.-But there was a problem; many of those soldiers didn't want to come back. You know now, soldiers are crying. They want to go back to mom and dad. I want to go back to my girlfriend. They are weeping. They are crying. But none of the soldiers who were fighting for Fisabillilah wanted to go back. So Umar bin Khattab had to force them. He sent some orders. He said, "You either go back, or I am going to exempt you. But you have to give nafaka to your wives; you have to provide her with sufficient money so that she won't be in any need. Otherwise, you divorce.

These are the teachings that show the care that Umar bin Khattab had for the Muslim family. He was eager to make sure that men and women were happy and that children were so glad.

The spirit of conquest under ʿUmar I

Abū Bakr's successor in Medina, ʿUmar I (ruled 634–644), had not so much to stimulate conquest as to organize and channel it. He chose as leaders skilful managers experienced in trade and commerce as well as warfare and imbued with an ideology that provided their activities with a cosmic significance. The total numbers involved in the initial conquests may have been relatively small, perhaps less than 50,000, divided into numerous shifting groups. Yet few actions took place without any sanction from the Medinan government or one of its appointed commanders. The fighters, or *muqātilah*, could generally accomplish much more with Medina's support than without. ʿUmar, one of Muhammad's earliest and staunchest supporters, had quickly developed an administrative system of manifestly superior effectiveness. He defined the *ummah* as a continually expansive polity managed by a new ruling elite, which included successful military commanders like Khālid ibn al-Walīd. Even after the conquests ended, this sense of expansiveness continued to be expressed in the way Muslims divided the world into their zone, the Dār al-Islām, and the zone into which they could and should expand, the Dār al-Ḥarb, the abode of war. Islam supplied the norms of ʿUmar's new elite as it was then understood. Taken together, Muhammad's revelations from God and his Sunnah (precedent-setting example) defined the cultic and personal practices that distinguished Muslims from others:

prayer, fasting, pilgrimage, charity, avoidance of pork and intoxicants, membership in one community centred at Mecca, and activism (jihad) on the community's behalf.

Forging the link of activism with faithfulness

'Umar symbolized this conception of the *ummah* in two ways. He assumed an additional title, *amīr al-mu'minīn* ("commander of the faithful"), which linked organized activism with faithfulness (*īmān*), the earliest defining feature of the Muslim. He also adopted a lunar calendar that began with the emigration (Hijrah), the moment at which a group of individual followers of Muhammad had become an active social presence. Because booty was the *ummah*'s primary resource, 'Umar concentrated on ways to distribute and sustain it. He established a *dīwān*, or register, to pay all members of the ruling elite and the conquering forces, from Muhammad's family on down, in order to enter into the *ummah*. The immovable booty was kept for the state. After the government's fifth share of the movable booty was reserved, the rest was distributed according to the *dīwān*. The *muqātilah* he stationed as an occupying army in garrisons (*amṣār*) constructed in locations strategic to further conquest: al-Fusṭāṭ in Egypt, Damascus in Syria, Kūfah and Basra in Iraq. The garrisons attracted the indigenous population and initiated significant demographic changes, such as a population shift from northern to southern Iraq. They also inaugurated the rudiments of an "Islamic" daily life; each garrison was commanded by a caliphal appointee, responsible for setting aside an area for prayer, a mosque (*masjid*) named for the prostrations (*sujūd*) that had become a characteristic element in the five daily worship sessions (*ṣalāt*s). There, the fighters could hear God's revelations to Muhammad, which were recited by men trained in that emerging art. The most pious might commit the whole to memory. There, too, the Friday midday *ṣalāt* could be performed communally, accompanied by an essential educational device, the sermon (*khuṭbah*), through which the fighters could be instructed in the principles of the faith. The mosque fused the practical and the spiritual uniquely. Because the Friday prayer included an expression of loyalty to the ruler, it could also provide an opportunity to declare rebellion.

The series of ongoing conquests that fueled this system had their most extensive phase under 'Umar and his successor 'Uthmān ibn 'Affān (ruled 644–656). Within 25 years, Muslim Arab forces created the first empire to link western Asia with the Mediterranean permanently. Within another century, Muslim conquerors surpassed the achievement of Alexander the Great, not only in the durability of their accomplishment but in their scope as well, reaching from the Iberian Peninsula to Central Asia. Resistance was generally slight and nondestructive, and conquest through capitulation was preferred to conquest by force. After Sāsānian Al-Ḥīrah fell in 633, a large Byzantine force was defeated in Syria, opening the way to the final conquest of Damascus in 636. The following year, further gains were made in Sāsānian territory, especially at the Battle of al-Qādisiyyah, and in the next, the focus returned to Syria and the taking of Jerusalem. By 640, Roman control in Syria was over, and by 641, the Sāsānians had lost all their territory west of the Zagros. During the years 642 to 646, Egypt was taken under the leadership of 'Amr ibn al-'Āṣ, who soon began raids into what the Muslims called the Maghrib, the lands west of Egypt. Shortly after that, in the east, Persepolis fell; in 651, the defeat and assassination of the last Sāsānian emperor, Yazdegerd III, marked the end of the 400-year-old Sāsānian empire.

After the battle of Nihawand, many Persians, men, women, and children were taken as captives by the Muslims. The captives were sold as slaves. One of these slaves was Firoz alias Abu Lulu. He was purchased by Mughirah Shu'bah the Governor of Basra. This Firoz was a craftsman, a carpenter, an iron smith and a painter. Umar did not allow non-Muslim adult captives to reside in Madina. Mughirah sought special permission for the residence of Firoz in Madina on the ground that as he was a skilled craftsman, he would be of service to the people. Umar gave the permission as a special case.

One day, Firoz waited on Umar and complained that the tax which his master Mughirah was exacting from him was too high. He wanted the Caliph to reduce the levy. Umar enquired what work did he do. He said that he worked as a carpenter, painter, and an ironsmith. He added that he could make windmills as well. Umar next enquired as to the amount of the tax that he was required to pay to his master. He said that he had to pay two dirhams a day. Umar said that keeping in view the lucrative nature of the jobs done by him, the levy of two dirhams a day was prima facie not excessive. Umar said that he would, however, write to Mughirah, and examine the question further in the light of what Mughirah said. That did not satisfy Firoz, and he went away sulking.

Umar wrote to Mughirah, and in reply Mughirah quoted facts and figures to establish that what he took from his slave was by no means excessive. When Firoz called on Umar again, Umar explained to him that as the levy was not excessive, no reduction therein was called for that made Firoz angry. In order to humor Firoz, Umar said, "I understand you make windmills; make one for me as well." In a sullen mood, Firoz said, "Verily I will make such a mill for you, that the world would talk about it." As Firoz went away, the Caliph told the people around him that the Persian slave had threatened him.

There were Persian children slaves in Madina. Seeing them, Firoz would say, "You have been enslaved at such a tender age. This Umar sees eaten my heart. I will take his heart out". He made for himself a dagger with a very sharp edge and smeared it with poison.

On the 1st of November 644 A.D. at the time of the morning prayer, Firoz went with his dagger to the Prophet's mosque and hid himself in a corner in one of the recesses of the mosque. When the faithful stood for prayer after straightening the lines, and Umar took up his position as the Imam to lead the prayer, Firoz emerged from his place of hiding and rushed at Umar. Firoz struck Umar six consecutive blows with his dagger, and Umar fell on the floor profusely bleeding.

Other persons rushed at Firoz, but he had the fury and frenzy of a desperate man about him. He struck right and left, and thirteen Muslims were wounded, some of them fatally, before Firoz could be overpowered. At last realizing that he could not escape, Firoz stabbed himself to death with his own dagger.

Umar's death

The second Rashidun caliph, Umar ibn al-Khattab, was assassinated in 644 CE while leading morning prayers in the Masjid al Nabawi in Medina:

- **Assassination**

Umar was stabbed six times by a Persian slave named Abu Lu'lu'a Firuz, who was angered by a personal quarrel.

- **Death**

Umar died three days later.

- **Burial**

Umar is buried in the Prophet's Mosque in Medina, alongside Muhammad and Abu Bakr.

- **Successor**

Before he died, Umar appointed a six-man council to select his successor, who chose Uthman ibn Affan.

Umar was a strong ruler and a major figure in the early Islamic community. He is known for establishing many of the Muslim state's political institutions, stabilizing the Arab empire, and creating the Islamic calendar.

Umar's legacy

The achievements of Umar ibn al Khattab are all the more remarkable considering that he lacked the advantage of birth, nobility or wealth that some of the other Companions enjoyed. He was born into the tribe of Bani 'Adi, a poorer cousin amongst the Quraish. In his own words, before he accepted Islam, he was at various times a petty merchant and a shepherd who would often lose his sheep. From such humble beginnings, he rose to weld together an empire greater in extent than either that of Rome or Persia, governed it with Solomon's wisdom, and administered it with Joseph's sagacity.

Umar's life requires but few lines to sketch. Simplicity and duty were his guiding principles, and impartiality and devotion were the leading features of his administration. Responsibility so weighed upon him that he was heard to exclaim, "O that my mother had not borne me; would that I had been this stalk of grass instead!" In his early life, he had a fiery and impatient temper, and he was known, even in the later days of the Prophet, as the stern advocate of vengeance. Ever ready to unsheathe the sword, it was he that at Bedr advised that the prisoners should all be put to death. But age, as well as office, had now mellowed this asperity. His sense of justice was strong. And except it is the treatment of Khalid, whom, according to some accounts, he pursued with an ungenerous resentment, no act of tyranny or injustice is recorded against him, and even in this matter, his enmity took its rise in Khalid's evil treatment of a fallen foe. The choice of his captains and governors was free from favouritism and [with only a few exceptions] singularly fortunate. The various tribes and bodies in the empire, representing the most diverse interests, reposed in his integrity and implicit confidence, and his strong arm maintained the discipline of law and empire. A particular weakness is discernible in his change of governors at the factious seats of Al-Basra and Al-Kufa. Yet even there, the conflicting jealousies of Bedawin and Koreish were kept by him in check, and he never dared disturb Islam till he had passed away. The more distinguished of the Companions he kept by him at Medina, partly, no doubt, to strengthen his counsels and partly (as he would say) from an unwillingness to lower their dignity by placing them in office subordinate to himself.

Whip in hand, he would perambulate the streets and markets of Medina, ready to punish offenders on the spot, and so the proverb,—"'Umar's whip is more terrible than another's sword." But with all this, he was tender-hearted, and numberless acts of kindness were recorded of him, such as relieving the wants of the widow and the fatherless. (190-191)The Shi'a, however, believe that he usurped authority that properly belonged to Ali ibn Abi Talib. Sunni and Shi'a hold diametrically opposite views of Umar. However, for the majority of Muslims, he is a revered and highly respected figure whose role in consolidating Islam, expanding the Caliphate territorially, combining the Qur'an's collection into a canon and laying down ground rules for the science of *hadith* were all crucially essential aspects of Islam's development as a religious-social-political system or comprehensive way of life. He is equally remembered for his piety and simple lifestyle. Many see him as third in merit, after Muhammad and Abu Bakr. He carried the responsibilities of power with humility. Although he had a reputation for recklessness, he governed wisely and with a strong sense of justice. The system he helped to create gave stability to the lives of countless people, resulting in the flourishing of Islamic civilization. It gave a strong sense that all activities must be acceptable to God, of whose presence people should be conscious at all times, for the whole world is a mosque. His view of the ruler's role remains relevant throughout the Islamic world today.

Throughout this remarkable expansion, 'Umar closely controlled general policy and laid down the principles for administering the conquered lands. The structure of the later Islamic empire, including legal practice, is largely due to him. 'Umar established the *dīwān* (a register of warriors' pensions that over time evolved into a powerful governmental body), inaugurated the Islamic Hijrī calendar, and created the office of the qadi (judge). He also established the garrison cities of Al-Fusṭāṭ in Egypt and Basra and Kūfah in Iraq.

The second Caliph after the Prophet Muhammad, upon him be peace and blessings, 'Umar ibn al-Khattab has a world-wide reputation for justice and simple life-style despite ruling a very vast area stretching from Abyssinia to Caucasia and from Egypt to Afghanistan. Every year during the Hajj season he summoned his governors to Makka and questioned the inhabitants of the cities about their governors. In one Hajj season, the inhabitants of Hims (Emessa) in Syria complained about their governor, Sa'id ibn 'Amir, and said: 'We have four complaints about him. First: He comes to his office late in the morning. Second: He does not attend to our wants at night. Third: He never comes out among us one day a week. Fourth: He sometimes loses his senses and almost goes mad.' 'Umar sent for the governor. When he came, he questioned him about the complaints of the people in their presence.

The governor explained the reason why he came to his office late in the morning:

It is not proper to explain it, but since you want me to, I consent to do it: I do not have any servants and my wife is ill. I knead the dough myself and make the bread, and only after doing other work at home am I able to leave for my office.

In answer to the second complaint of the people, the governor said:

Although it is not proper to explain this either, I will explain it since you want me to. I spend all my day among them to attend to their work and needs. When it is night, shall I not worship my Lord and accuse myself before Him for what I did during the long day?

The third complaint of the people was that Sa'id ibn 'Amir stayed at home one day a week and did not come out among the people. The governor answered that complaint:

As I said before, I do not have any servants and my wife is ill. I have only one suit of clothes and wash it on that day. That is why I cannot go out among them one day in the week.

The last complaint was that the governor sometimes lost his senses and almost went mad. The explanation was as follows:

'Umar, may God be pleased with him, was content with his governor's conduct and gave him one thousand gold pieces to meet his needs. However, the pious, righteous governor turned to his wife and said: 'Let us spend this for a day when we will need it more than at any other time. Let us distribute it among those poorer than us.'

The governor handed the gold pieces to one among his family to distribute them among the poor, which he did.

Almost all the governors of Caliph 'Umar were of a like quality in belief, conduct and understanding of administration. God-fearing, piety and righteousness were the lights by which they made their decisions and conducted their lives. It was the golden age in human history, or 'the Happy Time' as it is called in Islamic tradition.

Umar ibn al-Khattab's contributions

Umar ibn al-Khattab ibn Nufayl ibn `Abd al-`Uzza ibn Rayyah, *Shaykh al-Islam*, *Amir al-Mu'minin*, Abu Hafs al-Qurashi al-`Adawi al-Faruq (d. 23). Among the Companions who narrated from him: `Ali, Ibn Mas`ud, Ibn `Abbas, Abu Hurayra, and especially his son Ibn `Umar upon whose narrations Malik relied in his *Muwatta'*. He was described as fair-skinned with some reddishness, tall with a large build, fast-paced, and a skilled fighter and horseman. He embraced Islam after having fought it, in the year 6 of the Prophethood, at age twenty-seven. This was the result of the Prophet's explicit supplication: "O Allah! Strengthen Islam with `Umar ibn al-Khattab." In his time Islam entered Egypt, Syria, Sijistan, Persia, and other regions. He died a martyr, stabbed in the back while at prayer by a Sabean or Zoroastrian slave, at sixty-six years of age.

`Umar al-Faruq was second only to Abu Bakr al-Siddiq in closeness to and approval from the Prophet. The latter said: "I have two ministers from the inhabitants of the heaven and two ministers from the inhabitants of the earth. The former are Jibril and Mika'il, and the latter are Abu Bakr and `Umar." He said of the latter: "These two are [my] hearing and eyesight" and instructed the Companions: "Follow those that come after me: Abu Bakr and `Umar."

`Umar was given the gift of true inspiration which is the characteristic of Allah's Friends named *kashf* or "unveiling." The Prophet said: "In the nations long before you were people who were spoken to [by the angels] although they were not prophets. If there is anyone of them in my Community, truly it is `Umar ibn al-Khattab." This narration is elucidated by the two narrations whereby "Allah has engraved truth on the tongue of `Umar and his heart" and "If there were a Prophet after me verily it would be `Umar." Al-Tirmidhi said that according to Ibn `Uyayna "spoken to" *(muhaddathûn)* means "made to understand" *(mufahhamûn)*, while in his narration Muslim added: "Ibn Wahb explained 'spoken to' as 'inspired' *(mulham)*." This is the majority's opinion according to Ibn Hajar who said: "'Spoken to' means 'by the angels'." Al-Nawawi and Ibn Hajar said respectively in *Sharh Sahih Muslim* and *Fath al-Bari*:

The scholars have differed concerning "spoken to." Ibn Wahb said it meant "inspired" *(mulham)*. It was said also: "Those who are right, and when they give an opinion it is as if they were spoken to, and then they give their opinion. It was said also: "The angels speak to them..." Bukhari said: "Truth comes from their tongues." This hadith contains a confirmation of the miracles of the saints *(karâmât al-awliya)*.

The one among [Muslims] who is "spoken to," if his existence is ascertained, what befalls him is not used as basis for a legal judgment, rather he is obliged to evaluate it with the Qur'an, and if it conforms to it or to the Sunna, he acts upon it, otherwise he leaves it.

A claim was raised that since the hadith states "If there is anyone in my Umma, it is `Umar," it must follow that at most the number of such inspired people is at most one, namely `Umar. Ibn Hajar replied to this with the reminder that it is wrong to think that other Communities had many but this Community only one. Thus what is meant by the hadith is the perfection of the quality of *ilhâm* û inspiration û in `Umar, not its lack in other Muslims, and Allah knows best.

`Umar also had the unique distinction of having his views confirmed by the revelation in the Holy Qur'an: He said three things which were confirmed by subsequent revelations:

I concurred with my Lord in three matters: I said to the Prophet: "O Messenger of Allah! Why do we not pray behind Ibrahim's Station?" Whereupon was revealed the verse: ". . . Take as your place of worship the place where Ibrahim stood (to pray). . ." (2:125); I said: "O Messenger of Allah! You should order your wives to cover because both the chaste and the wicked go in to see them," whereupon was revealed the verse: "... And when you ask of them (the wives of the Prophet) anything, ask it of them from behind a curtain. . ." (33:53) Then the Prophet's wives banded together in their jealousy over him, so I said to them: "It may happen that his Lord, if he divorce you, will give him instead wives better than you, [submissive (to Allah), believing, pious, penitent, inclined to fasting, widows and maids]." (67:5) Whereupon was revealed that verse.

He was unique in his power of separating truth from falsehood and the Prophet conferred on him the title of *al-Fârûq*, saying: "In truth, the devil certainly parts ways with *(layafruqu min)* `Umar." He memorized Sura al-Baqara in twelve years, and when he had learned it completely he slaughtered a camel. Imam Malik stated that on his suggestion the words "I testify that Muhammad is the messenger of Allah" were added to the *adhân,* and likewise the words "Prayer is better than Sleep" to the *adhân* for the dawn prayer. However, the more correct report is that it is

Bilal who first inserted the latter formula in the call to the dawn prayer and the Prophet retained it.

`Umar ibn al-Khattab was the first Muslim ruler to establish a Public Treasury; the first Muslim ruler to levy a customs duty named `ushr`; the first Muslim ruler to organize a census; the first Muslim ruler to strike coins; the first Muslim ruler to organize a system of canals for irrigation; and the first Muslim ruler to formally organize provinces, cities, and districts. He established the system of guest-houses and rest-houses on major routes to and from major cities. He established schools throughout the land and allocated liberal salaries for teachers. He was the first to prohibit *mut`a* or temporary marriage, according to the Prophet's earlier prohibition. He was the first to place the law of inheritance on a firm basis. He was the first to establish trusts, and the first ruler in history to separate the judiciary from the executive.

He took pains to provide effective and speedy justice for the people. He set up an effective system of judicial administration under which justice was administered according to the principles of Islam. Qadis or judges were appointed at all administrative levels for the administration of justice and were chosen for their integrity and learning in Islamic law. High salaries were paid to them and they were appointed from the among the wealthy and those of high social standing so as not to be influenced by the social position of any litigants. The qadis were not allowed to engage in trade.

From time to time, `Umar used to issue firmans or edicts laying down the principles for the administration of justice. One of his firmans read:

Glory to Allah! Verily Justice is an important obligation to Allah and to man. You have been charged with this responsibility. Discharge this responsibility so that you may win the approbation of Allah and the good will of the people. Treat the people equally in your presence, and in your decisions, so that the weak despair not of justice, and the high-placed harbor no hope of favoritism. The onus of proof lies on the plaintiff, while the party who denies must do so on oath. Compromise is permissible, provided that it does not turn the unlawful into something lawful, and the lawful into something unlawful. Let nothing prevent you from changing your previous decision if after consideration you feel that the previous decision was incorrect. When you are in doubt about a question and find nothing concerning it in the Qur'an or the Sunna of the Prophet, ponder the question over and over again. Ponder over the precedents and analogous cases, and then decide by analogy. A term should be fixed for the person who wants to produce witnesses. If he proves his case, discharge for him his right. Otherwise the suit should be dismissed. All Muslims are trustworthy, except those who have been punished with flogging, those who have borne false witness, or those of doubtful integrity.

One day Abu Musa al-Ash`ari, the governor of Basra at the time, wrote to `Umar complaining that the ordinances, instructions, and letters from the Caliph were undated and therefore gave rise to problems linked to the sequence of their implementation. Because of this and other similar problems of undatedness, `Umar convened an assembly of scholars and advisors to consider the question of calendar reforms. The deliberations of this assembly resulted in the combined opinion that Muslims should have a calendar of their own. The point that was next considered was from when should the new Muslim calendar era begin. Some suggested that the era should begin from the birth of the Prophet while others suggested that it should begin from the time of his death. `Ali suggested that the era should begin from the date the Muslims migrated from Mecca to Madina, and this was agreed upon. The next question considered was the month from which the new era should start. Some suggested that it should start from the month of Rabi` al-Awwal, some from Rajab, others from Ramadan, others from Dhu al-Hijja. `Uthman suggested that the new era should start from the month of Muharram because that was the first month in the Arabic calendar of that time. This was agreed upon. Since the Migration had taken place in the month of Rabi` al-Awwal, two months and eight days after the first of Muharram that year, the date was pushed back by two months and eight days, and the new *Hijri* calendar began with the first day of Muharram in the year of the Migration rather than from the actual date of the Migration.

`Umar was the first Muslim ruler to levy `*ushr*, the Customs or Import Duty. It was levied on the goods of the traders of other countries who chose to trade in the Muslim dominions, at up to 10% of the goods imported and on a reciprocal basis. `*Ushr* was levied in a way to avoid hardships, and only on merchandise meant for sale, not goods imported for consumption or for personal use. Goods valued at two hundred dirhams or less were not subject to `*ushr*. Instructions were issued to the officials that no personal luggage was to be searched, and `*ushr* was applied only to goods that were declared as being for the purpose of trade. The rate varied for Muslim and non-Muslim citizens of the Muslim dominions. If the former imported goods for the purpose of trade, they paid a lower rate of `*ushr*: 2+ % , that is, the same rate as for *zakât*. Hence, this was regarded as part of the *zakât* and not as a separate tax. *Dhimmi*s or non-Muslim citizens of the Muslim dominions who imported goods for the purpose of trade paid a `*ushr* of 5%. In order to avoid double taxation, it was established that if the `*ushr* had been paid once on imported goods, and then these goods were subsequently taken abroad and then brought back into the Muslim dominions within the same year, no additional `*ushr* was to be levied on such re-imported goods.

NOTES

Adhan: Ritual call to prayer. It consists of three iterations of "God is the greatest" followed by two repetitions each of "I witness that there is no god but God," "I witness that Muhammad is the messenger of God," "Come to prayer," "Come to prosperity," and "God is the greatest." At the end, "There is no god but God" is repeated.

Ahl al-Kitab: Qur'anic term referring to Jews, Christians, and Sabaeans as possessors of books previously revealed by God. They are sometimes applied to Zoroastrians, Magians, and Samaritans. The books associated with Jews and Christians are the *Torah*, Psalms, and Gospels, all of which are recognized by the *Qur'an* as God's revelation. However, the *Qur'an* declares that they were repealed and superseded by Muhammad 's book since they were corrupted. The *Qur'an* recognizes the unique relationship of Jews with God. It grants both Jews and Christians a special legal status in Muslim communities as dhimmis (protected scriptural minorities), permitting them to practice their faith, defend themselves from external aggressions, and govern their communities in return for paying a special tax (jizyah). Many twentieth-century scholars are concerned that dhimmis enjoy only second-class citizenship in Muslim states. Some modern thinkers call for recognition of the ties binding the People of the Book together as a means of promoting interfaith dialogue and cooperation.

Allah: The Arabic name for "God". Worshipped by Muslims, Christians, and Jews to the exclusion of all others. Revealed Himself in the *Qur'an*, which is self-described as His book. Defined in the *Qur'an* as the creator, sustainer, judge, and ruler of the material universe and the realm of human experience. Has guided history through the prophets Abraham (with whom He made a covenant), Moses, Jesus, and Muhammad, through all of whom He founded His chosen communities, People of the Book (*ahl al-kitab*)

The establishment of the first Islamic state in Medina is one of the seminal events in Islamic history. This entry examines the historical roots of Bayt al-Mal, the early state treasury, its key revenue streams, and how its goals evolved. Among the revenue sources during the time of the Prophet of Islam were zakat, tribute, Mubashir, jizya, and spoils of war. Together, these funds were applied to eliminating poverty and promoting social welfare. During Caliph Umar's reign, the expansion of the state's borders institutionalized the Bayt al-Mal. As the state's wealth grew, challenges arose in managing funds and maintaining an official record-keeping system. The primary sources of revenue were taxation forms such as zakat, ushr, shari'ah, jizya, and others. Over time, additional sources such as import duties and revenues from state-owned property supplemented these. The institution of Bayt al-Mal still exists in some Muslim countries today.

Caliph: The Prophet's successors were known as caliphs, and their empire was the caliphate. (The Prophet was a political as well as a religious leader.) The first four caliphs are known as the *Rashid* (the "rightly guided" caliphs). Sunni Muslims consider the rule of the *Rashid* to be the golden age of Islam. Shia Muslims believe that the fourth caliph, Ali, was usurped by the first three caliphs and that his descendants were the proper heirs to the caliphate. (One sect of Shiis set up a rival caliphate in Egypt in 983. It lasted nearly 200 years.)

Dhimmi: Non-Muslim under the protection of Muslim law. A covenant of protection was made with conquered "Peoples of the Book," which included Jews, Christians, Sabaeans, and sometimes Zoroastrians and Hindus. Adult male dhimmis were required to pay a tax on their income and sometimes on their land. Restrictions and regulations in dress, occupation, and residence were often applied. In return, Islam offered dhimmis security of life and property, defence against enemies, communal self-government, and freedom of religious practice. In the modern period, dhimmi status has declined in importance as a result of the formation of nation-states and Western or quasi-Western legal codes.

Hadith: Report of the words and deeds of Muhammad and other early Muslims; considered an authoritative source of revelation, second only to the *Qur'an* (sometimes referred to as sayings of the Prophet). Hadith (pl. ahadith; hadith is used as a singular or a collective term in English) were collected, transmitted, and taught orally for two centuries after Muhammad›s death and then began to be collected in written form and codified. They serve as a source of biographical material for Muhammad, contextualization of Qur'anic revelations, and Islamic law. A list of authoritative transmitters is usually included in collections. Compilers were careful to record hadith precisely as received from recognized transmission specialists. The six most authoritative collections are those of al-Bukhari, Muslim, al-Tirmidhi, Abu Daud al-Sijistani, al-Nasai, and al-Qazwini. The collections of Malik ibn Anas and Ahmad ibn Hanbal are also important.

Hajj: The pilgrimage to Makkah, which Muslims with the physical ability and financial means should perform at least once in their lives. It is one of the five pillars of Islam. The hajj takes place during the 12th lunar month of the Islamic calendar and focuses on rituals around the Kaaba. A pilgrimage that takes place at any other time is called the *Umrah*. Around two million Muslims carry out the *hajj* each year.

Hijrah: The act of migration from one place to another. In Islam, the Hijrah refers to the Muslims migrating from Makkah to Medinah and also marks the beginning of the Islamic calendar. Islam: In Arabic, the word means "surrender" or "submission" to the will of God. Islam is considered one of the three major monotheistic world religions (the others being Judaism and Christianity).

Islamic calendar: The first year of the Muslim era is 622AD, the year of Muhammad's migration to Medinah. The Islamic calendar consists of

12 lunar months: years typically last 354 days, and leap years previous 355 days.

Islamic morality Islam differs from many other religions in providing a complete code of life. It encompasses the secular with the spiritual, the mundane with the celestial. Man is the vicegerent of God on earth: "Behold thy Lord said to the Angels: I will create a vicegerent (khalifa) on earth" (Q. 2:30). The satanic claim to superiority is the source of arrogance. Islam considers it the worst sin since, through arrogance, all other sins are committed. Freeing humanity from the original sin, empowering human beings, and giving them full responsibility for their actions is the message of the Qur'an: "Every soul will be held responsible for what it had done" (Q. 74:38)—is the essence of morality and ethics in Islam.

Istisqa: Salat ul istasqa is a prayer consisting of two rakaahs performed during times of drought to ask Allah for rain. It was first introduced in Medinah during Ramadan on the 6th of Hijrah.

Ash-Shaf'i states that it has been related to Salim ibn 'Abdullah, on the authority of his father, that the Prophet would say for Istisqa ': "O Allah, give us a saving rain, productive, plentiful, general, continuous. O Allah, give us rain and do not make us among the discouraged. O Allah, (Your) slaves, land, animals, and (Your) creation all are suffering and seek protection. And we do not complain except to You. O Allah, let our crops grow and let the udders be refilled. Give us from the blessings of the sky and grow for us from the blessings of the earth. O Allah, remove from us the hardship, starvation, and barrenness and remove the affliction from us as no one removes afflictions save Thee. O Allah, we seek Your forgiveness as You are the Forgiving, and send upon us plenteous rains." Ash-Shaf'i said: "I prefer that the imam would supplicate with that (prayer)."

Saad reported that for Istisqa, the Prophet would supplicate: "O Allah, let us be covered with thick clouds that have abundant and beneficial rain, frequently making a light rain upon us and sprinkling upon us with lightning. O Allah, You are full of majesty, bounty and Honour." This is related to Abu 'Awanah in his Sahih.

Islamic Studie Study of Islam and the Qur'an The field of Islamic Buddhism is both wide-reaching and dynamic. It includes the range of foundational documents, traditions, institutions, and history of Muslims in various countries and regions throughout the world from the origins of Islam to the present day. This interdisciplinary field, therefore, includes history, religion, philosophy, anthropology, Arabic language and literature, as well as literature in other languages, including Persian, Turkish, and Urdu, and remains responsive to discoveries, interpretations, ideologies and theories.

The Internet makes access to staggering amounts of information easy – but it also raises important questions: What are the major issues and critical developments in the field? Which sources are up-to-date, and which are obsolete? Which works are pivotal in defining the discourse at various stages in its development? Which sources are considered accurate and balanced, and which represent simply a given individual or group's position? These questions are essential to keep in mind when undertaking any new study, but they are particularly critical in a dynamic and contested field such as Islamic Studies. *Oxford Bibliographies* in Islamic Studies combats this overload by providing expert guidance to the field in all its diversity and throughout its developmental stages. Top scholars in the field have contributed to their areas of expertise so that users will understand how the field is organized and why it developed in the way it did. The articles present a guided tour through the critical literature on each topic, providing context for its development and a balanced overview of the significant issues within a given topic.

Jizyah: Compensation. Poll tax levied on non-Muslims as a form of tribute and in exchange for an exemption from military service, based on *Qur'an* 9:29. However, in the light of Sharī'ah or Muslim law, if a Muslim ruler fails to protect the life and property of nonMuslim citizens, this Muslim ruler has to return the *jizyah* to the concerned non-Muslim citizen. So, all non-Muslims must pay jizyah just as Muslims will have to pay the obligatory Zakat in order to help the poor. Moreover, non-Muslims will be absolved from military service. Still, if any non-Muslim citizen wishes to serve in the army, they may do so, in which case they will be exempted from the payment of jizyah. A great jurist, Al Mawardi, stated that "only those who are capable of paying are required to pay the *jizyah,* and this has meant that the sick and the disabled, the elderly, children, women and monks are not under a duty to pay"

Jihad: An Arabic word meaning "to struggle" or "to exhaust one's effort". The "effort" can mean preaching Islam and living virtuously in accordance with God's commands. But it can also apply to actual fighting to defend Muslims. Even military jihad, however, is supposed to be fought with respect for the rules of war.

Jerusalem: It is sacred to followers of three faiths - Islam, Christianity, and Judaism. From the seventh century, Jerusalem and the surrounding area were ruled by Muslims, who had primarily lived in harmony with the Christians and Jews of the city. However, in the late 11th century, the Christian Byzantine empire, based in Turkey on the pilgrimage route to Jerusalem, was at war with the Muslim Seljuk Turks. Christian pilgrims reported difficulties in visiting Jerusalem. The Europeans launched a series of largely unsuccessful wars called the Crusades to try and defeat the Muslims and take over Jerusalem and other nearby lands.

Ka'bah: The most sacred shrine of Islam, it is a cube-shaped stone structure in Makkah. Traditionally, Muslims believe Abraham and his son Ismail built the Ka'bah. On the outside of one corner is the sacred Black Stone, kissed by pilgrims. The angel Gabriel gave the Black Stone to Abraham, according to one Islamic tradition; according to another, the stone was set in place by Adam.

Khutbah: An address called a *khuṭbah* is delivered by a *khaṭīb* (orator) as part of a religious service. As a religious ritual with fixed rulings, the *khuṭbah* fulfils a religious mandate associated with specific occasions such as the weekly congregational Friday service, the two ʿĪd holidays, and the Day of ʿArafāt (the ninth of Dhū al-Hijjah) during *ḥajj*. The *khutbah* is also delivered on other occasions, such as a marriage contract ceremony or during an eclipse or excessive drought. In the Friday service, the *khuṭbah* precedes the prayer, whereas the prayer precedes the *khuṭba*h during the two ʿĪd services.

In a marriage ceremony, the imam also delivers *the khuṭba*h before officiating the contract. The *khuṭbah* during the marriage contract (*khuṭbatu al-nikāh*) is recommended but not obligatory based on the Prophet ʿs tradition. The marriage *khuṭbah* follows a simple format: the imam recites three verses (Qurʿān 4:1, 3:102, 33:70–71) and a Prophetic tradition (*ḥadith*) related to marriage. In addition to this, the imam can also remind the couple of their rights and responsibilities toward each other, invoking their sense of God-consciousness (*taqwā*).

Although the *khuṭbah* can take various forms, the most common form is the weekly Friday sermon, which is a prerequisite for the congregational Friday prayer. The word *jumʿah* (Friday), the name of the day during which the *khuṭbah* is delivered, is derived from the Arabic verb *jamaʿa*, which means to gather, to collect, and to unite. The institution of the *jumʿa*h prayer brings together Muslims in the congregation for the fulfilment of this weekly obligatory ritual. Hence, praying in congregation is a condition for the validity of the Friday service, which explains the relationship between the words *jumʿah* (Friday) and *jamaʿah* (congregation).

Islamic scholarship is not just based on the study of the Qurʿan. In a famous saying, Muslim scholars are told to "Seek knowledge, even unto China," In the Middle Ages, there were well-known Muslim scholars in many fields, from astronomy and mathematics to medicine and natural science, and in most areas their ideas were among the most advanced in the world. The Islamic scholars gained much of their knowledge from the ancient world. They translated the works of ancient Greek scholars, preserving information that had been lost or forgotten. The Muslim scholars then built on this with their original work, carefully recording all their discoveries.

Makka: Holiest city of Islam., birthplace of Muhammad, site of the Ka'bah and the annual pilgrimage, and the town Muslims face during prayer. It is located in what is now Saudi Arabia. In pre-Islamic Arabia, Makkah was a significant city on the trade routes, a pilgrimage site, and a site of worship of numerous pre-Islamic gods and goddesses. After the rise of Islam, it lost commercial prosperity due to changes in trade routes.

Medina: Also located in western Saudi Arabia, Medinah is Islam's second holiest place. Mohammed migrated to Medinah with 70 Muslim families in 622 when persecuted by Makkans and Muhammad's burial site. Originally known as Yathrib, it changed its name to "City of the Prophet" (*Medinat al-nabi*). A place where Muhammad began to set the course for Islam to develop into a religious and political society; first, he regulated the political problems of Medinah by gaining assent to the Constitution of Medinah, making all inhabitants into a single community. The early caliphs (successors to Muhammad) remained in Medinah, making it the capital of the new Islamic empire until 661. A pilgrimage to Medinah is often made in conjunction with the pilgrimage to Makkah in order to visit the tombs and shrines of Muhammad, his family, and the first three caliphs.

Merchants and Travelers: Trade has always played a vital role in the Islamic world. The Prophet himself came from a people who had long ago established the two great caravan journeys from Makkah, the Winter Caravan to Yemen and the Summer Caravan to the outskirts of the Roman Empire. When Muslim armies took over the territory, traders were quick to follow, opening up routes that led east to China, south into Africa, northwest to Europe, and southeast across the Indian Ocean. The faith of Islam was soon spread by merchants as far as Malaysia and Indonesia. Muslims did not only travel for trade. They also went in search of knowledge, on diplomatic missions, and, of course, to make the Pilgrimage.

Mosque: The Arabic word is *masjid*, meaning "place of prostration" before God. Mohammed built the first mosque in Medinah. A mosque should be oriented toward Makkah. In many of the world's Islamic societies, mosques serve social and political functions in addition to religious ones.

Muslim: In Arabic, "one who surrenders to God"; a follower of Islam. There are one billion Muslims in the world.

Pillars of Islam: The five pillars of Islam (*arkan al-Islam*; also *arkan al-din*, "pillars of religion") comprise five official acts considered obligatory for all Muslims. The *Qur'an* presents them as a framework for worship and a sign of commitment to faith. The five pillars are the *shahadah* (witnessing the oneness of God and the prophethood of Muhammad), regular observance of the five prescribed daily prayers (*salah*), paying *zakah* (almsgiving), fasting (*sawm; siam*) during the month of Ramadan, and performance of the *hajj* (pilgrimage during the prescribed month) at least once in a lifetime. Both Sunnis and Shiis agree on the essential details for carrying out the five pillars. In popular Sufi piety, the five pillars were personally internalized as acts of devotion and spiritual exercises. The shahadah became a constant recollection (*dhikr*) of God, and the obligatory prayers became a life of continuous prayer and meditation.

Qadi, also spelt Cadi or Kadi, is a Muslim judge who renders decisions according to the Sharī'ah, the canon law of Islām. The *I* hears only religious cases such as those involving inheritance, pious endowments (*waqf*), marriage, and divorce, though theoretically, his jurisdiction extends to both civil and criminal matters. Initially, Qadi's work was restricted to non-administrative tasks, such as arbitrating disputes and rendering judgments on the issues brought before him. Eventually, however, he assumed the management of pious endowments, the guardianship of property for orphans, imbeciles, and others incapable of overseeing their interests, and the control of marriages for women without guardians. The *Qadi*'s decision in all such matters was final.

Because the *Qadi* performed an essential function in early Muslim society, requirements for the post were carefully stipulated: he must be an adult Muslim male of good character, possessing sound knowledge of the Sharīah, and a free man. In the 7th and 8th centuries, the *Qadi* were expected to be capable of deriving the specific rules of law from their sources in the Qur ān, hadīth (traditions of the Prophet), and *ijmā* (consensus of the community). This view was later modified to allow the *Qadi* to accept as absolute the opinions of one of the four orthodox Muslim law schools.

The second caliph, Umar, was the first to appoint a *Qadi* to eliminate the necessity of his personally judging every dispute that arose in the community. After that, it was considered a religious duty for authorities to provide for the administration of justice through the appointment of *Qadi* s.

Fiqh: Conceptually, the human attempt to understand divine law (sharī'ah). Whereas sharī'ah is immutable and infallible, fiqh is fallible and changeable. Fiqh is distinguished from usul al-fiqh in terms of the methods of legal interpretation and analysis. Fiqh is the product of the application of usul al-fiqh, the total product of human efforts at understanding the divine will. A hukm is a particular ruling in a given case.

The Shari'ah(Religious Law)a

Islam differs from many other religions in providing a complete code of life. It encompasses the secular with the spiritual, the mundane with the celestial. Man is the vicegerent of God on earth: "Behold thy Lord said to the Angels: I will create a vicegerent (khalifa) on earth" (Q. 2:30). He endowed Adam with knowledge of all things, as the Qur'an relates: "And He taught Adam the names-all of them" (Q. 2:31). The Angels did not know those things. Accordingly, Adam was on a higher level than the angels. It was for this reason that God commanded the angels to bow in obeisance for Adam: We told the angels to prostrate before Adam, so they prostrated except for Iblis (Satan, the Devil), who is from Jinn. "He refused and was arrogant and became a disbeliever" (2:34). Allah said: What prevented you from prostrating (to Adam) when I commanded you? (Iblies) said: "I am better than him. You created me from fire and created him from clay" (Q. 17:12).

The satanic claim to superiority is the source of arrogance. Islam considers it the worst sin since, through arrogance, all other sins are committed. Adam and his progeny were honoured by God, as the Qur'an says: "We honoured the progeny of Adam ... and preferred them over many of what We have created with (definite) preference" (Q. 12:70). According to the Qur'an, there is no original sin. Adam repented from his mistake of eating from the fruit of the forbidden tree by the deceit and trick of Satan. (Q. 7:19–23). Adam and Eve both repented, and God accepted their repentance and were forgiven. The Qur'an has recorded what Adam and Eve said to God:

Qur'an: The holy book of Islam, recorded by the prophet beginning in the year 610AD. Muslims consider it to be the word of God. Islam teaches that the Christian and Hebrew scriptures are also holy books, though they have become distorted over time. The Qu'ran is the primary source of Islamic law, followed by *hadith* (teachings attributed to Mohammed that are not recorded in the Qur'an) and the *sunnah* (the habits and practices of Mohammed's life). The word Qu'ran means "recitation".

Rashidun (Rightly Guided Caliphs): For Sunnis, the first four successors of Muhammad: Abu Bakr al-Siddiq, Umar ibn al-Khattab, Uthman ibn Affan, and Ali ibn Abi Talib. All were prominent Companions of Muhammad and belonged to the tribe of Quraysh. The period of their rule is considered a golden age when Muhammad's practices consciously guided the caliphs. The]period saw the establishment of Arab Muslim rule over the heartlands of the Middle East, and preparation for conquests and expansion carried out under subsequent dynasties. Umar is portrayed as the dominant personality among the caliphs, establishing many of the fundamental institutions of the classical Islamic state. Uthman is generally held responsible for the canonization of the *Qur'an, which is what* it is known today. He is described as personally pious but lacking the character needed to withstand unscrupulous relatives. Uthman's murder by malcontents opened a period of fitnah (disorder, civil war), which brought about the disintegration of the previously united community, the takeover of the caliphate by the Umayyad family, and the end of the era of Arabia-centered Islam.

Shar'iah: God's eternal and immutable will for humanity, as expressed in the *Qur'an* and Muhammad's example (*sunna*h), is considered binding for all believers and is the ideal Islamic law. The *Qur'an* contains only about ninety verses directly and specifically addressing questions of law. Islamic legal discourse refers to these verses as God's law and incorporates them into legal codes. The remainder of Islamic law is the result of jurisprudence (fiqh), human efforts to codify Islamic norms in practical terms and legislate for cases not explicitly dealt with in the *Qur'an* and *Sunna*h. Although human-generated legislation is considered fallible and open to revision, the term sharī'ah is sometimes applied to all Islamic legislation. This was supported by formal structures of juristic literature and many specific statements from the tenth through the nineteenth centuries. Modern scholars have challenged this claim, distinguishing between sharī'ah and fiqh and calling for reform of fiqh codes in light of contemporary conditions.

Shia: The "partisans" of Ali, the fourth caliph, the Shias, eventually became a distinct Muslim sect. The largest Shia Muslim sect is the "Twelver Shia," named after the first 12 leaders (or imams) of Shia Muslims. However, Shia believe that the descendants of Ali, Mohammed's cousin and son-in-law, were the legitimate leaders of Islam. Shias believe the last imam is in hiding, and they await his return. Shias are the majority in Iran, and many can be found in Iraq, Syria, Lebanon, and Pakistan. There are more than 165 million Shia Muslims in the world. (Also known as Shii or Shi'ite Muslims.)

Shura: Consultation. Based on the Qur'anic injunction to Muhammad to consult with his followers (Q 3:159) and to Muslims to consult with each other in conducting their affairs (Q 42:38). Modern scholars consider shura to be the basis for the implementation of democracy. Liberal scholars argue that shura declares the sovereignty of people in electing representative leaders to democratic institutions designed to act in the public interest. For conservative thinkers, shura must be based on the principle of the ultimate sovereignty of God and geared toward the implementation of traditional Islamic law.

Sufis: Sufism is the name given today to the spiritual way at the heart of Islam. Those who follow it have their spiritual practices and a distinctive culture of poetry and music. Sufis aim to discover the inner meaning of Islam. They study under a spiritual teacher in order to come closer to Allah. Their practices sometimes include ecstatic singing and sacred dance rituals that have earned one group of Sufis the nickname "whirling dervishes.

Sunni: Unlike Shii Muslims, Sunni Muslims believe that Islamic leadership is vested in the consensus of the community rather than in religious and political authorities. Despite their differences, Sunnis and Shi'ites alike observe the five pillars of Islam. Like Judaism, Islam is a religion that requires people to live a certain way rather than to accept certain credal propositions.

Tawhid: It is the defining doctrine of Islam. It declares absolute monotheism—the unity and uniqueness of God as creator and sustainer of the universe. Islamic reformers and activists use it as an organizing principle for human society and the basis of religious knowledge, history, metaphysics, aesthetics, and ethics, as well as social, economic, and world order.

During the classical period, discussions of *tawhid* focused on philosophical considerations about God's essence and attributes and the validity of the political institution of the caliphate. The thirteenth-century **Hanbali** jurist Ibn Taymiyyah shifted the emphasis of *tawhid* to sociomoral issues. He interpreted *tawhid* as a declaration that God is the sole creator, ruler, and judge of the world, rendering human beings responsible for submitting to and carrying out His revealed will through religious practice, ritual, and actions. True faith is expressed in both individual and collective virtuous behaviour, linking the private and public (i.e., spiritual and political) spheres.

Ulema: Men of knowledge (sing., alim). Refers to those who have been trained in religious sciences (*Qur'an*, hadith, fiqh, etc.). In the colonial and postcolonial world, alim can also mean a scientist in the secular sense—formulators of Islamic theology and law in the classical age. In the modern era, the ulama's sphere of operation is confined to the mosque and the madrasa. As imam of the local mosque, an alim leads daily prayers, delivers the Friday sermon, and teaches children the basics of Islamic law and Qur'anic recitation. On occasions of birth, death, and marriage, he may also be called upon for prayers or for help in performing the rituals themselves. In rural areas, an alim may be the most educated or wisest man in the area but not necessarily formally trained; in urban centres, ulama generally possess some credentials or formal education.

Ummah: The worldwide community of Muslims irrespective of colour, race, language or nationality. A fundamental concept in Islam expresses the essential unity and theoretical equality of Muslims from diverse cultural and geographical settings. The *Qur'an* designates people to whom God has sent a prophet or people who are objects of a divine plan of salvation.

Usul al-Fiqh: Roots of law. The body of principles and investigative methodologies through which practical legal rules are developed from the foundational sources. The primary base of law is the *Qur'an*. The second source is the *sunnah*, which reports about the sayings, actions, or tacit approvals of the Prophet. The third source is the consensus (ijma) of all Muslim interpretive scholars in a specific age on a legal rule about an issue not covered in the *Qur'an* or *Sunnah*. Most Sunni scholars consider consensus binding; others, including Shii scholars, say such consensus is impossible. The fourth source is analogy (qiyas), or rule by precedent. Some Hanafis, such as Ibn Abidin and Maliki jurists, consider urf (custom) to be an additional source of law. In addition to these primary sources, several presumptions and principles aid the jurist in deriving interpretive rules: preference (istihsan), unregulated interest (maslahah mursalah), and the presumption of continuity (istishab). This field is also concerned with hermeneutic and deductive principles.

GLOSSARY OF ISLAMIC TERMINOLOGY

*adab: **manners***, proper behaviour

al-adl: equilibrium

al-ahsan: Compassion

Allahu Akbar: literally "God is most great," a phrase used in the Muslim call to prayer and other occasions to glorify God.

Baitul Ma!: Treasury

bida: Innovation

Caliph: from*Khalifat,* successor. Ruler of Islam

deen: religion, the life of holiness

Dunya Dunya: world, life of the world; the here and now—see

annihilation: Sufi concept, merger with God

fatwa: The legal guidance of a pious, just, knowledgeable Muslim scholar and jurist, based on the Qur'an, *sunnah* and Islamic Shari'ah

*Isaiah: m*ale sexual honour and jealousy.

Hadith: sayings—and doings—of the Prophet, his traditions

hajj: the annual pilgrimage; it is obligatory for every Muslim once in a lifetime

haya: female sexual modesty and shyness.

hijra: departure, emigration; from the Prophet's*shijra*to Medinah

ijtihad: independent judgment

ilm: knowledge. Hence

alim: scholar

ijma: literally means consensus of the people

Jahiliyya: age of ignorance; time before the coming of Islam

Jannah: Paradise, the reward for those who are judged to be good

Jinn: They are created by Allah from fire and are invisible to human beings. They can change their shape. They are also subject to the Islamic call. Among them are believers and non-believers.

Ka'bah - a cube-shaped structure in the courtyard of the Grand Mosque in Makkah, the focal point of the *ḥajj*(pilgrimage) and the location that all Muslims face during prayer.

miswak: Tooth stick.

muezzin: Caller to worship (see *adhan*)

muhajir: Emigrant; a person who migrates in the way of Allah.

Muhajirun: Emigrants; the title given to Muslims who migrated from Makkah to Medinah.

nasab: ancestry, lineage

qiyas: analogical reasoning

qiblah: The direction which Muslims face in prayer.

Rahman, Rahim: Beneficent, Merciful—names of Allah

rak'ah: A unit of salah, made up of recitation, standing, bowing and two prostrations.

Sadaqah: Voluntary payment or good action for charitable purposes.

Sahih al-Bukhari: The title of the books of *hadith* compiled by Muhammad(peace be upon him) ibn Isma'il al-Bukhari, a Sunni scholar. The collection is described as *Sahih* (authentic).

Sahih Muslim: The title of the books of *hadith* compiled by Abul Husayn Muslim ibn al-Hajjaj, a Sunni scholar. The collection is described as *Sahih* (authentic).

sahabah: singular *sahabi,* Companions of the Prophet

salaam: peace, colloquial: greetings. Hence, Islam, the religion of peace

salah: Prescribed communication with and worship of Allah, performed under specific conditions, in the manner taught by the Prophet Muhammad (peace be upon him), and recited in the Arabic language. Allah fixes the five daily times of salah.

al-Shura **consultation**; colloquial: consultative body

such-i-kul : peace with all; Sufi saying and motto

sunnah: literally: the path to be followed by the Prophet;

ahle-sunnah or followers of the *sunnah* and Sunnis

Sira: biographical accounts of the Prophet

surah: Division of the Qur'an (114 in all)

talaq: Repudiation of the wife.Male-initiated divorce. This is extremely easy to obtain. The husband's declaration of *talaq* causes the divorce to come into effect.

taqlid: the following of predecessors

taqwa: **piety**

tawhid: unity of God

tayammum*:* it is the Islamic act of dry ablution using sand or dust, which may be performed in place of ritual washing (*wudu* or ghusl) if no clean water is readily available or if one is suffering from moisture-induced skin inflammation or scaling

umrah: Lesser pilgrimage which can be performed at any time of the year

SUPPLEMENTARY READING

al-Baladhuri. Ahmad bin Yahya Futuh al-Buldan (Conquests of Nations).

al-Qarashi, Ghalib A.K. Awliyat al-Farooq fi al-Idara wal-Qada (Firsts of the Farooq in Administration and Judicial affairs), being a Ph.D. thesis, Muasast al-Kutub al-Thaqafiyah, Beirut, 1990.

al-Tabari, Muhammad bin Jarir Ta'rikh al-rusul wa'l Muluk (History of the Prophets and Kings), 10 Vols. Ed. Muhammad Abulfadl Ibrahim. Dar Suywdan, Beirut, copy of the Dar al-Ma'raf, Cairo 2nd edition, 1960-69.

Arnold, Thomas W. The Caliphate, Barnes and Noble, New York, 1966.

as-Suyuti, Jalal ad-Din The History of the Khalifahs who took the right way, being a portion of as-Suyuti's Tarikh al-Khulafah, translated by: A. Clarke, Taha Publishers, London, 1995.

Blankinship, Khalid Y. The History of al-Tabari, Volume XI: The Challenge to the Empires, Translated by: the State University of New York Press, 1993.

Donner, Fred M. The Early Islamic Conquests, Princeton University Press, 1981.

Jandora, John W. The March from Medina, A Revisionist Study of the Arab Conquests, The Kingston Press, Clifton, 1990.

Khatab, Mahmoud S. Bayan al-Aqeedah Wal-Qayidah (Between Creed and Leadership) Dar El-Fikr, Beirut, n.d.

Nu'mani, Shibli Al-Farooq, The Life of Umar the Great, Translated from the original Urdu by Zafar Ali Khan, International Islamic Publishers, New Delhi, 1992.aaa